Thank God I... 💜 💜 💜

Stories of Inspiration for Every Situation

Thank God My Wife Cheated
Thank God I Was Raped
Thank God I Was Sexually Molested
Thank God I Had Cancer
Thank God I Have Herpes
Thank God My Son Died
Thank God My Husband Was an Alcoholic

CREATED BY JOHN CASTAGNINI

ISBN–13: 978-0-9815453-0-1

Cover Design: George Foster
Interior Design: Desktop Miracles, Inc.

Printed in the United States of America

Publisher's Cataloging-In-Publication Data
(Prepared by The Donohue Group, Inc.)

Thank God I— : stories of inspiration for every situation / created by
John Castagnini.
  p. ; cm.
  Partial contents: Gratitude: the key to experiencing love and
fulfillment in all seven areas of life—Thank God my husband
cheated—Thank God I was raped—Thank God I am divorced—Thank
God I had cancer—Thank God I have a dysfunctional family—Thank
God my child died—Thank God my husband was an alcoholic.
  ISBN: 978–0–9815453–0–1
  1. Gratitude—Religious aspects. 2. Life change events—Religious
aspects. 3. Adjustment (Psychology) 4. Conduct of life. I. Castagnini,
John.
BF575.G68 T43 2008
                                                                   158.1

TABLE OF CONTENTS

Introduction 1

Gratitude (Thanking God): The Key to Experiencing Love and
Fulfillment in All Seven Areas of Life 5
  DR. JOHN DEMARTINI

Thank God I Was Homeless 15
  NICK ARANDES

Thank God I Had Breast Cancer 21
  C. OLIVIA PARR-RUD

Thank God My Mom Died 28
  JOHN CASTAGNINI

Thank God My Father Went to Prison 33
  LISA KAYE

Thank God My Husband Died 41
  LUAN MITCHELL

Thank God I Was a Racist 45
  BRUCE MUZIK

Thank God I'm Bald 51
  LAURA DUKSTA

Thank God I Was Abused 57
KAREN HOYOS

Thank God I Was Sexually Molested 65
MICHAEL A. WEIST

Thank God I Got Diabetes 71
JOHN KREMER

Thank God I Left My Kids 75
MABEL KATZ

Thank God I Was Raped 81
JAY GRAYCE

Thank God I Had Cancer 89
MARILYN JOYCE

Thank God I Had a Catastrophe 97
PIERETTE DOMENICA SIMPSON

Thank God My Husband Was an Alcoholic 104
KATHERINE SCHERER

Thank God I Had Depression 109
MICHELLE ARMSTRONG

Thank God I Went Broke 116
MYLES L. MATHIEU

Thank God I Had an Eating Disorder 121
PAULA D. ATKINSON

Thank God I Lost My Mind 125
BRITTANY LUND

Thank God I Had Breast Cancer 133
ANNABELLE BONDAR

Thank God I Am a Single, Motherless Mom 138
ALANA PRATT

Thank God I Was Sent to Prison 144
KEITH MCEACHERN

Thank God I'm an Entrepreneur 153
CHRISTINE KLOSER

Thank God I Died Giving Birth to Twins 158
CHARLOTTE G.

Thank God I Lost My Babies 163
DENISE LAURIA VENITELLI, LCSW

Thank God I Had Cancer 168
CASSANDRA GATZOW

Thank God I Had a Miscarriage 174
DR. SARAH FARRANT

Thank God My Friend Was Sexually Abused
by Her Grandfather 182
ELIZABETH PASQUALE, LMT, CST

Thank God I Lost My Home and My Love . . . and
Ended Up a Winner 187
BRUCE HOFFMAN

Thank God My Son Died 196
CHRIS ADAMS

Thank God I Had a Miscarriage 201
IRENE NICHOLS

Thank God I Have Cancer 205
KAI JACOBSON

Thank God My Mother Died 212
CHRISTINA PERRY

Thank God . . . for Every Moment in My Life 217
JANET ATTWOOD

Thank God I Met the Debt Collector 222
SHAWN WIEDERIN

Thank God My Husband Left Me Pregnant and
an Employee Molested My Children 226
DR. SHAKTI DEVI KAHEALANI KAWAIOLAMANALOA
SATCHITANANDA

Thank God My Boyfriends Dumped Me. 234
ERIS HUEMER

Thank God I was Fat, Tired, Broke, and Beyond Hope. 241
SANDY ELSBERG

Thank God I Was Fired by Fax 247
LARRY THOMPSON

Thank God My Best Friend Died 251
          SUSAN BURGER

Thank God My Wife Cheated On Me! 257
          JASON THOMAS KICINSKI

Thank God I Was Fat 265
          TRICIA GREAVES

Thank God I Lost My Father 270
          ROBERT JOSEPH IWANIEC

Thank God I Am the Product of Rape! 276
                    LADY

Thank God I Have Herpes 286
          UMOH NTUK

Thank God I Was a Polygamist's Wife................... 293
          WHITE DOVE

Thank God I Lost My Dream Job . . . and Found My Dream 299
          STEVE BHAERMAN

Introduction

IMPORTANT . . .
Please Do Not Skip This Section!

Why this book? What makes it so different? Not only are these answers important, they are integral to your understanding of the stories presented here. Please do not skip over this brief introduction in your eagerness to get to the meat of the book itself.

When I first thought to include **Thank God I Was Raped** as one of the stories for this book, the concept sent chills through my spine. Could anyone who's endured this brutal, horrifying experience really embrace these words? Over the years, I've consulted with countless women during their rape recovery. I chose the title after witnessing what transpires for them when *they* come to this conclusion of gratitude. What became quite apparent over a course of thousands upon thousands of conversations is that we only evolve past the mental trauma from such a happening when we can hold "the love for it in our hearts"

What is meant by "God"?

God — Certainly, the biggest three-letter word ever created. Grand Organized Designer best describes the God referred to in TGI . . .

The thousands of people sharing their stories in this series all perceive God in their own light. *Thank God I . . .* is about this network of people, willing to move beyond having the right "name" for God. Even the word "God" itself cannot finite the infinite. Rather, God refers to a system governing the brilliance of what is, and is not.

What this book series is *not* supposed to be.

This series does not condone or promote any of the acts the writers have experienced, nor do we suggest in any way that anyone *should* either commit any of these acts or subject themselves to any of these acts. This series also does not promote or label any specific kind of behavior as "right" or "wrong", nor were the stories written or the book published for the purpose of suggesting that anyone rationalize their actions or behavior.

In addition, the *Thank God I . . .* series does not promote or deny any religion. Rather, it honors the existence of religion and all things as part of a perfect creation.

What is *Thank God I . . .* about?

Our intention with this series is to convey this one key principle: **Perfection permeates *everything*.** Each time we fail to recognize this principle, the next lesson to come our way will once again offer us the opportunity to see the perfection and break through into freedom. In fact, finding perfection in the pain and pleasure of our own personal tribulations is the *only* way we will *ever* liberate ourselves from the bondage of patterns. Whether it comes in a day, a year, or a lifetime away, situations will come into our lives that will *force* us to become thankful for "what was," and to whole-heartedly experience "what is."

What is meant by "Thanking God"?

During the creation phase of this series, we were fortunate to have as our ever-efficient assistant, Cassandra Gatzow, a beautiful twenty-three-year-old writer and poet. Just prior to coming to work with us, Cassandra was diagnosed with cervical cancer. A little over a year and a half later, the cancer spread and she left this world before the first book launched.

After Cassandra passed, my heart was struck by the words she put to the page as she endured this experience. She wrote of her earth angels and her explorations as she left her body to "dance with her angels." She did not write about her passing, she wrote about *Thank God I . . . living* as she moved through her life's greatest test, and her life's ending. She viewed each person, each moment as precious. How fortunate she was, to see God in the now.

Imagine — this is what she wrote about her cancer:

> "Tears fill my eyes daily with gratitude for every moment and every breath. It has allowed me to go after my dreams, to live from my heart, and to be truly free. I thank God for my cancer and for allowing me to reach a place in me that I don't think would have been possible without this experience. I am now twenty-three and feel that I have stepped into my skin proudly. I have felt an inner peace that many don't find until later in life. I am truly grateful for all my earth angels and want to thank them for sharing with me this wonderful journey"
>
> . . . CASSANDRA

There are 4 million tasks to accomplish in order to bring the *Thank God I . . .* network to the standard of our vision. Thank you, Cassandra, for reminding me why *Thank God I . . .* was conceived in the first place.

Thanking God is about the above. Not just what is above this sentence; it is about what is *above,* guiding us at every moment. Beyond the pain, chaos, and confusion of our circumstance exists true perfection. Thanking God is about finding this perfection. This place of thanking God might seem nearly impossible to find, but it is the only place we will find ourselves.

Thank God I . . . is true "gratitude".

Sure, we all hear about the "good things" that people are grateful for in their lives. But, is this gratitude? *Thank God I . . .* gratitude is about a state of being. It is about a state of inspiration, non-judgment, and presence. *Thank God I . . .* gratitude is beyond the illusion of positive or negative. It is beyond the lies of "good" and "evil". *Thank God I . . .* gratitude is about finding God in every word, thought, and deed. *In* spirit, we are beyond the illusion of pain or pleasure and we are present *with* spirit. *Thank God I . . .* gratitude is about *equal love* for all that is, as it is, was, or ever shall become. *Gratitude* is loving what we *don't* "like" as much as loving what we *do* "like".

The diversity of authors and experiences

The intention of this series is to reach all of humanity, every single unique creation. We did not base the selection of contributions to this series upon any faith or religious orientation. Each selected author took a former challenge into their heart. The diversity of authors spans religions, countries, professions, age, race, nationality, and definitely experiences. They range from strippers to doctors, from politicians to stay-at-home moms, and whoever they are, gratitude rules. From alcoholism to molestation or rape, the law of gratitude prevails with each of our authors. Thankfulness for whatever is, or is not, ultimately rules every one of our kingdoms.

The vision of *Thank God I . . .*

Little did I imagine how lightning-fast *Thank God I . . .* would circle the world. This network includes thousands of contributors, reaching millions of people, sharing not only their stories, but also their answers! Beyond the books, and the online community, we offer worldwide conference calls, workshops, and seminars! The vision of this series will provide *everyone* within specific communities information in order to evolve past the emotions that are holding them back. The people and the project are revolutionary.

> "All things in nature proceed from certain necessity and with the utmost perfection."
>
> . . . BARUCH SPINOZA

Gratitude (Thanking God)

The Key to Experiencing Love and Fulfillment in All Seven Areas of Life

DR. JOHN DEMARTINI

What does it take to live "happily ever after"? Ask a hundred different people and you'll get a hundred different answers. While some claim happiness is simply being in a happy relationship, others believe winning a pile of money would allow them to live happily ever after.

But, what if I told you that the hope for "happily ever after" is one of the greatest psychological and social delusions of our time? Winning a pile of money or having a great relationship won't keep you happy indefinitely, and half the time it might actually do the opposite. This might come as quite a shock!

If you set yourself up with the expectation that you are magically only going to live happily ever after, you may find yourself checking into a lifetime residence at the Heartbreak Hotel. Happiness-ever-after is a fantasy. It's a fairytale, and from this illusion are birthed some of the most prevalent social concerns including stress, suicide, heartache, hopelessness, anger, resentment, and depression.

Everlasting happiness goes against our truest nature. The purpose of life isn't to pursue only happiness, but to love and be grateful for life's winding road, which includes both happiness and sadness, positive and negative, and supportive and challenging experiences.

As you progress along your life voyage, you will experience life's natural cycles of highs and lows. However, the secret is to not fly too high on the up cycles or sink down too low on the down cycles. *Instead, your purpose is to appreciate all of life's experiences (happy and sad) and grow from them by recognizing their inherent balance.*

In my signature seminar program titled *The Breakthrough Experience®*, people learn the secret of how to embrace the complete balance of life (no matter what form of high or low it takes). And through the use of *The Demartini Method®*, people uncover and find this secret. This profound methodology provides a simple means to help you instantly find the blessings in every curse and teaches you how to be grateful with whatever confronts you in life.

So while you may not be able to live happily ever after, you can become deeply grateful in all areas of your life — no matter what happens. Let me tell you how to accomplish this "attitude of gratitude" in the seven areas of life:

Be Grateful For Your Spiritual State

With gratitude, you can open your heart to love.

If you desire to love yourself, others, and your magnificent experience called life, then being grateful is one of the most important steps you can take. Gratitude helps you live the life of your dreams. It doesn't matter if you are more conventional in your spiritual or religious beliefs or more orthodox — you can become grateful for the unseen energy flow of life that surrounds and fills you (the energy that some call the soul, others term the holy spirit, while others refer to as the life force). Do not underestimate the power and depth that gratitude has in connecting you to your own inner vital forces which you can bring into your everyday life.

Action steps:

Put aside a little time every day to connect with your inner spiritual force. It is amazing how inspired you can become when you allow yourself to open your heart and mind to this inspiring inner world. Gratitude is the key that opens up the gateway of your heart and mind. It allows your love and inspirations to shine

Whether you say your prayers of gratitude each day, give thanks before meals, write up your wish list, tune in to uplifting music, or spend some quiet time in contemplation or meditation, a little time spent partaking in a daily spiritual ritual of gratitude is incredibly nourishing for body, mind and spirit.

Affirmation:

I am forever grateful for my loving energy of life.

Be Grateful For Your Mental State

With gratitude, your mind becomes the most amazing place to explore.

How wonderful to have a mind of your own. Your mind makes up your private world, the secret part of yourself that often remains a mystery to others. Whether your mind becomes a friend or foe depends upon how you master your perceptions, or how your unsettled mind's perceptions run you. Your mind is like a garden. If you don't plant flowers in your mind's garden, you will forever be pulling weeds.

It is unwise to take your mind's powers for granted. You draw information in and send information out by your thoughts and ideas. Your mind interprets, filters, and assimilates your concepts, strengths, fears, and desires. Being grateful for your mind's diverse rich gifts helps it grow and expand.

Action steps:

Learn something new every day. Keep a book of inspiration nearby. (My book *The Breakthrough Experience®* is ideal for this mind-enriching, gratitude-initiating purpose).

Affirmation:

> *I am grateful for my mind because it provides me with an ability to think for myself and serve others.*

Be Grateful For Your Vocational State

> *Gratitude has the power to transform your vocation into a vacation.*

Slipping into your cozy bed each night with a feeling that you have accomplished something worthwhile each day is something certainly rewarding. Feeling productive is one of the most uplifting feelings you can experience. It helps you sleep soundly and heal.

Being grateful for your present vocational state doesn't mean you must forever remain in your nine-to-five work role. Whether your vocation makes you a homemaker, a student, an athlete, or even a holidaymaker, it is important that you feel that you have been productive throughout your day's activities — no matter what the form. For example, if you love to fish, you might view a day of productivity to be a great day of fishing. If you are a businessperson, it may mean the opportunity to close some deals. If you are a homemaker, it could mean cooking dinner for your family. Ultimately, being grateful for your own form of productivity completes your package of life. Without gratitude, a great deal of fulfillment will be missing from your everyday existence. Productivity provides you with a sense of purpose, achievement, and satisfaction.

Action steps:

Each morning set yourself seven highest-priority action steps that will ensure your vocational productivity. Do these actions first, before any less-productive distractions arise. If you follow these seven action steps, then you will be certain to complete each day of the week with a sense of gratitude for what you have achieved, not to mention that your life is likely to make a quantum leap forward as well.

Affirmation:

> *I am grateful for the ability to feel productive and serve.*

Be Grateful For Your Familial State

> *With gratitude, the entire world suddenly*
> *becomes your loving family.*

Family means different things to different people. You have an immediate family, like your marriage partner, children, and parents, and you have friends who are involved in family structures of a more unusual kind. Your personal sense of family or close connection may even take the form of a pet or a distanced friend with whom you only communicate via email. You may even regard all those who reside in your community, city, or world as part of your extended family.

But even if you consider yourself a loner, you still will have closer or more distant connections to certain individuals, groups, or other structures (even if only in your fantasies). These connections can be intimate or less personal and may even consist of groups of people rather than individuals. Ultimately, you have a family.

Action steps:

Sometimes you may forget the role that others play (and have played) in making your life complete. So spend some time each day thinking of those whom you love, such as immediate family members or old friends. Recall what their presence on this planet (or past presence, if they have already left this planet) meant and still means to you, and how it has contributed to your fulfillment. Thinking grateful and loving thoughts about others will open up your heart and enrich your life.

Affirmation:

I am grateful for those whom I love and
those who love me in return.

Be Grateful For Your Financial State

With gratitude, you may materialize
more money than you even need.

Being grateful for your financial state can be a tricky "attitude of gratitude" to master because you may be constantly in the habit of affirming to yourself that you don't have enough money. Your money woes may be one of your biggest stress tests, and you may be facing financial shortfalls, or your finances or money management may be your constant concern or pressure. You can become one of those who can truly say they are grateful for their financial state. The sooner you are grateful for whatever you have, the faster you will attract greater financial abundance. Your very thoughts, like "I don't have enough money," can make your life a self-defeating prophecy. If your mind fills with angst over your financial situation, then you may miss receiving the many riches that surround you.

Action steps:

If you find yourself being too busy worrying about finances, or feel "less wealthy" rather than "more wealthy," then begin counting your blessings today and become grateful for what you have and for the money you are about to earn.

Affirmation:

I am grateful for the financial abundance that
surrounds me and is available to me.

Be Grateful For Your Social State

With gratitude, every day becomes a
socially fulfilling opportunity.

There's a certain reason for the saying "novelty breathes fresh-ness into everyday life." Variety and change create more balance in life. Doing the same things repeatedly is like re-reading the same pages in the book of life, and you soon become bored. Getting out of your routine, meeting people, sharing ideas, and finding out what works or doesn't work for others and yourself helps you expand.

Your social and leisure life is important because being with others gives you the chance to see your world through their eyes. Gratefully socializing helps you relax, regain enthusiasm and energy, and allows you to share quality time with others. Being grateful for the opportu-nity to share experiences, whether that takes the form of playing golf, taking a vacation, or nurturing and creating old and new friendships, is an important part of your everyday life. Of course, when you love your work as if it were play and love your vocation if it were your vacation, then you certainly have much for which to be grateful, and you become inspired at your work.

Action steps:

Go out of your way to plan "social days" in advance so you may enjoy the anticipation in this experience of gratitude. Be friendly and open to new people coming into your life, and go out of your way to develop friendships that will enrich your life. This may mean that you are not to wait for others to invite you somewhere, but that you are to take the initiative and organize get-togethers yourself. Make an effort every day to expand your social network and connections. Making a phone call or sending a card to someone you would love to have as a friend can set all kinds of new social wheels spinning.

Affirmation:

> *My life is wonderful. I do what I love and I*
> *love what I do with those whom I love.*

Be Grateful For Your Physical State

> *With gratitude, my body becomes both a*
> *temple and an amusement park.*

The greatest art form that exists on this planet is your human body. What a magnificently structured temple of sacred architecture your human-body form represents. But are you grateful for it? Sometimes you may be, but other times you may be taking your body for granted. Instead of complaining about the shape of your body ("I'm too fat, too thin, too short, or too tall"), be grateful for your body. You may be spending a great deal of time in front of the mirror focusing on what you perceive to be the imperfections of your body rather than gratefully focusing on its beautiful or handsome perfections.

If you are consciously or unconsciously going out of your way to break down your magnificent body by smoking, eating poorly, not exercising, or burning the candle at both ends, then begin now to be grateful for your lovely body and for the multitude of powerful gifts it provides. This gratitude attitude can make the difference between experiencing wellness or illness. What you may term as "illness" may actually be your body's clever way of intuitively guiding you back to balance and more meaningful and grateful actions.

Action steps:

Be acutely aware of your body. Do not just expect it to maintain its own well-being without any contribution or effort on your part. Think of your body as a gift. It serves to bring you fulfillment in life. Tend to your body and take care of it, as you would tend to or take care of your garden.

Affirmation:

> *My incredible body is a created masterpiece*
> *hand-signed by G.O.D.*

❤   ❤   ❤

Dr. John F. Demartini is the founder of the *Demartini Human Research and Education Foundation* and is the creator of *The Breakthrough Experience*®. He travels the world teaching *The Demartini Method*® and appearing on international radio and television shows. Dr. Demartini has been featured in newspapers and magazines throughout the world. As a private consultant, he has advised people from all walks of life.

Dr. Demartini has authored dozens of books, including the best-selling titles *Count Your Blessings — The Healing Power of Gratitude and Love*; *The Gratitude Effect* and *The Breakthrough Experience — A Revolutionary New Approach to Personal Transformation*. His website is www.drDemartini.com.

Thank God
I Was Homeless

NICK ARANDES

*I*n 1994, I held happiness in the palm of my hand as my career soared to great heights. I felt led to write out my thoughts as a commitment to a future where my actions would express my gratitude.

I wrote:

> "My purpose in life is to bring joy, happiness, and encouragement to every person whom I come into contact with. To devote my entire life to the development and growth of my spiritual, mental, and physical capacities so that I can serve as an example to others. To help everyone see the greatness that resides within them that will allow them to live their dreams so that they can share the fruit of their endeavors with their loved ones as well as humanity." — Nick Arandes

Little did I realize that those very words would become my greatest challenge.

In 1997, I left my stage career and moved to California to pursue a spiritual path. I remember feeding homeless people on Saturdays as a way of giving back. I found other activities to help out the hungry and homeless. I financially supported myself with income from inherited properties in my native island of Puerto Rico. Then the wheels turned on me. I discovered that one of the properties incurred tax debts dating from 1960. I sold everything and still owed over $45,000 in credit card debt.

To my shock, I found myself out on the streets, hungry, and with no money of my own. I was forced into bankruptcy. I worked at odd jobs in order to buy food. I temporarily turned to friends and family as I made plans to go back on the road as a comedian in order to secure a steady income. Performing as a stage comedian no longer fulfilled me but it was the only career I knew. I lived out of my car or slept on floors whenever I found someone generous enough to put a roof over my head. Then the anger set in. I questioned my spirituality, and my purpose in the universe. I switched between anger at God and doubting His existence altogether.

I had always taken pride in taking care of my physical health. Imagine how I felt when I found myself budgeting to make sure I could have at least three sandwiches a day. I walked into a store to purchase a gallon of milk and a $1.00 box of cereal so I'd have something to fill my stomach. It was no longer about the kind of food I would eat but about *anything* to fill my empty stomach, so I could focus on the life I really wanted to have. A life I knew I deserved . . . I just didn't know how to create it.

Then mysteriously something happened. Each time I was about to give up, a strange synchronicity showed up in my life, allowing me to go on. I didn't know why these things kept happening, nor did I realize that one of the most powerful laws in the universe revealed itself — the law of surrender. In other words, as I let go and trusted my life's process, I drew into my space more and more hidden blessings that allowed me to continue on my journey.

I always received just enough shelter, food, and opportunities — my basic needs met — but not my wants, and I still could not afford a place to live.

I attended churches and asked for prayers and advice. When it came to money, all the ministers and congregants would say the same thing: *"Make sure you tithe so that more can come to you."* Of course, I thought that if I tithed 10%, I would always have more. Yet, most of the time I ended up with less money. It seemed to me that what was really sustaining me was not my tithing but my surrendering. So I kept tithing because now I had another fear to add: the fear that if I didn't tithe, the little I had at the time would be taken away from me.

Three years later, I still couldn't afford a place to live. I looked back and wondered how I'd managed to make it through those times when it seemed impossible. Somewhere deep within I knew that there must be a Power, God, Source . . . Something watching over me. I just wished I could access it more so that instead of just making ends meet, I could experience the abundance I deserved.

Going deeper into my spiritual practices — reading books, listening to tapes, meditating — I did whatever I could to stay in that place of trust and faith. I discovered that everything that happened to me offered incredible insights, if I stayed with the process.

Two more challenges emerged. Firstly, going out on the road as a comedian merely to make ends meet did not fulfill me and instead added to my misery. Secondly, I developed an undiagnosable health challenge. I could not afford medical insurance, which put me at the mercy of the malady.

As I drove through the state of Georgia to Tennessee for a four-day tour, I felt a very strong inward push against my chest. I didn't know what to do. I lacked the money for medical treatment, and I couldn't quit the tour because I needed the money. In short, I felt trapped by my own circumstance.

The next day, while staying with a friend, I prayed. I knew I needed to make a leap of faith because I now believed it was a matter of life or death. I contacted my agent and told him of my condition and to cancel the rest of my comedy engagements after the tour was over. He understood.

I had no place to call home, no income coming in, and an unknown physical challenge. I sought out a doctor who discovered a tumor in my thyroid. He wanted to remove the thyroid, but something deep within told me "no." I walked out of that office, never to be seen by a medical doctor again.

In Florida, I stayed with a friend and attended a church party at someone's house where I met a man who owned a home-based sign company. It turned out that he had seen me performing a few months earlier at a comedy club in Florida. He needed a graphic artist, I had experience as one, and so he hired me. Soon I found an apartment, and my life improved. I left the road because of my health, which led me to the new opportunity. This taught me another very powerful secret — I am always taken care of. But the opportunity presented itself only after *I took the first step.*

Other opportunities arose in my life, mostly from trusting and taking leaps of faith. I had a place to live, my health was improving, and I had money coming in . . . although, only enough to make ends meet.

A dear friend in California called to invite me to be her guest at a three-day intensive seminar she planned to attend. The trainer, a multi-millionaire, taught about money and emotions.

I knew I needed to hear this topic; not knowing at the time that I was about to discover another universal principle. The lecturer elaborated on the subject of tithing.

He basically stated that tithing has nothing to do with percentages. We are to tithe from the heart without expecting anything in return. He even shared that he gives only 5%, and he's still rich. Then he made a statement that triggered something within me that forever changed the direction of my life.

He said, "You hear a lot that it is better to give than to receive, right? Well, in order to have a giver, there has to be a receiver. And in order to have a receiver, there also has to be a giver. In other words, that is a 50/50 exchange. Therefore, one cannot be better than the other one. And those who preach that it is better to give than to receive are *always* on the receiving end."

Something deep within me resonated with this, as if God had said to me, "See, Nick? You knew about this truth all along but would not listen to me. Well, now you've met someone extremely well off finan-cially, sharing the truth about tithing. So now you don't have to feel guilty anymore."

In just a few short hours after that realization, I wrote my first book, *The Truth About Tithing*. The endorsements I received were mind-blowing! All of a sudden, I felt as if I was on to something. Right after that, my experiences led to the creation of *The Truth About Karma;* followed by *The Truth About Western Medicine* as a result of my health challenge; and *The Truth About Selling*, as well as audio programs, articles, music CDs, and so much more.

Once I had the *experience*, or as some may say, once I had learned the *lessons* I needed to learn, everything necessary (resources and oppor-tunities) to bring my dreams into fruition came easily and effortlessly. Something greater than myself supported me in everything I wanted to create. This reminds me of Richard Bach's words in his amazing book *Illusions*: "Every problem has a gift inside. We seek problems *because we want their gifts*."

You may ask, *Why did I have to go through all of that?* Remember what I wrote at the beginning of this story regarding my desire for my life's purpose?

"To devote my entire life to the development and growth of my spiritual, mental, and physical capacities *so that I can serve as an example to others*."

So that I can serve as an example. A minister once said to me, "You do not want to teach people how to do it. You want to share with them how *you* did it."

My journey taught me about surrendering and about the power of trust, faith, and the ability to create and attract into my life whatever I want.

I can now assist others who are facing major challenges, because my experience now allows me to relate to them at a deeper and more compassionate level. When I coach someone facing any kind of chal-lenge, I can truthfully say, "I know how you feel, I've been there. And, I can share from personal experience how to get from where you are to where you want to go". As opposed to, "This is my degree, and according to studies, this is what you need to do". Not nearly as effective.

As I continued on this path, my finances grew, and they continue to do so. I continue to attract blessings into my life, which led me to create *FulfillYourDreams.com*, considered to be one of the most powerful video classes taught over the internet on manifesting miracles.

I am literally transforming lives all around the world! My dream came true and continues to evolve, all because of what I went through.

> . . . to bring *joy, happiness, and encouragement* to every person whom I come into contact with . . . .

To this day, I no longer fear risks because I know my Source and Supply. Some may call my life experience positive, others may choose to call it negative. Regardless of the label, however, all I can say is, *Thank God I was homeless.*

♥   ♥   ♥

Nick Arandes, homeless, broke, and with a thyroid tumor, discovered a miraculous way of achieving perfect health without any medical intervention. He also achieved financial success. These accomplishments led him to the creation of his "Manifesting Miracles Online" coaching course at ww.FulfillYourDreams.com. His books, including *All Your Dreams Are Meant To Be Fulfilled*, of which Louise L. Hay says, "You certainly paint some memorable images", *You Were Born to Manifest Miracles*, *The Truth About Tithing*, *The Truth About Karma*, *The Truth About Western Medicine*, and *The Truth About Selling* is available through www.TheRadicalKid.com. Nick is producer of *Dare To Make The Turn* and *Manifest Your Dreams*. An empowering trainer and speaker, Nick is a frequent guest on radio and TV. He facilitates an inspirational Sunday talk at www.SuccessAndMiracles.com, and you can view his inspiring music videos at www.CheckMyMusic.com.

Join the *Thank God I...* community online to share your story and chat with the authors at **www.thankgodi.com**

Thank God
I Had Breast Cancer

C. OLIVIA PARR-RUD

*T*hink you have cancer." The sobering words of the radiologist reading my mammogram shot through me. I went numb. "That's impossible! I'm a health fanatic! I'm not supposed to get cancer!"

I was wrong.

The next few days brought shock, then denial. My mind reeled. How can I manage? I'm the sole support of my family. I have a thriving consulting business. I'm scheduled to speak at numerous conferences over the next year. I'm in the midst of producing an international conference. And I'm negotiating with publishers about writing a book. Why? Why is this happening to me? I'm a spiritual person.

I felt so betrayed . . . .

How would you feel? I contemplated my dilemma; I realized that I had allowed a part of my life to spin out of balance. As an adrenaline junkie, I lived in a constant state of stress, stress that now wreaked havoc on my hormone levels. I was killing myself. The cancer was my escape. Wanting to know the reason, I searched into my past. At age five, I experienced my first abandonment. My grandfather came to our house to tell my mother. My father was dead. He died in a plane crash. My mother broke into sobs. I didn't understand, so I withdrew. As I matured, I grew taller than most of the boys and I became painfully skinny. I suffered constant mocking and criticism. I hated my body and withdrew even more. No one could get close to me. I became my own worst enemy.

I contemplated my impending mastectomy, and asked the doctor about breast reconstruction. If I'm going to suffer this experience, I might as well make the best of it. I'd already been through many surgeries with plenty of scars to show for it. This was familiar territory.

At age nineteen, I almost lost my leg in a near-fatal car accident. My spleen ruptured and had to be removed. I experienced excruciating pain and boredom over the next eight months going in and out of the hospital, either in traction or in a body cast. I lost more weight and sunk deeper into depression. The resulting deep scars and slight leg-length discrepancy gave me more reasons to hate my body. After six months of using a walker and another six on crutches, I finally returned to college. Then just three weeks into my fall semester, my sister summoned me home. My mother had lung cancer. The doctor estimated six months . . . but in fact, she died two weeks later. I totally shut down. I felt lost and alone. My brothers, sisters, and I were all so traumatized. We didn't know how to support each other. My health declined. Severe trauma, several surgeries, and a year on pain medication and drugs, left my body a mess. I went from one doctor to another with no luck . . . nothing worked. Lost, alone, and scared, I still somehow managed to finish college.

Then one day I met an angel, a work associate who suggested I try a natural remedy. I followed her advice and actually felt better. Now curious about natural medicine, I read everything I could get my hands on, and learned about the causes of disease. I took vitamins, ate organic foods, and drank bottled water. I bought organic body care products. I cleansed my body through herbs and fasting. The dentist removed all metal fillings from my teeth. I filtered my shower water. I sought out holistic healers and garnered great benefit from chiropractic treatments, massage, yoga, acupuncture, and other alternative healing modalities. I pursued a spiritual search. I planned to live forever!

On May 16, 1999, I scheduled a routine mammogram as the fibrous cysts in one of my breasts reduced size. I assumed the reduction meant the cysts were going away and wanted to know how long that would take. The thought of cancer never entered my mind. I was shocked and devastated to learn that I had a nine-centimeter tumor in my right breast.

My only treatment option, a mastectomy followed by chemo and radiation, sounded like an assault to me. After twenty-five years of pristine body care, how could I allow someone to pump poisons into my veins? Over the difficult next few weeks the doctors performed numerous tests to determine if the cancer might have spread to other parts of my body. Fortunately, it did not. I scheduled the mastectomy and reconstruction. Because of my busy work schedule and the need to support my family, I focused on getting this nightmare behind me.

I examined my life patterns that led to so much stress. As the main breadwinner, I always put my family first and pushed myself to the point that my life was completely out of balance. I realized that I couldn't give my family any support if I was no longer here. Looking within for spiritual guidance, I realized how I created stress by not aligning my spirituality with my actions. I couldn't create what I wanted if I didn't heal my deeper wounds. I spent my whole life running away from the pain of my feelings of abandonment. Now it stared me in the face.

I determined to focus on healing, and attended workshops that would create the space for me to grieve the losses of my father, my mother, my body, and my health. Because of these experiences, I saw my cancer as a gift. I needed to slow down and examine my life patterns. I recalled that someone at my mother's funeral fondly said, "Betty lived a full life. She burned the candle at both ends." I suddenly realized that I followed her same pattern. And I didn't want the same outcome. I sought help in dealing with my workaholism, stress, and underlying grief. The first gift came in the form of blessings from others. I experienced an unexpected outpouring of love. My mother-in-law's entire church prayed for me every day. My friends and family sent me love and healing thoughts. My husband offered support in many ways, and my kids grew strong and caring. I knew everything would be just fine.

The surgery took its toll, both physically and emotionally. I had just reached a point of acceptance of my battered body and now losing a breast became a real setback. During the major reconstruction, the surgeon pulled up muscle from my abdomen to form a new breast. When I woke up, I saw tubes everywhere. Although I felt pain, my new breast was pretty amazing. . . .

Following my cancer, surgery, and subsequent healing, I entered a deep process of learning to love my battered body. I fully appreciated my amazing body that survived accidents, childbirth, and surgeries. My dedication to natural foods and healing gave me the resilience to survive and rebound after each trauma.

However, as I strived to experience true vitality, new levels of grief emerged. At this point, I realized that my greatest sense of gratitude was yet to come. As I ventured into the next phase of my healing, I really thanked God I had gotten cancer. During August of 2005, I experienced a profound healing through gratitude. I attended a 10-day leadership-training program on a remote island in northern Canada. Along with nineteen other participants and four leaders, I immersed myself in a series of individual and group processes designed to facilitate healing and self-realization. Many terrifying and wonderful experiences filled the week, combining the best of traditional management training with Eastern spirituality and Native American ritual. The activities included a ropes course, several sweat lodges, group gestalt work, and a three-day vision quest. I moved through many levels of emotional and spiritual openings that allowed me to emerge in a state of fearlessness and deep reflection.

One of my most profound healing experiences came during a process through which I reached a deep state of gratitude. The final night, we each had the opportunity to work with our support groups to design an experience for ourselves. We were to formulate a personal performance that would allow us to stretch outside of our comfort zone. I thought of doing a simple performance on relationships. But after getting some rather sobering feedback from the leaders, I knew I was playing it too safe. So I decided to take the risk and embrace this opportunity. I loved and totally trusted this strong community of people, and I thought to myself that I might not get this opportunity ever again. The sharing process commenced after dinner. As they drew names out of a hat, I hoped to be drawn last. I wanted it to be very dark. Some of the performances were quite entertaining. I accepted the invitation to play a support role in two of the light-hearted skits. But deep down, I was still very nervous. My performance would not be funny. Fortunately, I was the second-to-last person selected.

When they called my name, I asked someone to turn down the lights while I slipped into a back room to prepare. I removed my jeans and put on a light wrap-around skirt and a blouse over my under-wear. I debated about keeping my shoes on. I wear a lift on one shoe, a remnant from my car accident, which I usually try to hide. But my chal-lenge was to learn to love my body with all its imperfections. So I kept them on, re-entered the room, and addressed the group. I shared how I had spent most of my life hating my body. And with all its flaws, I asked them to be my witnesses as I went through a process of loving my body. Someone started the music I selected. As the Moonlight Sonata began to play, I closed my eyes, went into a trance, and moved around like a ballerina in slow motion. I felt a new sense of flow and freedom. A few moments later, I sat on a chair, slipped off my shoes, and gently touched my feet and legs, feeling gratitude for their unwavering sup-port over the past fifty-four years. As I looked at the parts of me I had always wanted to hide, my tears flowed. I arose and again moved around as I slowly removed my clothes. I allowed myself to feel love for my body, the tears turned to sobs, a mixture of grief and gratitude. I felt terrified and electrified at the same time. Removing all but my panties, I moved gently around the room a final time experiencing such love, acceptance, and fullness that I felt truly transcendent. I knew the music well, as it was my favorite piece to play on the piano. So as the end neared, I gracefully lowered my body as I continued weeping. On the final note, several women covered me with a blanket. I felt full and empty at the same time.

Over the next few days, I felt a sense of lightness unlike anything I had ever experienced. I felt as if my heart totally opened to take in love from everywhere. I was euphoric for days. Over the next few weeks, I slowly grounded myself back into my normal routine. I am still in the process of integrating this experience as I learn to really love and accept my body and myself. And beyond that, I am learning to listen to my body for introspection and guidance. Through meditations in sunlight, I feel the lovely warmth caress my body and spirit. This empowers me to be more intuitive and self-directed in my healthcare.

Last year, I developed precancerous calcifications in my other breast. One doctor advised a partial mastectomy, which would basically destroy the breast. Another wanted me to take hormone-suppressing drugs that had the potential to ruin my skin, my moods, and my sleep. I viewed it all as another wake-up call to determine where my life might be out of balance. Thank God, I got this message again. Recognizing some of my old patterns, I asked myself why I was so driven. I hold a Master's Degree in statistics, have an international best-selling book; attend a PhD program for organizational development while running an active consulting business, support three kids in college, and am building a house in the mountains. I still modeled my crazed life after my mother.

I examined the driving force and realized that I mistake admiration for love. I felt an obligation to continue achieving. Then I thought about my friends and realized I'm never around to be a good friend to anyone. And, if some loved me only because I was successful, then they weren't really my friends at all.

I took a year's leave from school to create room in my life for more relaxation and fun. I'm still working on finding the perfect balance. I probably still work too many hours. But I do make time to be with friends. I eat a very healthy diet with lots of raw foods and juicing. I practice hot yoga twice a week. And most importantly, I look for gratitude in each and every experience. I can honestly say that I wouldn't want to go back and change a thing. I have three beautiful children, wonderful friends and family, and a career that I love. I look at each experience as an opportunity for growth. I feel joy and gratitude every day as I focus on a bright future with many dreams yet to fulfill. I thank God for the wisdom I gained through all my hardships that empower me to continue on this path.

❤   ❤   ❤

Olivia Parr-Rud is an internationally known speaker, trainer, and author of *Data Mining Cookbook* (Wiley 2001). She consults and trains worldwide through her company, OLIVIAGroup.

Olivia is a partner in 4 C Alignment, through which she conducts research into the link between organizational development and complexity science. She has been working with clients for several years in areas of communication, change management, team building, and leadership development. Her upcoming book, *Business Intelligence Success Factors, Aligning for Success in a Global Economy*, comes out in late 2008. She contributes regularly to the *Business Intelligence Network*, where she serves as an expert in organizational alignment and data mining. As well as being a cancer survivor, Olivia is a mother of three talented adult children. She currently lives in Philadelphia.

Thank God
My Mom Died

JOHN CASTAGNINI

*W*hat was the most terrifying day of your life?

On January 9, 2005, my mom, Lorraine Castagnini, left this world at age fifty-six. She was not just my mom — she was my best friend, whom I spoke with almost every day. After her death, a torturous new mantra took possession of me: "I tried so hard, but obviously not hard enough, to help her discover her road to health."

My mom loved being a mother more than she loved anything else. During my childhood, many of my friends didn't have a close relationship with their mothers, so my mom became a mom to each of them. I guess this petite Italian woman from Brooklyn enjoyed chasing little boys around the kitchen table with a wooden pasta spoon!

Mom truly knew me, in many ways better than I knew myself, straight up to the day she died. She would often quote the serenity prayer to me:

"God grant me the serenity to accept the things I cannot change,
The courage to change the things I can,
And the wisdom to know the difference."

For the final five months that my mom was on this earth, we were at extreme odds. We warred over a time of great confusion to me, and of my separation from my childhood sweetheart. The evening before Mom died, I didn't even see her as my mom anymore: I saw a woman whom the doctors turned into a legalized drug addict.

The day of her death, mortified and gasping between gushing rivers of tears, I bellowed, "That's it. She's gone. It's over." I allowed the doctors to kill her with those pills, and I hadn't done enough to stop them. It was murder, and her blood was on my hands. I had tuned out her cries for help. I could have . . . should have saved her. It was all my fault — I didn't take the time to hear her screaming, begging to be heard and loved. Instead, I fought furiously every day to learn, to achieve, to compete and create. As a result, I missed cherishing and treasuring this most valuable gift the universe shared with me. Now it haunted my mind: *I could have, I should have* . . . over and over. *Please cut off my head. I can't stop hearing it!*

I staggered under the grief, as if I had control of the death card. Oh, the ignorance. Consumed, confused, obsessed, and alone, this little boy wanted his mommy. Nothing and no one would stop me. I was going to find her. I recall the first sign of sun a month later, under Florida skies. I met a fiery woman named Lorraine. *Lorraine!* (It was not the most popular name.) She was fifty-six. *Fifty-six! Like Mom!* She was from New York City (*like Mom!*) and was another chain-smoker, too. (Mom loved those damn cigarettes.)

I stared through this woman and *knew*, with *absolute certainty*, that her birthday was January 9 (the same day my mom had passed). I was right. Now, what the hell are the chances of that? Here stood living, breathing confirmation that Mom was still around here somewhere. The mind's manifestation powers are truly amazing.

Eventually I stopped looking outside and delved deeper within. I constructed a beautiful scrapbook of our life together. It began with a few simple pictures and became a year of daily meditation in scrapbook build-

ing! I honored our precious moments and all she ever was to me. Finally, I
observed how I visited her pretty much every day. I deliberately lived four
blocks away.

I then re-read this poem I had once written and shared with her:

MY MOTHER

All you are to me, you will never know.
There is not enough paper in heaven to list it.
Simply know that my will to become one with the
Heavens through life's most difficult tribulations is your
*   greatest gift.*

This rock I build upon
In order to speak with God more every day,
It is the incessant tenacity I harbor,
Allowing me to twinkle, one day shine,
Eventually bursting into stardust.

I appreciate this will more than anything.
It brings me closer to now, and
Gives me the strength to hurdle every fear
Impeding my path to a greater understanding
And a more profound experience in living.

Magically, I found a new, deeper, more profound relationship
with her. I listened in ways I couldn't before. I heard her, and we *both*
discovered a new "one another," closer and deeper in our communication. Before, there was my mom; now, there is my mom and a free soul
guiding my spirit. I understood — this beautiful woman came to this
planet to be a mother. She wanted to die a mother. Her boys were turning into men, and dying was her only way of letting go. She couldn't
let go and stay here with us. She had to leave for us to really think for
ourselves.

This woman who birthed me
Gave me a second life in her dying.
She knew in order for me to grow
I would have to do it on my own.

Since her death, I try to listen more closely and open my heart wider to others, and myself, just the way she lived. Thank you, Mom, for this empathy and dedication to listening beyond just what I want to hear. Mom, I understand it was your time to leave. I understand and honor your freedom to change. I realize that no matter how hard I would have tried to shift our roles a bit, and tell you what I think you should do, you wanted to live and die "The Mother." Thank you for this gift of serenity for what I could not change. God knows, no one was going to change you.

By my facing this great challenge, your leaving so young and so suddenly, you instilled in me the courage to discover and change the only thing I ever really can: my own mind. Thank you for the courage to share our story, my work, with humanity. I will cherish this courage you bestowed upon me in every breath, until my very last.

Thank you for leading me further toward this path to
    wisdom.
Letting go and changing can be oh, so difficult.
I pray with you for your constant guidance,
For the wisdom "to know the difference."

Thank you, God, for my mom's life and all our precious
    moments.
Thank you, God, for my mom's death. It has brought to me
    this priceless wisdom.
Yes, Mom I finally understand the serenity prayer.

Thank you, Mom. Your dying helped me reach a place to
    create
This book series, where thousands of people are sharing their
    stories of gratitude and love.

Your lessons to me are helping to open millions of hearts,
Through their greatest trials and tribulations.
You're one powerful little woman in your life, and even
        more in your death.

I thank God, for in His taking you away from me, you are eternally closer. Yes, Mom, when you left I was lost, but thanks to you, I now am found. I was blind, but now I see.

♥   ♥   ♥

Having studied "spiritually" for almost two decades, and inspired by the great minds of history, John Castagnini conceived of the *Thank God I . . .* series in 2006. He states, "There is nothing I love more than to conceive an inspired idea, bathed in God's great laws, and to shower its manifestation." John attended chiropractic school, holds a degree in biology, studied various martial arts forms, and worked with Dr. Wayne Dyer and Dr. John Demartini. He has authored over a dozen books, written over 2000 poems, and is finishing his second music CD as singer/pianist under the title *150 Moons*. "My mission is to share bits of wisdom in this gift of life and hopefully create a masterpiece along the way. My dream is to unite great networks that help unify and empower the soul of humanity to assist one another in becoming the true identity of love."

Thank God
My Father Went to Prison

Close To My Dad Once Again

LISA KAYE

When I was a little girl, my dad and I were close. I always felt safe around him. At 6'3" and 215 pounds, my dad, a former pro heavyweight boxer, seemed to me to be invincible. Dad was very liberal in what he would allow us kids (my older sister, my younger brother, and me) to do. We grew up on a dairy farm, and he let us do things other parents wouldn't allow their kids to try for fear of their getting hurt.

Dad drove big, heavy farm equipment, often with a big wagon pulled behind. He'd let us kids hang onto the wagon and run on the road behind it. We climbed on the rafters of the barn, then jumped into a pile of hay ... or into his arms. We climbed onto the barn roof and slid down. Dad also let us watch a cow being butchered. He allowed us to do these things to prevent us from becoming wimps. I, in turn, saw him as a cool dad, a fun dad. Dad had a private pilot's license, as did Granddad, who owned a plane. Dad took us kids flying in Granddad's plane, and then executed thrilling maneuvers, doing loop-de-loops in the air, flying under power lines, and gliding over the

ocean. I remember, one time, he landed us in a field. We were close
back then. I loved him and looked up to him.

During the year my parents divorced, Dad and I grew apart. I was
in second grade then. Suddenly Dad was around a lot less often and
paid less attention to me. He dated other women, growing closer to
them, but at the same time, growing more distant from me . . . and
me from him. I had no idea who these other women were, but I saw
his involvement with them as a threat to the safety and intimacy of
the relationship I had with him. Now we saw him only every other
weekend, or even less often. The relationship between the two of us
slowly changed. Life went on. I moved along from second grade to
third, fourth, and fifth. Then I focused on getting my dad's attention
and some reaction from him. I was a good student, notably so in math,
which was high on his list of values. I became an athlete, knowing that
was also important to him.

However, he remained distracted by other events in his life, and I
didn't get to see him very often. In a sense, this had a positive effect on
me: I tried harder at both my athletics and my studies, in my ongoing
campaign to get his recognition. As I grew older, certain aspects of his
lifestyle and beliefs bothered me, and so, although our relationship
at this point was positive, I kept it at a superficial level. I no longer
allowed any emotional intimacy between us. One of the things that
bothered me about his life surfaced when a family member attended
high school, and Dad dated one of her best friends. Though she was
totally OK with this relationship — in fact, she thought it was fabulous
that my dad was dating one of her closest friends — I was mortified
that my dad, then forty-two, would date an eighteen-year-old.

I was no longer a virgin and would talk to this same family member
about sex and the guys in my life, but I wasn't comfortable telling
my dad. She, on the other hand, was very open with Dad about her
sex life, though I didn't think it was an appropriate conversation for
a young woman to have with my father. The friend wasn't the only
much-younger woman whom Dad dated. During my senior year, Dad
remarked that he thought my best friend was cute. Attracted to older
men, she followed through on the compliment without my knowledge,
and the two of them wound up sleeping together. Neither of them told

me at the time; I found out only later on. Then when I entered college, Dad asked one of the girls on my basketball team out. She told me about it and said that she thought he was a great guy, but she had no interest in dating him. I approached Dad and told him that his asking her out was unacceptable to both her and to me. I told Dad I didn't want him coming out and being supportive of the team anymore because his behavior embarrassed me.

The incident leading to the chain of events that sent Dad to prison took place in August of '98. Dad dated a woman I'll call "Renee," who had a six-year-old daughter. Renee left the child with Dad while she went out somewhere. Things were fine as they played together until they decided to play a kissing game. The little girl would say, "Kiss my foot," and Dad would comply. "Kiss my arm," and he did. "Kiss my cheek," and Dad kissed her cheek. The child, delighted, laughed and laughed. Then she directed Dad, "Kiss my ginie (vagina)." And he did that, too.

Renee came home, and soon it was bath time for her daughter. During the bath, the little girl happily told Renee about the game she played with Dad. Renee confronted Dad, who readily acknowledged kissing the little girl's vagina, but he added, "It was a game. We were just playing." Dad and Renee discussed not only what had happened but also the possible consequences. If the girl told her father, Renee's ex, would Renee lose custody of the child? Renee and Dad decided it would be better if Dad went to the authorities and told them himself.

Having no cell phone and not wanting to call from Renee's house, Dad drove to the nearest payphone, from which he called the police and gave them a forthright account of the occurrence. The police asked him questions over the phone, then told him they needed to talk to him more extensively. They sent a police car to pick him up at the phone booth and bring him back to the station house. To Dad, the whole thing was no big deal. "I just wanted to make sure you guys knew," he told the cops. But to them it was a big deal. They arrested him. At the county jail, he went through the whole arraignment process and they eventually offered a deal: If he pled guilty to rape, he could get probation and no prison time, but he would have to enroll in a sex offenders' therapy program called SOSA, as well as several other restrictions. One of these restrictions stated that he could not read or watch any form of pornography. Dad took the deal, pleading guilty to rape but not to child molestation. He enrolled in the SOSA program and attended weekly therapy.

Initially, Dad was very upfront with the three of us siblings about his arrest. He called my sister, our brother, and me and told each of us the details of his arrest. One day, after Dad had been on probation for a while, his probation officer showed up for a surprise visit. Checking the cookies on Dad's computer, he discovered that someone — and he had to assume it was Dad — had visited a porno site, a clear violation of the terms of his probation. The authorities confiscated Dad's computer and took him into custody. I have never asked Dad if he really had visited the porn site, or if some friend of his might have been the one who accessed it. But his probation officer and the court system were thoroughly persuaded of his guilt.

The court released Dad from custody on his own recognizance and told him to come back the following week. But instead of doing so, he took off. Afraid he'd get a ten-year sentence for violation of his probation terms, he decided to run from the law and head to California. For a year, none of us knew his location. But Dad's parents, elderly and with whom Dad was close, lived a few states away, and he would travel there periodically to check on them, in spite of trying to keep a low profile and stay out of sight. One day, a cousin saw him there and called the police. They arrested him. In November of 2000, he received the full ten-year prison sentence, which he currently serves.

When all this happened — his initial arrest, his taking it on the run, and finally the prison sentence — I tried to be understanding and forgiving. After all, everybody makes mistakes. Nonetheless, despite my attempt to forgive him, his actions were unacceptable and wrong to my way of thinking. During the year Dad hid from the police, he struggled financially, and he urged me to help him monetarily. I didn't want to get in trouble legally for helping a fugitive, nor did I agree with his actions, so I refused to help him.

Initially his conviction shocked, disappointed, and embarrassed me. I didn't tell anyone that my dad was in prison, or why. I was mortified and humiliated to have anyone think my father was a child molester. And it was not just for the sake of his reputation . . . I was also concerned with what people would think of me. A family member, on the other hand, told people freely, which made me furious at her. I felt strongly that having my father in prison for child molestation was something nobody should know about.

After Dad shipped off to prison, he'd write to me periodically. But I didn't care for writing and didn't do much of it . . . which meant I rarely wrote back to him. However, he did have access to the prison payphone. All calls had to be collect, but I didn't mind paying, so I accepted the charges, and we'd talk. We communicated in this way . . . though we had still not regained the closeness of my early childhood.

In 1997, I had my first child, another in 1999, and the third in 2001. Inevitably, my husband and I discussed what kind of relationship we would let our kids have with their granddad, considering his actions. (I should interject at this point that Dad never said or did anything of a sexual nature to either my sister or to me when we were children.) My husband was adamant that my dad should not be around the kids. I wanted my kids to have a good relationship with their grandfather. Naturally I didn't want him to do anything wrong to them, but I didn't think he would.

The point I particularly want to make here, though, is that Dad's incarceration proved to be a turning point in our relationship: We grew closer once again. There was something about his being in prison that made me feel safer, made me feel that I could have a better, more open relationship with him. I let my guard down with him. I knew he couldn't do anything that might embarrass me now — that was part of the equation — and for whatever other reasons, I found it easier to talk to him.

My marriage hit some serious snags, and in 2001, my husband and I started marriage counseling. I'd talk to my dad about the conversations with the counselor and the problems in the marriage that had led us into counseling in the first place. Dad became my confidante, someone with whom I could talk freely. Because he was in prison and talked to few people on the phone, I opened up to him more easily, and our conversations were more authentic.

In September of 2004, my husband and I discussed divorce, and I started an affair. My dad was one of the few people to whom I felt comfortable divulging either of these facts. I told hardly anyone other than my closest friend, but I felt I could tell my dad because he wasn't judgmental. He was open-minded about so many things that I knew he wouldn't try to talk me out of doing what I was doing, nor would he judge me, even though, in the eyes of society, I knew my actions would be judged as bad and wrong.

I told Dad all the details, knowing he was a male whom I could talk to about my husband and the divorce process. Knowing Dad was in prison made it safer to have these very private conversations with him. My life became so dramatic that Dad would call me regularly once or twice a week to learn the latest events. This gave me an outlet, someone to talk to, and so he became one of my best friends. I could talk to Dad about anything.

In January of '06, I started working with Dr. John Demartini. I attended different conferences, and learned more about the *Demartini Method®*, applying it more, and doing more of the collapses that he teaches. My dad still called me weekly, and when he did, I would tell him everything I was learning. He would ask me questions about it, so I shared more and more of what I was doing.

At the time, my kids were five, seven, and nine. The two youngest were girls, and they became more intent on finding out what Grandpa had done that had resulted in his going to prison. My dodge at first was to answer, "Because he broke the law," then later, when that wasn't enough for them, "He did something that wasn't very nice to someone." But they grew more insistent about learning the specifics. Finally, in the spring of '06 I had done enough work with John to know that I wanted to tell them. But I didn't know how to tell them in a way where they wouldn't think what he had done was wrong or bad. I wasn't negatively defining what he had done; my position with the kids was simply that their granddad broke the law and had to be punished for it. I asked for a one-on-one consult with John. I wanted to make sure I had no reactions of my own left, in viewing what Dad had done as bad, wrong, or negative. If I worked through it with John, I would be sure I had no emotional charges around it; then I could tell my kids and be sure they had no emotional charges around it either. I had been very open about the reproductive organs and the genitalia with my kids from the start. They were very familiar with words like "vagina" and "penis," knew where babies came from, and knew all about sex. They were educated enough to deal with the conversation as long as I was able to tell them. John and I talked about what Dad had done. A hundred years ago, it would not have been against the law, and another hundred years from now it might once again be legal. In other cultures right now, it's acceptable, including cultures where the father has sex with a daughter before she gets married.

I sat down to answer the kids' long-asked question as to what their granddad had done. As I took a seat, the phone rang. It was Dad. I put him on speaker as I prepared to explain, and I told the kids what he had done and explained how it had occurred in the context of a game. I added the explanation that it is against our state law to touch a minor sexually if you're over eighteen. I added that if they're both either over eighteen or both under eighteen, it's not a crime. So, under the circumstances as they had occurred, my father broke the law, "and that's why Grandpa is in prison." The kids were mostly blasé in their reactions. "Is that all?" they asked. And then they got up and ran off to play. The *Demartini Method*® helped.

If you do the *Demartini Method*® and collapse the negative perceptions you have around what happened, you can come to see that the little girl whose "ginie" he kissed wasn't "actually" harmed. She may or may not have experienced pain from the event, but both pain and pleasure serve equally. Everything serves, and it is our choice to discover how even our most challenging events serve us. In this case, society might try to make the girl feel harmed, but that is just a matter of perception. It was an event that played out between them, like shaking a hand or rubbing a back. There are as many benefits as challenges that came out of the situation and it is up to her to choose to find them. It may appear difficult to find these benefits, but they are there if you take the time to look. When this girl discovers that there were as many benefits as there were drawbacks to the event, she will no longer be a "victim." At that point, she will experience the truth of the event and become thankful for it. As an example of a benefit, consider that many girls and women don't understand the power and control their femininity has with men. However, if they become involved with a brother, uncle, or dad at a young age, they can learn about that power through these events. This was a lesson I didn't learn until I was 38 years old when I did the *Demartini Method®* on child molestation and worked directly with other women who had experienced it. I would not have achieved this understanding without the *Demartini Method®*.

In two years, Dad will be released from prison. I can't be sure what the dynamics of our relationship will be like then, but I know that as of now our relationship is vastly improved as a direct result of him being sent to prison. If not for that, I would surely not have regained my former closeness with my father or been able to confide in him as I've done for some time now. He's not a bad man, and he is a good dad. I love him, and I am grateful that we are once again close and able to talk to each other freely. I don't think we'll lose that when he is freed. I believe that, thanks to his being sent to prison, I have found my way back to my dad again.

❤   ❤   ❤

Lisa Kaye is a dynamic woman, who loves work, family, and friends. Her high-powered lifestyle includes travel, study, and extraordinary experiences. Lisa is a successful financial planner, a mother of three amazing kids, and a student of the mysteries of life. Today Lisa Kaye lives in beautiful downtown Seattle, WA, ready to create her next adventure.

Thank God
My Husband Died

LuAn Mitchell

*G*od has called me heavenward. — Philippians 3:14

The news was out. The headline of the cover story read, *Every day is special when life is a gift.*

That was the headline of an article written about the ordeal experienced by my late husband, Fred Mitchell. It went on to say that Fred "had a new way of thinking" after receiving a heart and double-lung transplant. A reporter by the name of Marg Ommanney wrote this lovely, sensitive article. I remember that when she interviewed my husband and me, we were concerned that a "cold, hard fact" reporter might not understand that we were grateful for everything and that we would remain open to be grateful for absolutely everything that God had in store for us.

Some said we lived in La La Land, that we could not possibly have all our faculties. "Just look at the guy," they would mock. "He already looks like death warmed over!" But they didn't know Fred, and they didn't know our undying faith and level of gratitude for it all. The article went on to say, "Those who fear Hell seek religion. Those who have been to Hell seek God."

My husband suffered from cystic fibrosis, North America's number-one genetic killer of whites. It attacks the lungs and digestive system. Few sufferers, it is said, live past the age of twenty-six. My husband was thirty-nine years of age when he was diagnosed. This was shortly before our marriage. The prognosis was chilling: Fred could expect to live only four, maybe five more years without a miracle intervention.

It was February 25th, 1990, when he underwent the grueling six-hour heart and double-lung transplant at the Stanford Medical Centre near San Francisco, California. He recovered completely after several bumps in the road. We attended regular cardio rehab sessions, and he was also taken back into the operating room for more corrective surgeries, but two more children later (we already had a toddler son), Fred served to be a great teacher of personal growth and keeping the faith — no matter what!

I have heard that "More tears are shed for answered prayers than for unanswered ones." I must say this quote of Truman Capote's rings true. When I find myself "wallowing and questioning," I remember when my husband would say, "Don't feel sorry for me. I give thanks for it all, honey. I am just the co-pilot. God is the pilot!" (Meanwhile, while being around a grateful guy like this, I would catch myself complaining about a simple thing like a hangnail and feel so embarrassed and ashamed!)

Fred reminded us of the truth of this life: that we are here to learn and to grow. With his thankful attitude, he was a great teacher to many. Fred would watch us all scramble for words and facial expressions as we observed the anti-rejection drugs he was on wreak havoc on his body, but they never quenched his spirit. With a sly grin, he would offer many tidbits of wisdom to soothe our souls. This one comes to mind: "You know people complain about stuff" . . . "I can remember lying on the operating room table, wondering if I would wake up or not." Then he would add, with his usual happy tone, "I think it is so important to live each day as if it is our *only* day — not our first or our last, but as if it is our only day!"

During his life, he attributed his new energy and "priority list" to some great medicine and to the Lord. Fred liked to be recorded even when he was not at his physical best. His voice rings on in video recordings, which I watch with our family even now, in amazement, as this strong-willed, grateful-for-it-all guy reminds us when he speaks his truth: "I really appreciate having a second chance. Despite the fact that I am back working hard again, this time I feel I have God with me. I really have a very strong belief in God. I thank him for my life. It is a miracle. I didn't do it — I let him do it."

He continues to hit home with me when his voice, still in print and recorded on tape, shares his advanced wisdom. He tells us, "I feel I have been through hell, yet my spiritual connection — my belief in God, in forgiveness, in love, in being non-judgmental — is growing."

The "sick guy" then gently "lowers the big blow" — at least, that is how it feels for me as his widow, when he says from beyond the grave, "Every moment is special to me. It is just a joy to be alive, to be able to hug my wife again, my kids, my family." Talk about a reality check! I'd had a "bad day" — how dare he say it is all good?! Oh gee, I wanted to be more like him. I wanted to see the good in everything too. I really did. I decided others needed to learn from him also!

I brought in a big screen to my husband's funeral wake (everyone thought I was nuts!), and then I surprised them all and played some of the footage. *Wow!* The people were stunned. They spun their heads around in disbelief when a dead man shared his gratitude for it *all* . . . not for this part and that part, but gratitude for it all . . . at his own funeral. Fred said to the assembled crowd from the large screen, "People say they feel sorry for me, what I've gone through. I say, *don't!* I wouldn't trade what I've been through for anything. It's a whole new start. It's such a wonder." His death sparked new life. Some of us are like the living dead, but that day, none of us was.

Today:

My late husband would be proud to see the children today, and how they have grown. But even more than that, he would love my living husband — the man I found, the man I would have never been with if my first husband would have stayed on Earth and denied his

calling. They now have an "earth daddy," and an "angel daddy ,"
Reese, is a great father to these blessed children, his only children. I
feel so blessed! Reese is their new living hero, and he has respect and
admiration for the courageous and faithful man named Fred, the man
we have both sat and learned from in this life, whom we have watched
together in recordings and read about in print . . . and seen still present
on this earth in the lives that remain better because he lived, because he
shared, and just because.

Fred Mitchell speaks to us this day. He says to us all, "Faith in
God — that has been my salvation." So I say now in this moment, Yes,
I too thank God. I thank God that my husband died, for it has renewed
my faith in God, because Fred taught us all when he kept his faith,
when all others were losing theirs.

And so, the way I see it, we need to share his wisdom with the living.
Then there is real hope for the whole world. Fred encouraged laughter,
so in his honor I will close with this quote on death and dying: "I'm not
afraid to die. I just don't want to be there when it happens." — Woody
Allen

❤   ❤   ❤

From America to Australia and Madrid to Mexico, inspired audiences
are leaping to their feet after hearing LuAn Mitchell's message of genuine hope, unwavering faith, and personal commitment to action. LuAn
is a woman who has overcome adversity on every front, and she can
show you to do the same. Her life is a story of tragedy and triumph,
emerging every time to reach the pinnacle of business, family, and personal success.

Thank God
I Was a Racist

BRUCE MUZIK

I pulled up to my new home and felt terror in the pit of my stomach. But, I knew I had to go through with this. I saw the same fear in Dad's eyes. "Are you sure you really want to do this?" he asked. I nodded and got out of the car. Next door, two people sat on empty beer crates, drinking beer, on the otherwise deserted street. I wanted to move into my new home quietly, with time to adjust to my new surroundings. But it was too late. The beer drinkers came over to find out why Dad and I were unloading boxes from my truck.

Another local arrived to watch, and within minutes, twenty-five staring people surrounded us, faces as black as night. One of them, a woman, came forward, "Umlungu ('white man,' in the Xhosa tongue), what you doing?"

"I'm moving in," I told her warily as I pointed toward the dilapidated "shantytown" house that was my home for the next thirty days. I sensed her confusion as she turned to the others and translated what I'd said into Xhosa, their native language. As if in slow motion, the looks upon their faces turned from curiosity to disbelief. The crowd murmured in unison as they grappled with the concept of a white man moving into their black community in the township of Guguletu, the African equivalent of a ghetto or shantytown. Unsure of my real motives, the woman introduced herself to me as Maureen, my new neighbor. "What do you mean you are moving in?" Maureen asked.

I decided to tell the truth, as difficult as it was for me to admit. "I recently discovered that I'm a racist," I told her boldly, not wanting her to know how terrified I was, "and I'm moving into Guguletu to learn about your culture and conquer my fear of black people." A look of shock crossed their faces.

Two weeks earlier, I'd stood in front of a room filled with a hundred and ten people in a personal development course, clutching a microphone. David, the wonderfully powerful man leading the course, said, "How many black friends do you have, Bruce?"

"Uh, three," I lied, not wanting to admit that, in fact, I didn't have any close black friends. It wasn't that I didn't like black people; it's just that I never made the time to get to know any of them on more than a superficial level.

"You mean to say that you live in a country where eighty percent of the population is black — that's 40 million people — and you are friendly with only three of them?" David asked incredulously, pacing his words for maximum effect. A hush fell over the room as David patiently waited for his words to sink in and for me to answer.

Put that way, it did sound ridiculous. I laughed nervously as the reality of David's question revealed my hypocrisy. For years, I'd despised the apartheid regime in South Africa, and when the country finally had its first democratic elections in 1994, I rejoiced and proudly claimed my title as a New South African. Now, nine years on, I still did not have any black friends.

"I think I'm just scared of getting to know them", I admitted.

The apartheid government of the "old" South Africa conditioned us to believe that black people were third-class citizens, while white people were first-class citizens. In my growing up years, the media taught us to fear black people. On a subconscious level, this fear became normal for me, even though consciously I knew it to be wrong. I grew up in an area surrounded by imposing brick walls with electric fences to keep black people out. Black people perpetrated most of the crimes reported by the newspapers. I learned to lock the doors of my car to make sure that nobody hijacked it, and although never spoken aloud, nobody ever expected a white person to hijack a car. My local beach had an intimidating fence down the middle, separating the huge, sandy "white" beach from the much smaller, rocky "black" beach. We had buses for whites and buses for blacks. At one point in time, black people could not walk on the streets after 7 P.M.

"So, Bruce, would you like to get to know some of your fellow black South Africans?" David asked. I nodded introspectively, and David continued, "How are you going to do that?"

"Well, I guess I can go and talk to them. I can chat with the car guards outside my office, and I'll even sponsor some of them to do this course if they want to," I replied, excited at the prospect of completing this uncomfortable conversation and getting back to the anonymity of my seat in the audience.

"Well, that'll make you feel good for a few days, but it certainly won't change your life or your attitude to black people, will it?" I knew David was right, but I felt awkward and put on the spot. Aargh! Where was he going with this? "What's the best way to get to know someone?" David asked.

"Live with them?" I answered tentatively.

"That might do it. Why not go and live with some black people and get over your fear of them?" This suggestion was too much for me. Was he insane? How could a white guy go and live in an African township? How ridiculous.

I thanked David for his advice and returned to the safety of my seat. The rest of that day was hell for me. He'd challenged me to go and live with black people, and I'd chickened out. I was a coward, and I knew it. I hated the feeling. That night I slept restlessly and awoke early to return to the course. At breakfast, my landlady, whose luxury three-story mansion I was house-sitting at the time, informed me that she'd be traveling for six months and planned to lock up the house. She gave me six weeks' notice to move out and find a new place to live. This was just too synchronous to be coincidence. Yesterday I'm challenged to live with black people, and today I am asked to move? Slowly it dawned on me that perhaps the Powers That Be wanted me to take David up on his challenge and move to an African township.

Now, two weeks later, here I was moving into an area called the "Kak Yard" (crap yard), which earned its name because its crime-ridden streets were once inhabited by the "scum" of society in the township of Guguletu, just outside Cape Town. As far as I know, I was the only white man for miles among tens of thousands of black people.

Maureen looked visibly shocked to hear my admission of being a racist. She translated to the now-baffled and suspicious locals who, after a few seconds of silence, proceeded to laugh as if this was the funniest joke they had ever heard. I later found out that some of them suspected I was a part of a secret police operation sent to infiltrate and spy on them.

"Can we help you carry your boxes into the house?" Maureen offered, catching me off guard.

Oh, crap! Now I am truly screwed. I thought to myself. If I don't let them carry my boxes, they'll be offended and reject me from their community. That's just what I don't want. However, if I do let them carry my boxes, they are going to steal them. I caught myself mid-thought as I recognized my racist conditioning taking control of my mind again. This was just what I had come here to conquer. "Sure" I replied "why not?"

Several white-toothed, grinning new neighbors walked toward me and proceeded to haul my boxes off my truck into my new home. As I walked into my "new" dilapidated home, we were greeted by hundreds of cockroaches and a damp moldy smell. Although definitely several steps down from the luxury mansion I had been living in, I wasn't bothered. I wanted an authentic African experience, and this was definitely it!

Maureen and my new neighbors stacked my boxes neatly in a corner of the living room, and the celebrations began. The welcome party that ensued was unlike any I've experienced. For the next two hours, they hugged, kissed, questioned, fed, and generally treated me like the prodigal son returning home. My neighbors' unconditional generosity and love overwhelmed me. I'll never forget the image of two enormous African women sprinting down the road, their voluptuous bodies heaving in slow motion as they closed in on me shouting "Umlungu, Umlungu!" ("Whitey! Whitey!") News had already spread that a white man was moving in, and they were coming to say hello. Before I could escape, they ran into me, almost knocking me over with their huge, welcoming hugs. This was going better than I'd expected.

For a moment, I knew how celebrities must feel. I hoped to make friends, but never in a million years could I have predicted this kind of welcome. During those first two hours in Guguletu, I peeled away layer upon layer of racial conditioning, and I learned more about South African culture than most white South Africans learn in a lifetime. I went to bed that night listening to the foreign sounds of Guguletu street life. I couldn't decide if I was scared or if I was excited, but decided I was probably both.

The next morning, I woke up with a familiar feeling growing in the pit of my stomach. The reality of my circumstance sunk in, and I wanted to hide away in bed all day. I forced myself to go outside and eat my breakfast sitting on the front steps of my house. As I watched the locals scurry off to work, a small child, dressed in a school uniform, walked past me. He stopped dead in his tracks when he saw me, obviously shocked to see a white face eating breakfast in his township. "Do you live here?" he asked.

"Yes," I replied.

He looked away, paused for a second, then turned to me and said with wisdom beyond his years "Welcome home." He turned away and continued his walk to school. Tears rolled down my cheeks as thirty years of racial prejudice evaporated in that instant. I was home. A few days later, while I supported a local football team in Guguletu, a spectator came up to me and announced, "You need a Xhosa name. From now on, you will be called Xolani."

"What does that mean?" I asked curiously.

"Xolani means bringer of peace," he replied, smiling. I liked it. From that day on, I stopped introducing myself as Bruce. I was now Xolani. I felt proud to have an African name, and I loved seeing my neighbors' delight when I introduced myself as Xolani. One month came and went. Living in Guguletu was such a meaningful experience for me that I stayed for six incredible months.

I returned with new eyes to my old life. During those six months, my community and I both learned that despite the difference in our culture and skin color, we are all the same. I learned about community when my neighbors risked their lives to save mine, fighting off a gang of thieves who attacked me one night in an attempt to steal my phone. I learned about love when, while I was drinking at a shabeen (an illegal bar in someone's home) on the other side of Guguletu, Maureen arrived, having walked 2 kilometers at night through the most dangerous part of Guguletu, just to check up on me and make sure I was OK. I learned humility and determination as I turned hundreds of beggars away empty-handed, instead offering to teach them to earn their own money. In six months, only one accepted my offer. I learned about trust when I accepted Maureen's offer to look after my house and possessions as I traveled abroad to visit my family. I came back to find my house in better shape than when I had left!

Those six months changed me, changed my community, silenced my prejudices, and brought me humbly to my knees. I now have so many black friends I couldn't begin to count them. In retrospect, I thank God I was a racist, and I thank God I had the opportunity to learn these lessons — to learn what home, community, and Africa truly are.

❤   ❤   ❤

Bruce Muzik, founder of Designer Life, is an internationally acclaimed speaker, master communicator, success trainer, and an expert in how to use the human mind to bring about desirable circumstances in your life. He approaches his craft uniquely by blending leading-edge quantum physics with practical spirituality, providing real-world successes for his students around the globe. Bruce has owned and run a successful recording studio business, written a number-1 hit song, and trained with some of the greatest minds in the personal development world including Mark Victor Hansen, Dr. Tony Quinn, Robert Allen, T. Harv Eker, and many more. You can visit his website at www.designer-life.com.

Thank God
I'm Bald

LAURA DUKSTA

round the age of eight or nine, I clearly remember learning two lessons in Sunday school that would direct the course of my life. Firstly, Jesus taught that we are all brothers and sisters; and secondly, because of that we should love each other. Though I credit and thank my Catholic catechism classes for these nuggets of wisdom, it was clear to me, even at this young age, that these lessons were preached but not necessarily practiced.

I knew that I was meant to one day travel the world, meet my brothers and sisters, and spread the message of love. As my beloved mentor, John Demartini, says, life is a lot like a slingshot. I found the truth of this, and know that a mission of this magnitude will create a lot of tension. The further you are pulled back in life, the greater your ability to propel. Unfortunately, in life, as with a slingshot, sometimes you're pulled way back and you drop out instead of soaring. Who knew that in order to successfully fulfill this mission, I would go through the experience of losing my hair to a condition called Alopecia Areata? Alopecia Areata is stress-triggered, and I was "blessed" with some very stressful situations from verbal, emotional, physical, and even sexual abuse, coupled with a traumatic move in the fourth grade that took me away from my ocean side home to the country.

At the age of eleven, I lost all of my long brown, wavy hair. It began with a small, nickel-sized patch on the back right corner of my scalp. Though I now had this odd, very smooth patch, it was easy enough to conceal, and I just hoped that it would go away. It didn't, though . . . in fact, over the next six months my hair fell out to the point that I became an eleven-year-old girl with a really bad comb-over! The situation was anything but funny. I didn't know what to do. I was scared, embarrassed, confused. Friends and family didn't know what to say, or how to help. And for the most part, neither did the doctors. Once I finally received the diagnosis of Alopecia Areata, the advice from a Boston Children's Hospital doctor was, "There is really nothing we can do. Get her a wig, and no one needs to know." These words still ring in my mother's ears. She knew this was terrible advice and that things like this should be talked about. She tried to force us into family therapy, but faced incredible resistance from me and from my father, who at that time was a raging alcoholic.

Finally, she settled for the doctor's advice. I got a wig, skipped a couple of days of school, and went back pretending nothing ever happened. I thought I was acting the same, and didn't realize at the time that I was becoming introverted, miserable, and distrustful of life. I believed this to be the worst thing that could ever happen. I felt there was something wrong with me and that no one would want to be my friend. I believed I would never have a boyfriend or be able to do all the things I dreamed of doing. I loved to sing and perform, but I stopped. I quit gymnastics, swimming, and going on roller coasters — situations that might cause my wig to move on my head or fall off. I became someone who watched life rather than participate in it. I withdrew deeper and deeper into an undiagnosed depression. I completely shut down.

Now, I want you to know that I wasn't having a pity party. Early on, I realized that there were worse things that could have happened to me. I wasn't sick, hadn't lost a limb or the use of one of my senses. There were much worse fates than going bald, and I knew it. In my teens my sense of compassion and understanding for others expanded. I could, to some degree, put myself in the shoes of others experiencing challenges in their own lives. My ability to love expanded. People often say that you cannot love others until you learn to love yourself. Well, I guess there are exceptions to most every rule. I championed so many other causes and people before I could even begin to think about loving myself. In high school I became an activist against racism . . . I did not understand how people could discriminate against others just because of the color of their skin! This continued in college, where I earned a minor in African-American studies, and became an advocate for women's rights. My degree in sociology allowed me to explore the patterns of society and human behavior, which I found fascinating.

Did I mention I was introverted, withdrawn, and ashamed of my own existence? I was now in college, and I had never seen myself bald. Yes — in ten years of wearing a wig, from age eleven until age twenty-one, I never looked at myself in a mirror without the wig on! I dated a guy for almost two years in high school, and we never spoke about it. Talk about denial! It wasn't until my fourth year of college that I looked at myself wigless in the mirror. I dated a guy who asked if he could see me without my wig on, and I agreed. I cried for what seemed like hours in his arms, and only then did I move over and look at myself in a mirror. I'll never forget that moment. I remember saying to myself, "Crap . . . it's not so bad . . . now what am I supposed to do?" I'm not sure what kind of scary monster I was expecting to see. . . . Still, I put my wig back on and went back to hiding out. I became a little more comfortable talking about my baldness during my college years with my friends, but I still hesitated to raise my hand in class, not wanting to draw attention to myself. I often dodged questions like "How do you keep your hair so straight?" by answering "Just a lot of hair spray."

It was a miserable time of lying and denial. From a young age, I drank heavily, trying to avoid the stares and the feelings of inadequacy I felt. After graduating from college, I moved to South Beach, a trendy part of Miami, and bartended in a world where many others were trying to escape from reality as well. My heavy drinking continued, and I added drugs, like ecstasy and acid, to the mix. I had no self-esteem, and through these drugs, believed I could experience a sense of belonging. Since everything serves some purpose — and yes, the drugs were certainly detrimental to my health and safety with the potential to get me into a lot of trouble, — I also experienced a sense of love and acceptance for myself and others that I didn't know existed.

After a while, by the grace of God, I realized that I could get to this place without the use of these unhealthy and artificial "helpers". I could create this love and one-ness through other means. This brought a new chapter to my spiritual path. Actually, my path veered one night when I found myself praying for my sister. She was a very young mother now pregnant with her second child and having problems with her husband. As I prayed, something clearly answered me and said, "Your sister is fine. Pray for your nephew." I acknowledged that this was strange, but as I did, the whole idea for a children's book about love flooded my mind. It became one of those ideas that I just knew I had to make happen.

I bartended for six years and had no idea how to transition into being an author. Several months after "The Prayer," I was on the cusp of turning thirty. Just weeks before my birthday, I told my friends, "Throw me a party. I have an announcement to make!" We chose a nightclub called Life in New York City, and in July of 1998, I had what has now become known as my "Coming Out Party as The Bald Chick."

Wow, . . . I had no idea that the prayer and the idea for *I Love You More* were the catalyst for this unexpected unveiling of my head. Now, looking back, I can see how consumed my life had become with the fact that I wore a wig . . . were people wondering? . . . when and how should I tell someone? . . . was it going to fall off if someone put their arm around me unexpectedly? . . . yikes!

Though it took much adjustment for my new life as The Bald Chick, I also experienced an incredible sense of freedom. A weight had literally been lifted off my shoulders! I came upon Wayne Dyer speaking on TV, which led me to the teachings of Emerson, Troward, Thoreau, Science of Mind, Unity, Landmark, and ultimately to Dr. John Demartini. I reconnected with my childhood desire to travel the world, meet my brothers and sisters, and spread the message of love. I realized that I could do this through writing and publishing my first book, *I Love You More*. It's amazing to look back on my life now and know that everything that happened, all the abuse, trauma, and neglect, both from others and self-imposed, was a catalyst for me to learn to love others more fully. For me the biggest lesson was learning to love myself and allowing others to love me.

I now know that our biggest challenges become our biggest blessings when we are willing to embrace the gifts they present to us. I would never trade having my hair for this life experience. Not only did it teach me lessons of love, understanding, and compassion for humanity, but it now allows me the opportunity to go into schools and share with young people one of the most simple yet powerful lessons . . . Just Be Yourself. It's one of those very simple though not necessarily easy lessons, one that I think we often spend our whole life learning to embrace. Also . . . I'll let you in on a little secret: As an author, being bald makes me both memorable and marketable. Talk about coming completely full circle!

But seriously, when I share with people the true power and freedom that comes from learning to love oneself, these are not just empty words. I am a living expression of this truth. I have a program now that I bring into schools titled *"Self-Esteem Through Love: Empowering Our Children to Shine."* I am able to share with young people and adults universal truths that I have reawakened to and implemented along this journey of self-discovery. Coming from a powerful, bald woman standing in front of them, they hear the lessons at a deeper level than they might if coming from a teacher, parent, or guidance counselor.

One of my favorite verses from John Keats's poem "Ode on a Grecian Urn" says, *"Beauty is truth, truth beauty — that is all ye know on earth, and all ye need to know.'"* When I read these words shortly after choosing to shed my wigs and become The Bald Chick, they resonated throughout my soul. What I didn't know was that, by embracing my truth, bald head and all, my beauty would shine through. The world agrees because I cannot count the times I am told, over and over again, often by total strangers, how beautiful I am. I know this is the outcome of learning to not only be myself but to love myself as well. My light and beauty now beam from within. It also doesn't hurt to have named my company I Shine, Inc. I tell people that when I answer my phone all day, "Hello, I Shine, this is Laura. How can help you?" I can't help but glow!

I now get to fulfill my mission of generating the conversation of love around the world and am committed to doing so with my company, I Shine, Inc., through books, music, speaking, TV, film, and the web. Thank you, God, for allowing me the opportunity to play such a big game this time around! I am a living example that when people realize that they are loved . . . anything is possible! Thank God I am bald . . . I can't imagine my life without this experience and the blessed opportunity to spread, live, and embody the messages of love, beauty, truth, gratitude, and courage!

♥   ♥   ♥

Laura Duksta is president of I Shine, Inc. and best-selling author of *I Love You More*, (BookSense winter pick for 2007-2008) endorsed by Wayne Dyer, John Demartini, Jack Canfield, Mark Victor Hansen, and Alan Cohen. She has been featured in numerous media publications including *USA Today*, NBC 6, *The Sun-Sentinel*, *Miami Herald* and *Boca Magazine*. A sought-after speaker, she's presented her programs to thousands of students, parents, educators, authors, charitable organizations, and entrepreneurs nationwide, including to Gilda's Club, the Juvenile Diabetes Foundation, New School network marketing (Xango), as well as dozens of schools and community groups. She has committed her life to making the world a brighter place by empowering people to shine! You can contact Laura at Laura@LauraDuksta.com or visit www.MySpace.com/ILoveYouMoreBookTour. Her book *I Love You More* is available from Sourcebooks/Jabberwocky, at Amazon, and at all other major and independent book stores and gift galleries across the country.

Thank God
I Was Abused

KAREN HOYOS

*M*any times we look back in life and remember those difficult times, the ones we couldn't understand because there was no reason they should have been happening; painful situations with no solutions, no way out. From these circumstances, people tend to form into two groups. First, are those who choose to bury themselves and their circumstances and choose a lifetime of anger and bitterness. Yes, some have taken this hurt to the grave. And then there is the second group, those who choose to learn and grow from their worst moments and turn them into the best blessing of their lives.

I choose to be part of the group that's thankful, the group that's unstoppable, the group that elects to share their stories and make a difference in the lives of others, no matter how big the challenge they've confronted in one moment or another. And so I can say, "Thank God I was abused."

My story starts in a beautiful country called Colombia, a place of passion, full of life, full of fiesta, a place filled with gorgeous women. When I was just an eighteen-year-old girl, young and beautiful, I was at the head of my class and captain of the cheerleading squad. It seemed as though the whole world admired my combination of beauty and brains. I walked in the clouds, hungry to conquer the world. I wanted to be an actress, a singer, a ballerina, a writer . . . anything that would put me in the public light, sounded exciting.

As the oldest sister, naturally I was the protector of my younger siblings. This lasted until my mother immigrated to America with my stepfather, who entered my life when I was five. They went out in search of the American dream, to seek a better life, while I stayed behind to complete school and graduate. This I did with honors.

It was a very meaningful day for me, because even though I was away from my family, I was proud to have kept my promise and accomplished what I had given my word to do. Now it was time to go to the States and launch myself to stardom. But something surprising happened that night: My boyfriend of many months, who was also many years older than me, proposed that we get married. I was surprised and so moved that I told him I would think about it. After giving it some thought, I agreed to first live with him, to which he agreed.

I then found myself purchasing a phone card, instead of a plane ticket, so that I could call my mother to tell her the news. My mother cried a lot. I didn't understand why she felt this was incorrect, why this was wrong. After all, I was an adult. But eventually, my generous mother, with a heart of gold, respected my wishes and gave me her blessings.

All my magnificent dreams slipped away, no longer were they my priority. I didn't see that my once-beautiful, abundant man, who enlightened me with his presence, turned into someone else, no longer the same person he'd been. My life turned into an endless round of cooking and cleaning. I no longer dreamt of stardom. Going to the States seemed totally out of the question.

My boyfriend told me what to wear, though he stopped buying me clothes. I secretly asked others I knew for money to buy a blouse or a shirt, so I could wear something new like other young ladies. At every turn we fought more and more. He always wanted to go out alone and leave me home. One time, after a big fight, I told him I wanted to leave. He locked me in the house. When he returned, he spoke to me horribly and yelled so intensely that the neighbors called the police. That night I cried bitter tears of sorrow and regret. I had no idea why this was happening to me. The situation I found myself in was appalling; I couldn't believe that I would continue to tolerate this kind of treatment. I didn't know then that these were the symptoms of a destructive pattern that I would continue to tolerate in my life.

From somewhere I gathered up strength — I don't honestly know from where it came, but probably from my prayers and from thoughts of my mother, which are blessed. I told my boyfriend that either he would come with me to the United States, or I'd go without him. For the first time in a long time, he agreed to my request.

The day I reunited with my mother, my siblings, and my stepfather, in New York City, was the happiest day I'd had in over a year. Naturally, my family had no idea of what had been going on in my relationship with my boyfriend, and they opened their home to us. At first things went relatively well for him and me, but soon it became evident that he had grown lazy. He never helped with the expenses of the house, the expenses of living; he wouldn't even get a job. And so, my parents provided and paid for everything. After a short time, I managed to get a job, and with the help of my family, I asked him to move out. He could continue a relationship with me, I told him, but he had to move. Finally, I felt free. No one had a hold over my life or me any longer. Or, at least, that's what I thought.

It was a hot August afternoon in the borough of Queens, in New York City, one of those days when the beautiful sun left an orange glow in the sky. I worked as a secretary for a company that sold religious products. I was thrilled to be making my own money and had registered in a modeling academy, at a place where the 'stars' studied. Nothing could stop me now! My relationship with my boyfriend grew distant, and I experienced feelings of completeness and power as I stepped onto the road to my dreams. One day, my very personable boss introduced me to Eric, a young man with a radiant smile. I had never believed in love at first sight, but when I met Eric, suddenly I knew I loved him. My heart raced a million miles an hour, my stomach was astir with the proverbial butterflies, and I felt as if I could talk to this man forever. He was so young, yet he had a mysterious air

about him. In my nineteen years, I had never known the feelings he
caused within me. Eric was twenty-six, divorced, with a daughter, and
he impressed me. He experienced so much already, at so young an age!
He had such responsibility.

In a short time, we began dating. I officially cut off my old boyfriend. I had eyes only for Eric: I breathed for him; I wanted to be close
to him. It was something unexplainable. He was very romantic, and
although he didn't have much money, when he drove me around in
his $500 car, I felt I was in glory, as if I were being driven around in a
limousine. We walked together by the bay, and I received as a gift from
him: a full moon, the stars, the sun, and many songs, not to mention his
dreams of traveling around the world. It was pure romance. Everything
was simply perfect. I was madly in love with him. After a few dates,
I shared with him my dreams of being an actress. He said nothing in
reply, but I didn't let that bother me. We would go out dancing, and
I noticed he would get upset for no apparent reason. I figured he was
probably jealous, but I ignored it. I told myself he was stressed, and I
thought I could cure the problem with a kiss and a hug. I figured, after
all, we all have defects. In less than a month, he asked me to move in
with him. It wasn't a marriage proposal, but it didn't matter — he was
a free spirit, a dreamer, and he didn't need a piece of paper to formal-
ize our love. I still perceived him as being so amazing. I said I would
continue my studies in Manhattan; he quickly let me know it would be
him or modeling, but never both. I had to choose. He explained that we
could not have a happy, healthy home while I studied, that it would be
too difficult, and we would have no privacy if I entered into the public
light. To him, it was simply impossible. To me, it made sense. I would
never take the risk of losing him. I really began to believe it was impossible to have it all.

We started living together, but I didn't feel fully self-expressed,
and I soon experienced anxiety. As for him, he had frequent mood
swings — happy, angry — and never explained these radical changes
to me. I excused his behavior, blaming the mood swings on the new
changes in our relationship. He was Colombian too, and said he wanted
to go to Colombia to visit his family. I didn't want to leave my family,
but I agreed, because he promised it would be for only one month. We

arrived in the middle of the December feast. His family was famous for their coffee business. They received us very affectionately with a big party. Everyone danced, ate, and drank, and Eric introduced me as his wife, although we had never actually married. Soon, everyone accepted me and welcomed me with open arms.

I noticed that Eric had begun to carry a gun. A gun, I thought. Why, my love, why do you have a gun? When I asked him, he said, "Only to protect you. We are in a tough region. I want to take care of you." Although I was not comfortable with it, I trusted him and took his vow to protect me seriously.

The New Year was coming, midnight was approaching, and everyone was getting drunk, including Eric. I felt left out and alone, and I missed my family dearly. Excusing myself, I went to the bedroom and cried tears of loneliness. One of Eric's younger cousins came into the room to look for something among his luggage. He left about three minutes later. Shortly after that, the young cousin returned to get something else, then quickly left again. Suddenly Eric burst into the room with a look of anger, and then abruptly I felt a blow to the ear. I fell to the bed and looked up only to see that he was using the gun he had sworn was to protect me with. He was using it in a fury to hit me with, instead, seeming to try to kill me. He yelled obscenities at me, calling me "You bitch! You're a whore! You're a hussy!" He said he wanted to kill me. "You're going to die!" he screamed, ranting insanely. I cried, begging him, "Stop! Please stop!" but no one could hear me. It was a nightmare! He said I had been sleeping with his cousin, and for this, he would kill me. I prayed to God to calm him and wake him from his drunken stupor, so that I could return to my family and my dreams . . . .

God heard my anguished prayers, and finally Eric put down the gun. He stopped screaming and told me I had to leave and put my luggage in the car. As I ran to the car, I was desperately screaming about what had just happened to me, but no one responded. No one cared. This was part of the culture, to ignore the situation, to behave as if nothing were wrong. Some men get drunk, some men act foolish, and so the family behaved accordingly and just watched. In the middle of this, he forced me into the car. Then suddenly, as we drove, he begged me for forgiveness; said he loved me, and promised he would never act this way again. Never, he promised. Never. Never. I don't know why, but foolishly I believed him again, although a part of my mind screamed out against it, warning me to leave this crazy man. But there was a part of me that understood him, and this part was much stronger. I convinced myself that it was true, that he would change. I loved him, and I believed that love could triumph over anything. So I decided to stay and to keep this incident from my parents. But despite his promise, Eric became extremely jealous and controlling, and instead of getting better, he got much worse. I could not look at any man, despite race, age, or where he came from. In Eric's eyes, they were all out to steal my love from him, and if I looked at a man, I was an accomplice. Life turned into an inferno — truly hell.

Although his business was doing well, he delayed our return to America. Months went by, and he provided me excuse after excuse. I bought the excuses. I tolerated his excuses, tolerated his behavior. I allowed his abuse, and I became mediocre. I had no respect for my own word, no integrity as a woman and a human being. I simply fell apart. Eric brought me many material things to cover up his behavior. I began to drink and smoke. My happy spirit was lost in a superficial life, as his abuse became more and more frequent. The ultimate incident took place one night when we went out to a restaurant, and he drank, and drank, and drank. I went to the coatroom and asked for my coat, and again I felt a blow to the ear. There he was in his rage, his jealousy out of control again, and this time in front of everyone!

The people there helped me and sent me home, and security chased him, but he got away. When he got home, he shot through the ceiling and through the door, which I was cowering behind in terror. I thought this was the last day of my life. There was nothing else I could tolerate, and this was the end.

I believe in miracles, and the mere fact that I am alive is one. Through an act of God, Eric finally fell asleep, drunk. My guardian angel had again rescued me, and I knew I had to make a decision. In each moment of decision, our life changes for good or bad, and we create our own destiny. I knew that God had saved me for a great purpose, which I would soon discover. With the unconditional support of my family, who finally found out the whole truth of my situation, I was at last able to leave Eric and come home. Although I was free, I was a prisoner of my own mind. With my heart empty and my self-esteem on the floor, I convinced myself that all men were the same. I felt a lot of anger and hate in my heart. I didn't believe in anyone or anything, much less myself. I had become a victim.

Like a perfect gift from the universe, a friend invited me to an Anthony Robbins seminar. I had no idea what a seminar was, nor had I any clue that something existed such as personal development. I was looking for answers, for signals, for hope, so I said, "Okay, let's go." That day changed my life forever. This magnificent man believed in me, more than I believed in myself. During the four days, he helped me transform my life as I discovered my essence, my love for others, and I discovered forgiveness. I knew at that time that my life mission was to inspire humanity. I learned that no matter what has happened in your life, no matter what the circumstances, you could make your dreams come true. I decided to dedicate my life to transforming the world — this was my true life's dream. It was part of my soul, and my whole being. It filled me completely.

With no experience, only my story of abuse, I started down a road of transformation, of health and plenitude. I left the role of victim and took responsibility for everything that had happened. I was generous with Eric and complete in my relationship with him; knowing that people can't give what they don't have, more importantly, I honored myself. This allowed me to create new, deep relationships with all those who had suffered because of my circumstances. I participated in all seminars that gave me power; I started to share, with my Latin community, my testimony of the transformation in my life. My heart was full of gratitude. I started to live and to follow my dreams. In actuality, my words started to touch and inspire millions of people through my seminars, and my products, through television, radio, magazines, and newspapers. I expressed my message across the globe and discovered that you could definitely have it all.

Today, I do what I love the most: contribute. My life is extraordinary because one day I was abused. As a mother of twins, I am reminded each minute to be thankful for my existence and give profound gratitude to

God because I lived. I wouldn't change a thing because everything turned into a plan, a master plan, a universal plan, to inspire the world, and to make an infinite change in humanity.

So now I invite you to let go of your past and be grateful to all who have done you wrong and harmed you in your past. Surrender to love and thankfulness. Gratitude is the perfect pass to make your dreams a reality. Today and always, with my hand on my heart, I scream to the universe, "Thank you, God. Thank God I was abused!"

♥   ♥   ♥

Karen Hoyos is one of the most recognized success coaches and speakers. Applying the principles she teaches, in only ten months her message reached over 40 million people through her seminars, top television show appearances, published articles, and best-selling products. This Colombian native is the president of Karen Hoyos International, revenues from which help support her foundation for abused children in Latin America and Africa. Today, Karen Hoyos is frequently asked to refresh, awaken, and expand the minds of people around the world, changing their lives forever.

Thank God
I Was Sexually Molested

MICHAEL A. WEIST

I was fourteen years old that winter of '76. In the twilight, snow gently fell a foot deep; perfect for going "hitching," a game my friends and I played often. We hid in the bushes until a car stopped at the stop sign. Then we'd sneak out, grab onto the bumper, and enjoy the thrill of a sneaky ride!

That night, two friends came over to go hitching. After a few rides, a sedan pulled up and a man stepped out of the car, pointed a gun at us, and told us to freeze. Frightened, we stopped. Then he told me to get in the car. The car looked like an unmarked police car. He made me sit for what seemed like hours while he pretended to call the police on the CB radio. CB's were just becoming available to the general public, and I had seen them only on big trucks and police cars.

When the police didn't come, the man drove through town in the direction of the police station. As he drove, he started to talk to me. He told me we could make a deal. I could either go to the police station and get into trouble, or I could do something else. I asked, "What else?" but he didn't answer. However, he changed the direction in which he was traveling, and while I didn't know where we were headed, I knew it didn't have anything to do with the police. Something was terribly wrong.

He drove about fifteen minutes outside of town to a state park, closed for the winter. After parking the car, he ordered me to climb into the front seat.

Fear gripped my whole body. After telling me to take off my pants, he proceeded to do things physically to me that I had never imagined. My mind stopped thinking of anything but pain and fear.

When he finished, he told me to climb into the back seat. I put on my pants and crawled back as quickly as I could. Scared and embarrassed, I stared out the window as he drove out of the park. As we got closer to downtown, he began to talk, and I heard the anxiety in his voice. At a stop sign I contemplated jumping out of the car and running away, but I was afraid of what he might do. The closer he got to town, the more distressed he became. After telling me I couldn't tell anyone, he offered me a deal: If I didn't tell, then he would take me home. I agreed. (He never did say what he would do if I told.)

Before crossing the main bridge, he suddenly turned onto a side road. My heart raced — I knew he didn't plan to take me home. He drove to a dark, secluded, and very private dirt road alongside the river. As he turned onto this road, he stopped talking. Fear gripped me. It was the kind of place you'd take someone to kill them and dispose of the body. I sat behind him, and so, hidden by the seat, I tried to get the nerve to jump out of the car. My mind raced, I have to do this, I have to do this. I was trying to talk myself into jumping out of the car that moved at about 25 to 35 miles per hour.

Just then, I spotted the darkened lights on top of a police car as it drove past. Suddenly the lights flashed as the car spun around, heading back toward me. I felt as if some ne had taken all the weight off, allowing me to breathe again. The police officer walked up, revolver pulled. My captor ordered me to say nothing or I would be hurt, but when the police officer shone his light into the back seat and asked if I was okay, I said, "No!"

I later learned that our neighbor witnessed the man forcing me into the car and had reported it. Without her, who knows what would have happened. She has my gratitude! He went to jail; I went to the hospital. They took samples of everything! It was uncomfortable and embarrassing; everyone's expressions reflected uncomfortable sadness, from the hospital employees to my family. You could tell they didn't know how to respond — how could they? Even the police exhibited discomfort. They told me that in jail they would treat a man like him in subhuman ways. Within a couple of days, I went back to school, and I thought that then things would get better.

But they didn't — life got harder! The front page of our small town newspaper blared that an abducted youth suffered sexual assault, and the perpetrator was in custody! When I read it, my heart jumped. In a small town, people talk! I felt like I was in jail. The school administrators and teachers knew of the incident, and so did many of the students. Somehow, the news got around at school, and though most people said nothing, some gave me strange looks. The second day, a student stopped me in the hall, smiling at me, and asked, "How could you let a man do that?" Embarrassed and ashamed, I didn't know how to respond. Though I just walked away, I wanted to hurt him. It was the first time I felt deep pain and hatred, and it scared me. I was taught to turn the other cheek, that I was better than that, but I really wanted to hurt him!

I associated being in society and in school with pain. I hated being there, not caring about anything or anyone. On the outside, I faked my emotions, but on the inside, I withdrew more and more as the days passed. I turned to drugs and alcohol to bury the pain. I had the ability to walk through school, acting aware, but in reality, I retreated to somewhere else in my mind. Communication with my parents became a challenge. They didn't know how to communicate with me, and though I wanted and needed their support, they didn't know how to express it. I began to hate my parents and cast blame on my father.

Dating, sex, and sexuality scared and confused me. (At that age, I know, almost every kid is confused or scared.) But I feared that the experience would "make me homosexual"; and to make things worse, occasionally a homosexual man would show interest in me. Quite simply, homosexuality is not my choice. At age nineteen, I hit the lowest point in my life and realized I couldn't continue with life the way it was going. My excessive drinking and inability to move forward with my life brought me to a point of contemplating suicide. The first step I took toward resolving these problems was to find a counselor. A good first step. Tom proceeded to peel away the layers of the onion of my life, but it happened slowly, ever so slowly. I went to counselors erratically for the next nine years but came to realize that even though they could be a mirror for my recovery, I needed more.

At age twenty-eight, I came across hypnosis and found it helped more than counseling. Later, I worked with Scott McFall, a phenomenal practitioner in the field. I felt better about myself and learned what worked and what didn't. I learned self-hypnosis, which helped a lot. I discovered I could change the way I responded by changing my thoughts. I read and devoured more books than I had read in the first twenty years of my life. Reading opened up a doorway. I accepted more personal responsibility and reduced my tendency to blame. In my late twenties, I went to the top of a mountain and prayed. I forgave my father for all the things I perceived him doing to me, and felt better about him and myself. It was a step toward resolution. I had been blaming the world, both for my past and my present, and became aware of how this left me stuck and repeating the same lessons. I started to read poetry, philosophy, physics, science, sociology, finance and economics. I learned that our philosophy runs our lives, and to truly run my life I needed to declare my philosophies.

I married a beautiful woman, my lifelong friend, Lisa. We had a child together. At that time, I trained with a spiritual man, Jerry Stocking. He taught me to discover how enlightening life is. He was challenging and empowering, and is one of the most aware men I have come across in my life. He peeled back even larger layers of the onion. He was great at revealing the illusions and fantasies I chose. But the biggest challenge I encountered was that the more I chose to heal myself, the more my marriage fell apart. Torn between keeping the marriage, or growing and healing at the expense of my marriage, became a dilemma that did not feel good. The pendulum of my life arced between bottomless lows and celestial highs. Jerry Stocking taught me to be thankful for my family and friends, who reflect love, and to be even more grateful for my enemies and the people who upset me, for they teach me more than anyone else does.

The divorce was more difficult than we thought it would be, and we both aged as we went through it. I'm very grateful for Lisa and my son, Dillon. They continued to teach me a lot. Both of them reflected back to me the things about myself I had refused to face.

Next, I met an ordinary man living an extraordinary life! John Demartini lives life searching for the truths in this world and teaching them. He teaches the most profound change model I've come across so far. I have training in clinical counseling, NLP, and clinical hypnotherapy, to name a few. Of the ten or fifteen models of change I've trained in, John's work is by far the most life changing I've experienced! His scientifically proven method is a step-by-step way to free yourself from the internal binds that we experience. Through his teachings, I learned that the man I thought victimized me was, and is, a blessing in disguise! I discovered how I manifested that experience in order to grow, learn, and love.

Twenty years ago, I expressed hatred, anger, betrayal, fear, confusion, depression, and victim blame from my experience. No one could have shown me anything but that. Now, without a shadow of doubt, I see the perfect order and divine perfection of that event. I am grateful for the experience and to the man who taught it. I appreciate what he did on that night over twenty years ago. Everything he did showed me how I did not love myself fully. I realize this and am thankful.

Being molested at age fourteen led me on a journey of self-discovery, a career, and a mission! Since 1993, I have been on a path to change the world one person at a time. In my clinics, I work with clients and teach them how to transform their lives from feeling stuck, trapped, and unable to accomplish their goals, to becoming healthier, wealthier, and more well-balanced people; living more of their full potential. As a teacher, healer, philosopher, and speaker, I'm blessed to have the opportunity to use my God-given talents, skills, and abilities to work with hundreds of clients, families, and companies to help them "align their minds with the divine through time to allow people to feel fine"!

This is my choice, this is my path.

♥   ♥   ♥

Michael A. Weist is the owner of Life Change Centers in Green Bay and Appleton, Wisconsin and of the Wisconsin School Of Hypnosis. He is a speaker, author, teacher, and healer. Michael helps transform people's lives using innovative technologies, life-changing systems, and time-proven philosophies. He is a practitioner of the Demartini Breakthrough System®*, N.L.P., and hypnosis. Visit his website at newhypnosolutions.com.

*The Demartini Method® Dr. John F. Demartini © 1988 Property of the Demartini Human Research & Education Foundation www.drdemartini.com

Thank God
I Got Diabetes

JOHN KREMER

I am a night person. I love working at night when the world settles down, all is quiet, and there are no interruptions. That strategy worked well for me for many years as a writer, but eventually it caught up with me.

To keep going late at night — when the earth is so still and silent — I'd snack on junk food, often eating an entire box of cookies or bag of candy. As a result, I gained some 50 pounds over a 20-year period. It was so gradual a change — just a few pounds a year — that it didn't seem so bad. Of course, it was.

I bore the brunt of the weight: walking was harder, muscles ached, getting out of bed got harder and harder. But I loved working at night so much and I couldn't stop the snacking. Truth be told, I was addicted.

I tried diets and would lose a few pounds here and there, but I always gave up on any program within a week or two. Dieting simply wasn't for me. Too many rules.

Then one May, a number of things began going wrong with my body. The key was my eyesight. I began having trouble reading the words on the computer screen as I wrote. It started with me having to wear my glasses on the tip of my nose so I could read the words clearly. That worked for a while, but within a week or two, I couldn't push my glasses any further down my nose in order to read.

I discovered another solution for a time. Silly as it seems, I found that I could read the screen if I wore my glasses upside down. That odd strategy worked for another few weeks, but then even that stopped working.

I feared it was old age, that I was losing my ability to see, that my eyes were deteriorating right in front of me. I went to the optometrist and got a new prescription. Again, I could see, but three weeks later, the same problem crept into my routine. I knew I was going to have to see the optometrist again. That was scary. My eyesight was literally degrading minute by minute, hour by hour.

Before I could see the optometrist again, other parts of my body began breaking down. Over the same period of time, I had been getting major calluses on my feet. I thought it was from walking around barefoot so much, which I did when it was hot — and it had been a very hot May and June. One particular dried and cracked callus didn't seem to want to heal at all, no matter how much lotion I slathered on it. This also worried me, but again, I was too busy to do much more than put lotion on my feet several times a day.

I placed the blame on getting older. I was then fifty-five and just figured that it was the cost of aging — a little sooner than I expected. Not having grown old before, I really didn't have a yardstick to go by, except to see other friends also complaining about growing aches and pains.

Then, in late June, I started having another symptom. I had to urinate all the time. Now, on one hand, this was good because it enabled me to drink more water — something my wife had been encouraging me to do. But after a week of urinating on the hour or sometimes more often, I grew concerned that there might be something more going on. So I made an appointment with the doctor (it really takes me getting knocked over the head to visit a doctor). Long story short, he told me I had diabetes.

All the symptoms were there: the rapidly changing eyesight, the cracked and dried skin on my feet, the excessive urination, and other signs I'd ignored. I just didn't know. No one had ever told me.

Diabetes, as it turns out, is not just an inconvenient set of symptoms. It is a life-threatening disease — one that can kill you quickly if ignored.

My doctor described to me my options: drugs, diet change, more exercise, and eventually insulin. None of these options sounded inviting to me. But I did not want to die, so I started making changes.

Thank God, I got diabetes.

I didn't want to start taking drugs because, once you do, you really have to keep taking them for the rest of your life. Since I've never been good at taking any sort of pills, whether vitamins, other supplements, or prescription drugs, I knew that really wasn't a viable option for me.

So, slowly, I changed my diet. I ate more vegetables. I cut down on snacks, way down. I drank more water. That wasn't enough. Finally, I discovered Weight Watchers®.

I've never been able to stick with other diets because they always felt so restrictive. Don't eat this. Don't eat that. Don't eat at night. Don't do this. Don't do that. Too many do nots!

With Weight Watchers®, though, I only count points. As long as I stay within my points, I can eat anything I want, whenever I want. That works for me. Ultimately, we all have to find those little somethings that work for us.

Now my blood sugar is under control. My skin is back to being baby soft. I can see my computer screen without strain. I can read road signs again at night. Most important, I now feel good, even invigorated, as I walk up and down the arroyos near my home in New Mexico. They are steep, but I'm a kid again. My body still complains some, but I am able to move again, get out of bed without that old morning stiffness, and — joy of joys — keep up with my dogs as we walk and sometimes run the arroyos.

I thought I was getting old. I thought I was slowly dying. I thought I had little hope but to go out with a whimper and a sigh.

Thank God I got diabetes. It changed my life. My energy is back. My depression is less. And, I've lost 25 pounds so I'm halfway there to losing those 50 pounds I had gained over so many years.

I still work at night. I can't seem to get away from the deep silence I love so much. But I don't snack anymore. I can't. I want to live.

And, thanks to my diabetes, I am.

❤   ❤   ❤

John Kremer is an acknowledged expert on book publishing and marketing. Besides being the owner of his own publishing company (Open Horizons in Taos, New Mexico), he is also the author of a number of books on publishing and marketing, including *1001 Ways to Market Your Books: For Authors and Publishers* (6th Edition), *The Complete Direct Marketing Sourcebook*, *High Impact Marketing on a Low Impact Budget*, and *Celebrate Today*. He is the webmaster of BookMarket.com, QuotableBooks.com, and TouristTrains.us.

Thank God
I Left My Kids

MABEL KATZ

When I received the invitation to write this chapter, I first checked to see if spiritually it was the correct thing to do. And, of course, I wanted my kids' approval. This is a delicate subject, and I wanted to be sensitive to their feelings. As it turned out, my oldest son, Jonathan, now twenty-four years old, responded, "Mom, if this will help create more opportunities to share your message with people, go ahead. I'm okay with it." Lyonel, who is nineteen years old, said, "Mom, it's sad. But go ahead. I'm okay." So I'm taking this opportunity to share with you how some things that we may consider "wrong", "incorrect,", or "bad" can be right for us and our loved ones, even if we don't know it until after the fact.

When I separated from my husband, back in 1998, he wanted to be the one to stay in the house with the kids. I'd never heard of any woman who had done such a thing! The mother and children are supposed to stay in the house and the husband is the one to leave. I was outraged and extremely upset. How could he propose such a thing? I'd been good to him, supported him so that he could do and be whatever he chose, and since I make a good income as accountant, I always helped him financially.

Fear-filled, I left my marriage of more than twenty years, leaving behind my husband and my children. I started a new career and signed a lease, taking on a huge financial responsibility without backup funds. Fortunately, my faith and confidence in myself allowed me to act in spite of my fear. An inner voice told me that I could do it, but this security did not come spontaneously. I acquired it by working on myself — reading books, taking seminars, and daring to face and accept the things that I needed to change. By trusting in the universe, I was willing to feel the fear of the unknown and do it anyway.

Fortunately, at the time I was already practicing the ancient Hawaiian art of problem-solving, Ho'oponopono. Ho'oponopono teaches us how to "clean" and "erase" old memories or programs that attract things that don't work for us and allow what is perfect and right to come at the perfect time in our lives. But often "we don't know that we don't know." As soon as I began my cleaning and erasing regarding my husband, the following thought came to me: "He's actually helping me. He doesn't know it consciously, but he's helping me. I need to be by myself in order to do what I came to do." At the time, this was a very novel and scary thought, but, because I was doing my cleaning, I trusted and decided to let go and let God.

Prior to my leaving, my kids fought and put each other down constantly. After I left, they became more responsible and their relationships grew. They became good friends who cared for each other. They were also closer to their father and a great source of companionship to him. In fact, they helped him through a difficult transition. In the end, my decision to leave was best for everybody, even though I didn't know it at the time.

When my mother came to visit from my birthplace, Argentina, she asked, "Mabel, I don't understand. Are you abandoning them?" My response was, "Mom, I know this is not what we learned as the "right thing" to do, but don't you see they're fine?" Her reply was, "Yes, but I don't understand. Don't they suffer?" She was also worried because they didn't call me. I told her, "Mom, that's a good thing. It means they're okay."

I never set up visiting days or times with my sons. I gave them no guilt trips. They saw me only if they could, if they wanted to and they always called me if something was wrong. I would ask them, "Does this work for you?" This way, they learned to ask that question of themselves and of others. I let them know that I loved them no matter what. I told them that love doesn't depend on what they did or didn't do, or on their behavior. It didn't depend on whether or not they got a college degree. These statements surprised them . . . they looked at me with wide-eyed wonder as though I was telling them the strangest thing they had ever heard in their lives.

At the time I left, I could never have imagined a relationship like the one we now have. My oldest son, Jonathan, calls me every day to tell me that he loves me. He says I'm on his best friend list! By my actions, I taught them it's not selfish to put ourselves first. I showed them that by being themselves they would find happiness in who they are. Without self-love, we cannot love anyone else. By refusing to accept this, we deceive others and ourselves. It is essential to learn to love and accept ourselves exactly the way we are. It doesn't work to do things solely for others. If something doesn't work for us, it won't work for anybody else.

Especially as mothers, we tend to believe that we must relinquish what is important to us and sacrifice for our children. However, the best gift we can give them is to love ourselves. With our example, they can learn to love themselves. When we are in the correct place, we became an example to others. The more we try to obtain love by doing things and behaving in certain ways for others, the more we distance ourselves from the possibility of experiencing the very thing we so desire.

I now know that my decision showed my children that it is important to do what works for us. When we dare to follow our dreams and go through our fears, we reach the other side of the tunnel and see the light. We then recognize truth. We feel triumphant and present with ourselves, as we look back and see that the journey wasn't as terrible as we had imagined. When we stop attaching ourselves to the results and worrying about situations, when we abandon the need to have opinions and pass judgment, and when we become aware that we know nothing and surrender and accept the process of life, then, and only then, can we experience the flow of the universe. It is at this point that things start to happen in the easiest way. I often tell my children that their job is to be grateful. When we are grateful, things just come to us effortlessly.

Before I started my self-transformation process, I lived my life trying to be perfect: the perfect mother, the perfect spouse, the perfect accountant. What a relief to find out that I didn't need to be perfect! When I left my kids, for the first time in my life I was able to love and accept myself just the way I was. Love toward our own being is the most powerful tool of transformation. Love begins with us. It's useless to look for it elsewhere because we can only experience it if we have it within. Unless we love and accept ourselves unconditionally, we cannot love truthfully. If we don't allow our children to be themselves, we love possessively . . . , and they become slaves of our thoughts, opinions, and perceptions. I was raised in this old tradition and became a people-pleaser. I needed to know that people liked me. I now know that if I hadn't had enough self-love and trust, I would never have been able to make the decision to leave my family. I would have put other people's ideas and approval first, and, although unhappy, I would have stayed married. I would have become an angry mother and made my kids' lives miserable. Fortunately, I faced my fears and chose the path that taught my kids to follow their hearts and be themselves.

In my case, it was essential to show my sons how a person can change, no matter their age, sex, or religion. When we started taping my TV show at home, my son Lyonel would help. He often came to me and said, "Mom, I am so proud of you." What else could I have asked for? Many people say our kids are our gurus. I believe that we definitely have been with them in other lifetimes, and they come only to give us another chance. They give us the opportunity to take 100% of the responsibility. Our children come to teach us something, not the other way around.

When situations are present in our lives, it's very easy to see them as problems, tests, or punishments, instead of blessings and opportunities. Usually, the first thing we do is judge. We have opinions and tend to think that we know what is right and what is wrong. Through my experience with my family and countless others, I have learned that God knows what is right for us, and that if we get out of our own way, we tend to "miraculously" be in the right place at the right time.

In Ho'oponopono, we use two very important tools for transformation. These are "thank you" and "I love you." When we repeat any of these, we erase, clean, and let go of the memories that don't serve us anymore and allow inspiration to enter our lives with the perfect ideas and solutions to our problems. The best thing is that, while we are erasing and cleaning, whatever we erase from ourselves, we erase from our families, relatives, and ancestors as well. That is why things start changing without you having to be present. We definitely affect relationships in ways our intellect cannot understand.

Remember: Our kids don't listen to us. They observe us and learn from our example. My sons saw the differences between their father's path and mine, which gave them opportunity to see and decide what works for them. My decision to leave my kids helped us all grow in ways that I could have never imagined. Our judgments and opinions of situations and events have to do with our own insecurities. Our fears do not allow us to know who we are or to understand the power we have to create and manifest in our lives. When we trust and believe in ourselves, we recognize that every moment is perfect.

> *"Your children are not your children.*
> *They are the sons and daughters of Life's longing for itself.*
> *They come through you but not from you,*
> *and though they are with you, yet they belong not to you.*
> *You may give them your love but not your thoughts.*
> *For they have their own thoughts.*
> *You may house their bodies but not their souls,*
> *for their souls dwell in the house of tomorrow, which you*
> *   cannot visit, not even in your dreams.*
> *You may strive to be like them, but seek not to make them*
> *   like you.*
> *For life goes not backward nor tarries with yesterday.*
> *You are the bows from which your children as living arrows*
> *   are sent forth.*

The archer sees the mark upon the path of the infinite, and
He bends you with His might that His arrows may go
swift and far.
Let your bending in the archer's hand be for gladness;
for even as he loves the arrow that flies, so He loves also the
bow that is stable."

KAHLIL GIBRAN

♥   ♥   ♥

Mabel Katz is the author of *The Easiest Way. Solve your problems and take the road to love, happiness, wealth, and the life of your dreams.* Her passion is sharing the power people have inside themselves to change their lives. She hosts her own TV show, *Despertar* ("Awakening"), and travels around the world "awaking people's consciousness" with her lectures and seminars. Mabel is president of Your Business Inc., where as a business consultant she helps others create successful businesses. For more information, please visit www.mabelkatz.com or www.businessbyyou.com.

Thank G-d
I Was Raped

JAY GRAYCE

*S*everal years back, if someone told me I would be making such a statement as "Thank G-d I was raped," I would have considered them cruel and crazy. So, I'm aware of how disturbing this may be for some people to hear or understand. I didn't wake up one day and ding!—suddenly find myself thinking, "Hey, G-d . . . thanks for the rape." It was so-o-o not like that, my friends. It was quite the opposite. I could not understand why G-d would let this happen to me. I went through unspeakable pain and anguish, and I saw my family's hearts break for me. Yet here I am writing about my rape, and I really am earnestly thankful to G-d for it! How did that happen? I'll tell you a bit about myself before the rape in hope that you'll see how life so cleverly prepares us for our personal tragedies. It took me some hard, painful years to figure this out. So here is a brief history of my background:

For the first thirteen years of my life, I suffered from a chronic illness. Going through the hardship made me want to help those who were in need. I worked as a crisis counselor, advocate, and support group facilitator for survivors of violent crimes. For ten years I worked directly with victims of sexual assault, rape, incest, elder and child abuse. Working with such heavy situations is draining, and I felt the signs of burnout. Taking a leap of faith, I resigned from my job, and co-founded a consulting business in New York City, where I'd always lived. But after several years I felt I owed it to myself to get out of my comfort zone and go to live on the other side of the country.

The several times I'd visited San Francisco, I enjoyed the aesthetics and the laid-back attitude of the people there. My family and friends were apprehensive about my moving to a place where I had no friends or established means of income. I understood their concerns, but I was determined to make a life for myself in California and I went ahead with the relocation. This was during the dot-com explosion, and most people were willing to pay a disturbing amount of money in cash to get an apartment, something I obviously was not able to do. So after I had found a full-time consultant job, I still needed a part-time job to make ends meet.

I applied for evening and weekend bartending jobs and got a Sunday interview appointment at a high-end restaurant. It was not far from my place. This made me happy because commuting would be easy and the tips would be good. Being new to the city and wanting to take precautions (I am a New Yorker, after all). I asked a new friend to go with me and wait while I interviewed. My counseling experience made me think about safety issues. The restaurant was both lovely and busy, and the hostess directed me to the manager. After I gave him my resume, he told me to sit at one of the tables while he tended to customers. Finally he got back to me and proceeded with a friendly and informal interview. I had already learned that in San Francisco even employers were super casual and laid back. The manager even introduced me to his wife, who was dining with some of their friends. He finally offered me the job and insisted that my companion and I stay and try some of the cuisine so I could become familiar with the food. I thought, *How generous!* and was happy to get the job.

After some time, the restaurant manager asked me to go to his office to fill out some forms. I told my friend I would be right back. The manager went over to his wife's table and said something to her, then motioned for me to follow him to his office. He was walking quite a bit ahead of me, and I had to take large steps to try to catch up with him. Losing track of where he had gone, I asked an employee, who pointed to the manager's door. When I knocked, he called to me to open the door and come in.

This is when my true journey began.

I opened the door but didn't see him. Suddenly, I felt a hand around my face, covering my mouth. He pulled me down to the cold, hard floor. I could not believe it! *What was happening?* I screamed, but no one heard me. The office was far from the noisy dining room, and no one heard my pleas for help. He held me down and took off my clothes. I struggled, he was too strong . . . so strong that the bruise of his hand-print on my right arm remained for a couple of weeks. He raped and sodomized me, and I immediately knew that he had done this before because he was so methodical and quite confident that he would not be caught.

Time stood still, and I began to experience what many survivors of trauma describe as an out-of-body experience: as he raped me I felt like I was watching a movie of someone being raped. But that someone was not an actor . . . it was *me*, and *it* was *real*. I am not sure how much time passed, but when he was done with me, he calmly got himself together while I lay there bleeding, shocked, and in disbelief. Slowly and painfully, I got up to put on my clothes. He turned to me, kissed and thanked me, and walked away. Yes, he did! I could not believe it myself, and it happened to me.

I was no longer the person I was before I opened those doors. The person before would have thought the same thing that some of you are thinking now, which is, "Why didn't you run after him and try to kick his ass?" I tried to fight him off during the rape, but at some point I disconnected. I was in shock and felt broken. Then denial set in . . . I just could not accept what had happened to me — after all, I did every-thing I thought I could to do to be safe. I had someone go with me to the place of the interview, and I told her that I was going to the office and would be right back. The place was crowded, and an employee sent me to the manager's office, so this person knew I was in there with the manager. (Much later, I found out he was his lookout.)

Why didn't the red flags come up? How could I let this happen?

The whole thing was like a nightmare. I don't remember going back into the restaurant's dining room. I finally found my friend, who was waiting for me. She was upset and began to yell at me because I'd taken so long that she thought I'd just forgotten about her. Then suddenly I blurted out, "I was raped." Naturally she freaked out — she was very upset. We left the restaurant, and she wanted to call the police. But I said no, and we got a cab home.

Once home, we talked about it, and I decided to call the police. I knew that in rape cases the victim is basically the evidence, so I didn't shower or change my clothes, although every cell in my body wanted to scrub the rapist off me. I could smell him on me, and it made me want to throw up and peel off my skin. The police came, took my report, and drove me to the hospital. They were insensitive and dismissive. I spent about seven hours waiting for a rape crisis nurse to do my rape kit. In the interim, the investigators interviewed me several times. I was in pain and exhausted. When the nurse finally checked me, she said that in all her time doing this type of work, mine was the most terrible physical trauma she'd encountered, adding that she would be more than willing to testify to that in court. She was very kind and compassionate.

I took emergency contraception, an HIV cocktail as a precaution against possible exposure, and an STD test. For weeks I was weak from the side effects of the HIV cocktail. I was relieved and grateful that my test results were all fine, but can you imagine how awful I felt during those weeks, not knowing if I was okay?! I tried to get counseling, but the referrals I got were not helpful, and I couldn't afford to pay for therapy on my own. I told no one but my sister; I simply worked like a robot, just existing. I didn't know what to do. I didn't eat and couldn't sleep — I just worked — until about a bit over a month after my rape, when I ended up in the emergency room with a severe asthma attack, during which I was pronounced clinically dead for about four minutes. Actually that was the only time I had felt any peace since the rape. Then I was brought back to my so-called life, and I was not happy to be back!

Why? Why would G-d be so cruel as to have me go through the agony of physically dying? Why did I experience what I call a cosmic tease? I felt the deliciousness of being on the other side. I had peace, absolute love, and joy when I was dead, and then *bam*! I got the Cosmic Boot™, (which I wrote about in detail in my soon-to-be-published book, *Death Didn't Want Me Getting the Cosmic Boot*™).

I returned home to finish my recovery and wanted to know about my case, but the investigator was dismissive and unresponsive. I tried many times to find out what was going on, but couldn't get any answers. It took me many months, with the assistance of an advocate, to find out the status of my case: It was closed. The investigator in charge said that I never showed interest in pursuing the case — a completely false statement on his part.

It took years for me to finally have the satisfaction of knowing that my rapist was behind bars for the crime that he committed against me. Even though I was relieved when they put him away where he cannot hurt anyone else, I remained inundated with a rage that was destroying me. After a while of searching, I found a therapist in California who helped a bit. Meanwhile I was trying to live my life, which I did very poorly. I was a walking, talking, breathing ghost, and no matter what I did to help myself, nothing worked. I remained stuck in "Why did this happen to me?" and unable to make progress in my healing process.

I went through all the stages common to someone who's had a traumatic incident: denial, shame, self-blame, anger, and so on. Clinically I knew why I felt and behaved in those ways. But that didn't help me from feeling it. I had worked with rape survivors for many years, and I had taken a self-defense class. I felt that somehow I should have known better, that I should have been able to stop it. I should be able to "get over it" because I knew what steps to take to heal. My life was a complete mess, and I felt no zest for life. I had no direction with work and no personal social life.

After several years in San Francisco I moved back to New York City and my family found out about the rape — I was no longer functional. I stayed home, unable to go out by myself. I wore baggy clothes and hats, so that no one could see me — even if it were hot outside, I would cover my body. Back in therapy, I still had to take anti-depressants and anti-anxiety medication in order to become functional again. The medication helped, but rage still filled me. I simply felt hopeless. I finally decided to end all the pain, so I overdosed on the pills. I ended up in the emergency room, where they gave me an enormous amount of charcoal to help rid my body from the toxins of the pills. I have to tell you there's nothing more mind clearing than seeing the image of yourself with your mouth and teeth stained with thick black coal goop. The thing about hitting rock bottom is that you have only the top to go to. It took me some time to ask myself why I was still in such pain and despair. I knew I was stuck, but how do I give myself the nudge to begin healing?

I thought about when I worked with my clients, and what they shared with me. I remembered the feedback that they gave about me — how compassionate and non-judgmental I was with them. I seriously began to meditate on why I was able to show compassion for others but not for myself. On one of my many sleepless nights, I opened a big box of my old journals and started to read both the pre- and post-rape ones, and I sobbed uncontrollably. I finally allowed myself to grieve for the person I had been before the rape. I decided to bury most of my journals symbolically, which allowed me to say goodbye to that part of me that I felt was gone.

But after a while, I realized that part of me was not gone. What the rapist had done had changed me forever. That was a fact! But now it was up to me to decide **how** it had changed me. *Was I going to be a lost soul? Someone scared of her own shadow? Someone who did not trust her judgments anymore? Was I going to continue to see only the ugliness of life and marinate in bitterness?*

I re-read the journals from after the rape and tried to objectively see the things that I was going through. I really tried not to judge anything. I just recognized all the things that I had been doing that were not allowing me to heal. I finally did for myself what I was able to do for the clients I worked with: I showed compassion and worked on not being judgmental. By doing so, I ended up forgiving myself. Through doing these things, I became less angry, and started the process of letting go of the rage I felt toward my rapist. He overpowered me that night. But I realized that I could have that power back by not letting what he did prevent me from having a happy, fulfilling life. So I simply began to forgive him. This does not mean I wanted to hang out with him and send him holiday cards. But holding on to the rage was not hurting him — it was hurting me. I know it sounds cheesy, but just because it's cheesy doesn't mean it's not true.

I wondered if my working with victims of violent crimes years ago had been a way for G-d to help me prepare for my own personal tragedy. I know it might sound strange, but I do believe this to be true. Once I took those *huge* steps of self-compassion, forgiveness, letting go, and re-claiming my life, I reached out to others more and talked openly about my rape. In time, I could again go out by myself and I started literally taking off the layers that I carried. An artist friend of mine knew about my rape and told me about a radio show called The Rape Declaration Forum in New York on radio station WBAI, which his girlfriend hosted and produced. He suggested that perhaps I would want to go on and talk about what had happened to me. It's a live call-in show, where people can share their story on the air. I decided to do it, and Rebecca Myles, the show's host, invited me to be in the studio while she played my pre-recorded interview.

I went to the studio; it was my first time doing any radio, and I was nervous. After Rebecca played the tape of my story, people called in to share their own stories, saying that in my telling my story I had inspired and helped them. It truly was *powerful*. That's when I *really* began to thank G-d that I had been raped! The pain and anger that I had for myself, my rapist, and G-d had transformed to inner peace and purpose. I was able to see the person I am now — a woman who has survived a personal tragedy and has found her *power*. I have the power to claim my life. It is *me* and not *my rape* that defines it.

I know that compassion and forgiveness starts with *me*. I know that being in a state of gratitude allows me more things to be thankful for in my life. I have the courage now to be true to myself. I now embrace the writer and artist in me by way of my poems and books. I am an activist and public speaker, spreading the message of self-empowerment and inspiration. The biggest blessing for me is that I found my purpose: to do radio broadcasting. I was graciously asked to co-host *The Rape Declaration Forum* at WBAI with Rebecca Myles. I also produce and host my own radio show, *The Jay Grayce Radio Variety Show*, on Tribecaradio.net.

It is a place of gratitude that allows me to see and understand the great opportunities that can come from my struggles. It has taken me a long time to understand that. I really did not believe that I would find joy in my life again. So for anyone who is lost in despair, I would suggest that you feel what you are feeling. But please also be patient and compassionate with yourself. And I thank G-d for allowing me the honor of having *you* read my story.

❤   ❤   ❤

Julian J Grayce was a crisis counselor, advocate, and group facilitator for crime victims for ten years before she decided to go in a different career direction, in which she has been an entrepreneur and artist. She is now the creator/producer and host of *The Jay Grayce Variety Show*™ for Tribecaradio.net. Julian also is the co-host of *The Rape Declaration Forum* on New York's WBAI, 99.5 FM. She serves on the board of directors for NPOs and is an activist for victims and animal rights.

Thank God
I Had Cancer

MARILYN JOYCE

*I*n most ways, it was a day like any other back in 1985. I awoke at 5:00 A.M., did my concentrated hour of yoga and meditation, and hurriedly showered as I began, in my already over-full brain, to organize my busy day ahead. With two teenage kids to rouse from their usual deep sleep, breakfasts were always a challenge as I continually yelled those all-too-common words, "Get up *now*, or you'll be late for school!"

However for me, this morning was different. As I stood in front of the bathroom mirror after my delicious, steamy shower, deep in contemplation, I noticed that the little blue spot under my eye (from an extremely hard baseball that hit my eye when I was eleven) was not the same. Today it was shiny, hard, and kind of a mixture of black and purple, depending on how the light. It definitely would have been beautiful as the fabric of a dress for me, since those are my best colors. But on my face, it was not a pretty picture! How had I not noticed this before? I guess like most moms, I rarely had the luxury of time to gaze in the mirror at my face when the day ahead always had so many demands to meet. A quick make-up job, and then I was off and running.

That particular morning I'd awoke feeling on top of the world. I had arrived! My own professional association invited me to be a keynote presenter at our annual conference. As I showered, anticipation and a sense of incredible possibilities filled my thoughts. I planned my speech and visualized the room packed with more than a thousand of my peers. The thrill of this picture left me almost breathless. Until I looked in the mirror! Would *you* want to stand up there on a stage with that ugly thing on your *face?* No question about it . . . this had to be removed pronto!

That began a journey that I shall always remember. Here I was at the peak of my career and feeling like I had achieved amazing success, only to be slapped in the face with a diagnosis of cancer. Melanoma, to be exact! I had no idea how serious this illness could be. But, as if that weren't enough, a week after I got out of the hospital from this diagnosis, I was rushed into the hospital again with uterine cancer — *stage four.* I was only thirty-five years old! The women in my own family impacted by this were more than double my age when diagnosed.

Of course, I went through all of the same feelings everybody else goes through. *How could this be possible?* I was vegan, practiced yoga, meditated daily, used the most environmentally friendly products I could find, worked hard, and had the respect of my peers and business associates for always doing more than what was asked of me. I appeared to have more energy than most people I knew, and on the surface looked, very healthy. In other words, I went into complete denial, followed by immense, almost seething anger, and eventually felt like a completely hopeless victim. My frequent lament was — you guessed it — "Why me?"

Four years later, I found myself at the lowest point in my life, and health, imaginable. My finances were low — well let's just say *nil* — and I had not been able to eat solid foods for months. I could only suck on ice chips in order to stay hydrated. My body wasted away simply from lack of nourishment. And, just as most of my seriously ill patients have done, I tried everything anyone suggested, from anywhere and everywhere in the world, in search of that magic bullet.

By 1989, I weighed eighty-eight pounds and was in a wheel chair. They said I wouldn't live more than another week or so. That's when the miracles began!

In an effort to get me out of the house, my family and friends dragged me off, or rather wheeled me off, to a local home show. There, a rather handsome young man with a Vita Mix machine (which I now fondly refer to as a 2-horsepower lawn mower for food!) introduced me to cantaloupe ice, with seeds and all included. After two months of this concoction, I had obviously outlived my prognosis by six weeks. *Hope* swept through my entire being. I was on my journey back to health. I included other fruits as tolerated, then vegetables, and eventually tofu, soy, and whole grains — in other words, whole foods in a whole food form; back-to-basics real food nutrition.

There's much more, though. You know how we say that illness, or wellness, is a whole body experience — emotionally, mentally, physically, and spiritually? Well, that same weekend, a close friend took me to a Bernie Siegel event — a *full day* seminar. Whew! Absolutely one of the least comfortable days of my life that I can remember! Not only on a physical level, but on every level imaginable. I faced so many things about myself and my life that I had avoided, ignored, buried, or denied, and otherwise never addressed. Cancer personality? Living everyday with endless *shoulds*, *coulds*, and *woulds*? "People pleaser" be damned! I had things that had to get done! Taking time out for myself? There weren't enough hours in the day for anything other than family and work responsibilities! Love my life and have fun? Life is an uphill battle, with no rest until you die! Stop constantly *doing*, and start *being*. *Being*? What in heaven's name was this crazy doctor talking about?

On the first break, the kind doctor came over to me and asked me my story. Reflecting back, I am quite certain that the huge block on my shoulder (*block* versus *chip*) expressed itself most clearly that day. I had a most definite victim perspective of the whole situation. Poor me. It's not fair! After all I had done for others, always putting them first — that's right: *the great big martyr story*! Everything bad that could happen to anyone happened to me! Everything and everyone was doing it to me! I had no control and was at the mercy of all of the odds against me. Poor little defenseless damsel in major distress! Ever meet anyone like that?

None of this deterred the doctor. His kind, compassionate, and loving gaze truly warmed my heart. He actually listened to me without interruption. And then he asked me a strange question: Did I see cancer as a friend? I was horrified! A friend? Indeed not! He assured me that my response was appropriate, asking what we normally do with a friend. We keep a friend around, of course. So did I see cancer as my enemy? "Absolutely!" I responded. His response to his own question of "What do you do with an enemy?" was that we also keep an enemy around. I sat expressionless, not sure how to reply. He continued saying that we do this from a negative stance; always looking for ways to get even with them, to get revenge for one thing or another, or just by constant feelings of anger, hate, resentment, or frustration toward them. I had never thought of it from that perspective before. And, without question, I had spent most of my life with complete anger and resentment toward my mother, whose mental illness and excessive violent outbursts resulted in massive turmoil throughout my entire life.

The last, and most provocative, question was — are you ready for this one? — "Can you see cancer as your teacher?" *I'm sorry*, I thought. That was just stretching this whole experience way too far for me at that moment. "Well," he asked, "what do you do with a teacher when you have learned all that you can from that teacher?" Oh my goodness. *I got it! You release that teacher and move on to the next teacher. You let go of that teacher, filled with all of the learnings and growth that you have gained, so that you can then be open for the next level of learning and growth in your life.* So then, the big question for me became, "What is this cancer journey trying to teach me?" As Dr. Siegel was wrapping up our precious moments together that wonderful and fateful day, he tried to hug me. He truly is a great hugger! I completely contracted and flinched. Smiling, he said, "Imagine if a hug a day could keep the doctor away, what might ten hugs a day do?" Quite frankly, hugs were never something I felt comfortable giving, or receiving. Well, at least not until that incredible day.

After the seminar completed, we left that hustling, bustling room, abuzz with an unprecedented level of enthusiasm, anticipation, and joy.

My heart raced with excitement, and my mind swam with all of the conceptual frameworks introduced by this amazing doctor. And the question kept racing through my already-full mind: "What is cancer trying to teach me?"

That evening I attempted to journal again (something I had done off and on over the years), in an effort to find the answer to this challenging question. I started a new type of journaling book: my book of gratitudes. What you focus on expands in your life. So, if you focus on what you are grateful for, you will attract into and create in your life a lot more to be grateful for. Without a doubt, this was a most difficult process I attempted that evening. I did not fare well at all. There was not one thing that the *block* on my shoulder would allow me to see as something to be grateful for in my life! I gave up and went to bed, completely fatigued from such an intense day of inner work, yet filled with calm anticipation for the potential healing of my body and soul.

Very early the following morning I awoke with answers to my question. That's right. Answers with an "s"! Life had become so full of commitments, perceived obligations, constant busyness, and a mile-long list of things that I was tolerating — constantly "*shoulding*" on myself — that I experienced absolutely no joy or love for, or in, my life. And I was definitely not having any fun! I was very clear that all of this had to change. *How* was another story. The morning was extremely overcast and depressing. When I pulled out my gratitude journal to once again try to come up with five things I was thankful for, my mind drew a complete blank. Then I remembered the good doctor saying that if I could think of only one thing to be grateful for, just write that down five times. At that very moment, the sun forced its beautiful bright smile out from behind those dense dark clouds, just for a very brief few seconds. Wow, what a sight! Overwhelmed with gratitude for that exquisite moment of brilliance, I immediately wrote it down — not once, but five times. "Thank God for the brilliant sun shining upon me and helping me to heal my resilient body!"

A month later, I was writing at least a hundred *different* gratitudes in my journal, each and every day. A year later, I recovered. And to prove that I was on the mend, I ran a mile — in thirty minutes. Slow, yes, but a huge step forward from where I was! It's been over seventeen years now, and my life is brim full of wonderful new adventures and tremendously loving friends and associates. I love my life — and I have lots of fun! Every day, I awaken filled with gratitude for the opportunity to just be here, to live my purpose, and to experience purpose for life in general.

Some important laws I've learned, through my journey with cancer, for creating a healthy, abundant, and meaningful life, include:

1) Surround yourself with loving people who express gratitude daily for their own lives.

2) Take five — five minutes — throughout the day to just be still and experience the stillness deep within: emotionally, mentally, physically, and spiritually.

3) Live in the moment. The past is like a canceled check, the future like a promissory note, and you cannot do anything about either one. *Today* is cash in hand. Spend it wisely. It is the "present" you have been given, to unwrap and thoroughly embrace and enjoy — moment to moment! So, you see, you can change your life in an instant.

4) Live every day filled with gratitude. Write at least five things, large or small, that you are grateful for each day in your own Gratitude Journal. Focusing on the good in your life creates more of the same.

5) *Gratefully* take responsibility for your own life, and learn to discern. Ask questions. Go to the source. Awareness and knowledge, balanced with some wisdom and a generous dose of discipline, are the cornerstones of a healthy life.

6) Stop "*shoulding*" on yourself! You have choices. Make them based on your own — no one else's — dreams, desires, goals, and personality.

7) Celebrate to accelerate (as my close friend Tim says). Gratefully honor yourself for your successes and a job well done. What you focus on expands!

8) Use balanced affirmation statements and visualization, along with "*feelization*," to achieve success in anything you do. *Feeling*

your success as you visualize it, before you have actualized it, opens you up to receiving/creating your desired results.

9) Write a long list of all the people you want to meet, and another long list of all of the things you want to do and places you want to go, before you die. People who do this generally live long, healthy lives. They have too much to do before they go!

10) See the sunny side of life. Laugh a lot, especially at yourself. Read *Anatomy of an Illness* by Norman Cousins. And watch a lot of funny movies!

11) Do what you love, and love what you do. Be in integrity with who you really are, not who you think you should be to please others. Discover your mission and live it with purpose. This is your birthright!

12) Gratefully be of service to others with love and generosity. Recognize the privilege it is to be alive and to be able to co-create, with others, a world filled with love, compassion, and gratitude for everything this life has to offer.

What I discovered during that often frightening, and most definitely challenging, journey of self-discovery, is that when I live according to my purpose, with *sincere* gratitude for *everything that occurs every day*, my life is filled with more love, joy, and abundance than one could ever imagine. And, as much as I realize that this is a cliché, it is amazingly true that within every seemingly dark cloud exists a miraculous silver lining. We just had to be open to see it — and then to act on it. What do you have to lose? Why not start right now with whatever is directly in front of you that you feel is an unfair hand of fate, and ask for the lesson. Then *feel* and *express* (in your Gratitude Journal) sincere and deep gratitude for the answer you receive — that answer may just save your life. It saved mine!

❤   ❤   ❤

Dr Marilyn Joyce, RD, The Vitality Doctor™, is an internationally acclaimed inspirational keynote speaker, seminar leader, trainer, writer, radio and television personality, and one of the world's leading authorities on overcoming and preventing degenerative illnesses five minutes at a time. For over thirty years, Dr. Joyce, Registered Dietitian, has been inspiring audiences around the world with her lively, information-packed seminars and workshops, which are loaded with powerful, proven, quick, and easy strategies for creating outstanding health and vitality. As a television and radio personality on such shows as *Doctor to Doctor*, *Leeza* and *Jenny Jones*, she has touched hundreds of thousands of lives. Marilyn is the author of *5 Minutes to Health*, *I Can't Believe It's Tofu!* and the soon-to-be-released *Instant Energy!* She is the former Director of Nutrition for the Cancer Treatment Centers of America, and is herself a five-time cancer survivor — now thriver! For more information visit: www.marilynjoyce.com.

Thank God
I Had a Catastrophe

SURVIVING THE ANDREA DORIA SHIPWRECK

PIERETTE DOMENICA SIMPSON

*W*e're going under! We're going to die! It's another *Titanic!*"
As a nine-year-old girl sheltered in a small village within
the Italian Alps, I was blissfully unaware of life's perils. I hadn't heard
of the *Titanic* and certainly didn't understand the concept of dying on
a sinking ship. But this was 1956, and many fellow passengers recently
saw the classic 1953 film, *Titanic*. Their ominous words paralyzed me
with fear. In the sudden darkness, panic ensued. I heard various expla-
nations for our predicament: "A boiler exploded! An elevator crashed!
We hit a mine! We hit an iceberg!"

As I much later described it in *Alive on the Andrea Doria! The
Greatest Sea Rescue in History*:

> We swayed rigidly from an abrupt jolt accompanied by a thun-
> derous noise. Those who were on the outer deck witnessed
> startling fireworks created by grinding steel — sparked by an
> unidentified vessel slamming into our hull at full speed. They
> watched in horror as the perpetrator tried to withdraw from

the hole it had created, slicing through thick walls of steel that had once protected passengers from the dangers of the ocean. In the Social Hall, these gruesome theatrics were magnified by the crashing of hundreds of bottles that landed on the bar floor, as if thrown there by the devil's rage.

Every fiber in our spines reacted to the scraping, screeching, and crunching noises from an indefinable source. The entire floating city began to lean dramatically toward the starboard side. When the lights finally flickered and stayed on, they revealed passengers lying on the floor, screaming from shock or injury.

Poor immigrants and wealthy passengers were struggling to survive the most calamitous collision in history between two passenger liners: the Swedish liner *Stockholm* and the luxury liner *Andrea Doria*.

My grandparents and I gripped each other with each episode of loud, creaking noises that plunged us to a lower depth — along with our dream of immigrating to the New World! To make things even worse, hideous fumes blurred our senses. My grandmother muttered something about surviving the war just to die on a beautiful ship carrying our life's possessions. I focused on the thought that New York was only one sleep away and that my mother had waited eight years to see me again. Fortunately, the *Andrea Doria* stayed afloat. We sat straddled on the sharply inclined floor for a few seemingly endless hours. Then our somber prayers were interrupted by sharp, hopeful voices. "Look, the rescue ships! We're not going to die!"

I wondered how we would reach the French liner *Ile de France*, which reminded me of a bobbing amusement park with its lights twinkling in the distance. As our ship seemed to be capsizing, we hurriedly lowered ourselves on ropes and nets thrown over the railing by the crew. Abandoning ship, 1,663 people embarked on overloaded lifeboats, leaving behind forty-three passengers crushed in their cabins or washed out to sea. Finally, we reached the *Ile de France*, who welcomed us aboard with a Jacob's ladder dangling several stories down the side of its hull. I didn't think I could make this death-defying climb and cried unmercifully. But there was no alternative. I made the ascent with a man climbing behind me, feeling the dreadful experience of being suspended a mile above the sea. *How would my grandparents make the climb*, I worried.

The next morning, my family watched the interment of everything dear to us as it became engulfed by a giant whirlpool. I cried over losing my first communion dress.

Thus did I immigrate to the land of promise. We survived a great ordeal; now everything would be all right, I thought; after all, with my grandparents alive, my lifeline was still intact. We finally arrived in Detroit on July 27, 1956. When I "met" my mother, of whom I had no memory, since she had left Italy during my infancy, I heartily embraced her. After many tears of joy and gratitude for having survived the seemingly unsurvivable, we went to live in a home a fraction of the size of our old farmhouse. It took all of one day before the blending of two families resulted in one troubled unit. The surfacing of old wounds, adapting to a new culture, all exacerbated by the *Andrea Doria* trauma, created an unhappy existence. And that unhappiness lasted for years to come, made worse by the guilt that besieged me for dragging my poor grandparents into a quagmire of turmoil.

Ten years later, petrified by how to survive on my own, I left this tattered nest. Instead of feeling the love of four parents, I felt only confusion about which ones were my parents. Incredibly, under these trying conditions, I met the man who would become my soul mate. Richard, also a college student, became my mentor and constant companion. In our marriage, I finally rediscovered the loving protection that I felt while growing up with my grandparents in Italy. Richard was my blessing . . . until he suffered a massive heart attack at the age of twenty-nine. Subsequently, I became his mentor and caretaker. But sadly, just six years later, at the age of thirty-five, Richard died after suffering a second heart attack.

Now widowed and only thirty-three years old, I had already experienced the loss of everything that had been dear to me: separation from my homeland, my grandparents, my new American family, and now my best friend. *How could I survive another abandonment?* As I pondered that question, hoping for an answer, the silence was resounding. This depleted me of all hope and desire to live. With grief counseling, I again arose from the ruins of my life and tried to create a new life for myself. Ten years later, I even remarried. But once again, it seemed that fate was bent on testing my endurance: after seven difficult years of marriage, my husband and I divorced. Although it was the right decision, I resented a Universe that seemed to be determined to bar me from my happiness.

But fortunately, not everything in my life was tears and sadness. During this difficult period I met my natural father, who lived in Italy. He accepted me fully as a daughter; finally I had a father! I welcomed this strange phenomenon of a real father's love. He guided me with his wisdom and introduced me to my new extended family, who offered me the sense of belonging that I so desperately yearned for. But, as if my string of challenges were to become eternal, after only a few years, my father passed away. I was now fifty years old and once again feeling desolate, abandoned, and without a lifeline.

It became imperative to find a new source of strength to help me create a vision. I turned to the wisdom of friends, yoga, mindfulness meditation, and spiritual teachers such as Dr. Wayne Dyer, Eckhart Tolle, and Louise Hay. I learned how to surrender to my past, live more in the moment, and neutralize the pain of abandonment. This process required reading, listening to tapes, reciting mantras, meditation, prayers, and journaling. I grasped the concept of taking control of my life and that I had within me the wherewithal to direct my life, instead of it directing me! Mostly, I learned about the power of focused thinking and using thought as my strength. I also took inventory of all my accomplishments, which, to my amazement, were numerous: I put myself through college, became a semi-professional violinist, named "Michigan Foreign Language Teacher of the Year," and inducted into my school district's "Teacher Hall of Fame." I also maintained solid friendships. But more importantly, I realized that I had surmounted numerous life challenges — while remaining physically and mentally intact! How could I have neglected to recognize this earlier?

With a thankful heart, I focused on shedding old baggage by concentrating on the benefits of my experience; I replaced long lists of resentments with a concrete list of objectives that I sought concerning relationships, career, and personal well-being. I was very specific, and I still refer to my list regularly, realizing that I'm crafting a new life for myself based on my wishes. Nevertheless, this self-development process did not include facing the guilt I felt over having uprooted my grandparents, just to have them hand me over to a new family. Along with this subconscious denial was the denial of the *Andrea Doria* as a major event in my life. During nearly fifty years, the tragedy surfaced only in casual conversation. In 2004, however, I astonished myself when I chose to write my first book, a work of historical non-fiction titled *Alive on the Andrea Doria! The Greatest Sea Rescue in History.*

I plunged feet-first into this project in order to have the book published by the fiftieth anniversary of the tragedy: July 25, 2006. I had only a couple of years to do extensive technical research both in Italy and in the U.S., and to locate and interview dozens of surviving passengers, crewmembers, and maritime scientists. This left a very short time to find a publisher, initiating my search for one only eight months before the book had to be published. But my two and a half years of intense work resulted in my signing contracts with not just one but two publishers: one in New York and the other in Milano, Italy. Even though writing a book required immense sacrifice, the process taught me some invaluable lessons: The first is that, in spite of all my former challenges, I have the courage to be a risk-taker. Second, I am blessed with the indomitable immigrant spirit — the ethics that made this country great: hard work with trunks full of perseverance lead to realized dreams. Finally, and along the lines of self-growth, I learned that I could rewrite my life script and see it through any perspective I wish.

I learned by writing my autobiography for Chapter 1, with the guidance of a book called *Your Life As Story.* Author Tristine Rainer explained:

When I view myself as the heroine of my own story, I no longer complain about the conflicts in my life and in myself. I am no longer a victim of circumstances. No longer am I caught within

the psychological paradigm of neurosis. Instead, I am full of
anticipation for my journey into the unknown. I'm a protago-
nist in a world of unending dilemmas, which contain hidden
meaning that it is up to me to discover. I am the artist of my
life, who takes the raw materials given, no matter how bizarre,
painful, or disappointing, and gives them shape and meaning.

What a revelation! I realized why I had embarked on being an
author of my personal *Andrea Doria* story. The autobiography allowed
me to recount my past while viewing my complex life through a new
filter — all while making sense of the scattered pieces. I could reinvent my legend with me as the heroine instead of the victim. But more
importantly, I wrote because I had the courage to face my past head-
on and have the reserve to go one step beyond to focus on altruistic
reasons. I followed my calling and conscience of restoring honor to my
fellow Italians, who were unjustly blamed for the collision and sinking,
correcting a part of history through my book. Would I have had the
privilege of serving humanity on such a large scale without the *Andrea
Doria* tragedy? It is unlikely.

The pride of writing and publishing has led me to believe that the
Universe has been "conspiring" in my favor, after all. It seems to have
brought me many defeats, so that each fight will fill me with a greater
sense of fulfillment in victory. With this in mind, I face new challenges
in appreciation for Eleanor Roosevelt's words:

> You gain strength, courage, and confidence by every experi-
> ence in which you really stop to look fear in the face. You are
> able to say to yourself, "I have lived through this horror. I can
> take the next thing that comes along." You must do the thing
> you think you cannot do.

I am grateful for the catastrophe that taught me resilience, thereby
bringing my life full circle: I am embracing heartily my Italian roots
and reconnecting to my American family, creating new lifelines in the

process. Being the author of one's catastrophic experience can be a painful process, but the results are revealing and enlightening I realize that retelling the *Andrea Doria* story ran parallel to my inner struggle: when I felt weak, I buried it; as I grew stronger, I faced it, thus becoming its heroine. Do I still feel pain for my grandparents' ultimate sacrifice of leaving their homeland, then forgoing me as a "daughter"? Certainly, but I surrender to its reality with more grace when my mother's praise reminds me of the blessings: "Your grandparents would be so proud that your book vindicates your fellow Italians for the *Andrea Doria* tragedy." Moreover, I've released the pain held within the series of abandonments, embracing new relationships with excitement.

Overall, I feel better prepared for treading on rough waters, grateful for having taken many lifeboats to transcendence. I'm confident that with future challenges, I will steadily climb another rope like the one that dangled along the side of the *Ile de France,* accepting another good fight in the miracle of life. Knowing that the *Andrea Doria* was my training ground for courage, I will gratefully say, "Thank God that traveling on the ill-fated liner steered me toward a life journey that I claim as my legend!"

❤   ❤   ❤

Pierette Simpson is the author of *Alive on the Andrea Doria! The Greatest Sea Rescue in History* and *L'Ultima Notte dell'Andrea Doria.* A survivor of the sea disaster, Simpson is an authority on this shipwreck and researches others; she speaks internationally on the topic. Being multilingual, Simpson enjoys foreign travel and is a supporter of the arts. For more information and to contact the author: www.pierettesimpson.com and www.andreadoriabook.com.

Thank God
My Husband Was an Alcoholic

THE POWER OF GRATITUDE:
A SENIOR CITIZEN'S STORY

KATHERINE SCHERER

This story begins with the end — the end of my marriage. It was the summer of 1989, a long way from my wedding day in 1957. As I walked off steam around the neighborhood, contemplating a separation from my husband, I thought about my dreams of being married forever and living happily ever after. Those were my dreams, all right, but now I reached my boiling point about my husband's refusal to work. He was willing to let our sons do the work while he sat in the bar, and on top of that, he criticized and demeaned them. How dare he! We owned our home, raised four children, and owned a successful business. My daughter was nineteen, my three sons were married with children of their own, which made me a grandmother. But now finally it was clear to me that I couldn't tolerate his behavior anymore, and I couldn't make my marriage work. How unfair that I had to start over again at my age — I was almost a senior citizen, for Pete's sake.

For years I did everything I could to hold my marriage together. I took care of the house, handled our finances, ran our business, and sold new construction. I still cared about the marriage and struggled to keep everything under control. I was exhausted, close to a nervous breakdown, and desperate. Things were getting more difficult when they should be getting easier. *Why couldn't my husband realize that his drinking was out of control?*

I had heard about Al-Anon. It was a place where family members of problem drinkers could go for support. I decided to try it. Soon after attending my first meeting, I met with a counselor and learned that I was married to an alcoholic for thirty-two years without even knowing it. I didn't know that alcoholism is a disease. And like so many others, I thought a person had to be lying in a gutter to be considered an alcoholic. In the early years, my husband always went to work, drinking mostly on the weekends. In fact, I often joined him in a drink. We bowled in a couples' league, had friends at the bar, and they considered us as fun people. It seemed pretty normal at the time. It was just "social drinking." Sure, he had outbursts that were pretty scary when he drank too much. But when I got upset enough about them, he cleaned up his act, and for a long time after that things would seem okay again—until the next time.

Now, he wasn't willing to clean up his act anymore . . . and I wasn't willing to live with his drinking anymore. By the end of the summer, I saved enough money to cover three months' rent. I took very little with me: the bedroom set, wicker furniture for my living room, an old kitchen table and chairs, dishes and utensils for four, a bowl or two, and a few pots and pans. And of course, my five boxes of books and tapes. I was an avid reader for over twenty years, and these authors were my friends. (I had given up my personal friendships many years ago to avoid the shame and embarrassment I felt about his drinking.)

In 1990, when my divorce became final, I was fifty years old. My now-ex stayed in the house, and I moved out, giving up many of my meaningful treasures. I worked full time, walking construction sites, hiring and firing employees, and doing everything I could to save a business that wasn't my dream. My resentment continued to fuel my anger. I was too old to be doing this stuff. I should be thinking about retirement soon. I should have someone to love me and take care of me. I should have more money. I should, I should, I should. On the outside I may have appeared strong, able, competent, and put together. On the inside, I was scared — scared about being on my own and about the future.

I often thought back to when my mother told me my dad was an alcoholic, back when my husband first showed signs of maybe having a drinking problem. She told me that just before I was born, she issued my dad an ultimatum to quit drinking or she would leave him. He quit drinking for the next few weeks, but then he died from a fall at work. I was only three weeks old, and my brothers and I grew up supported by the state. I watched my mother exhaust herself cooking, cleaning, washing clothes, and working part-time.

Looking back, it seemed like my life was too much like hers — too much pain, suffering, hard work, and bitterness, even though I tried so hard to make it different. I was an emotional mess, but I tried to fool myself into believing that I was better than other people because of my accomplishments. Denial is very powerful.

I was indignant at the thought that any of this could be my fault. I felt sorry for myself and hammered away at his mistakes and short-comings. I thought I had a right to be angry and was hard pressed to let it go. I spent most of my life trying to please him. Now it was time to take care of me. I went to Al-Anon meetings, continued the counseling, read self-help books, and listened to tapes constantly. I examined my own attitudes and activities and found out about co-dependence. I prayed the Serenity Prayer, read *One Day at a Time*, and used the Twelve Steps. Every Al-Anon meeting was full of talk about tolerance, kindness, patience, courtesy, humor, gratitude, and love. I had a very high tolerance for suffering, little expectation for love, and I couldn't see much humor in any of this. I was okay in the patience, kindness, and courtesy departments. I was thankful for many things, but unlike some of the people at Al-Anon, I couldn't find one single thing to be grateful for in being married to an alcoholic for thirty-two years. The years of blaming, accusing, and attacking had done me in.

I made a few friends. They were younger than I, but we all had the same story: We were just trying to survive. We accepted each other without judgment, and that felt good. I learned that I didn't cause this disease of alcoholism, I couldn't control it, and I couldn't cure it. That was a relief. I learned that I suppressed deep feelings of anger and resentment from feeling second to alcohol for so many years. I overcame those feelings and gained a new understanding. I gave up my pride and surrendered to God's will. I embraced change, and little by little I improved myself and my life. I believed in my worth as a person — but I still did not know gratitude.

At a meeting of the marketing committee at our church, I met Eileen, who would later become co-author with me of our book, *Gratitude Works: Open Your Heart to Love*. We became fast friends and soon realized that we were both on a quest for healing. We had lots of energy, which we shared with the church community by putting together a successful holistic health conference. We traveled together and, among our endeavors, we attended a "Compassion in Action" three-day workshop in Chicago to learn more about hospice work and compassion. (Eileen previously studied with Elisabeth Kübler-Ross.) We attended workshops on forgiveness by Colin Tipping and Fred Luskin, authors of *Radical Forgiveness* and *Forgive for Good*. I learned that my resentment and anger hurt me more than anyone else. It was time to stop punishing myself. In each workshop, I released more anger and I learned to forgive.

Eileen and I were nearing sixty, but there was something in us that wouldn't let us accept that we had done everything we could do with our lives. We both had a desire to do something that would make a difference, although we had no idea what. One day we watched *The Oprah Show* and heard her guest suggest that people write down five things each day that they were grateful for. Something about that idea spoke to us, and we decided to try it. It wasn't long before we were discovering new things to be grateful for every day. It amazed us how everything seemed connected to everything else. We were in awe of the beauty in the world all around us that we hadn't noticed. This simple exercise shifted our consciousness, and we felt transformed.

Gratitude. It was that simple. We found what was missing from our lives.

Before I knew gratitude, my thoughts always focused on the negative. I looked at what was *not* going well instead of what *was* going well. The glass was always half empty. If you've ever heard the statement, "I hate when that happens," that was me. I didn't ever think about what might be *right* with my life and the world because I was so focused on what was going *wrong*. Then the great and wonderful gift of gratitude arrived. It helped me renew, reflect, and reconnect. It raised my energy vibration, and I felt healthier and happier. Since I truly embraced gratitude, everything that I thought was so bad about my life I now view in a new light. Many incidents of the past that seemed so terrible now seem humorous or even beneficial. Every moment of my past contributed to my finding gratitude, and gratitude was my vehicle to love. For most of my life, I did not know gratitude and I did not know love. Through the simple practice of writing down five things a day that I was grateful for, I found love.

A counselor once told me that education is the only thing that helps to break the chain of alcoholism in a family. What better way to start than with education about gratitude? Gratitude is the legacy I will leave my children, my ten grandchildren, my two great-grandchildren (and one more on the way), and all future generations through my writings and teachings. Gratitude has truly opened my heart to love.

I thank God that I am an independent senior citizen and that I have lived long enough to know gratitude. I thank God for the opportunity to share my story with the world in the hope that others will find gratitude sooner than I did.

Katherine Scherer and Eileen Bodoh are the authors of *Gratitude Works: Open Your Heart to Love*, an inspirational book that helps readers access the healing power of gratitude, and the e-books *Gratitude Works Journal* and *Gratitude Works Prayer Book*. Their mission is to touch lives with the spirit of gratitude.

Thank God
I Had Depression

MICHELLE ARMSTRONG

*I*t was a day not unlike any other day. I awoke that morning with the usual feeling of dread and anxiety about the day to come. I sighed deeply. I was so sick of my life. If only I could escape the pain, the emptiness, the endless stream of torturous thoughts, and the solitude I felt. If I had the energy to kill myself, I would have. Another deep sigh, and I recall thinking, *I'll just stay in bed today. Why bother getting up? What's the point? It's all just too hard. There's no point to anything anyway. Nothing makes any sense. Who cares whether I sleep all day or not? Who cares if I just lie here and die?* My body ached. I was so tired . . . It was exhausting just to breathe. God, my life sucked.

I rolled over and dragged the covers over my head, irritated at the audacity of the sunlight hitting my face through a crack in the heavy drapes. I hated the sun. It always looked so chipper. It seemed to be laughing at me. I angrily stuck my tongue out at it, wishing it would go away and leave me alone. I wanted to cry. The feelings wouldn't come. I felt numb. Sighing another painstaking, long sigh, I curled up in a tight ball beneath the sheets and decided to stay where it was safe. I felt no need to be responsible for anything except feeling bad. But a loud knock at the door disturbed my safe and quiet sanctuary. "Who is it?" I droned, knowing full well it was my housemate. "Bathroom's free," she sang out so enthusiastically I would've hit her if I could've mustered up the energy. "Okay, thanks," I said with about as much intention of using the bathroom as my cat would have of doing laps in the pool. I was too tired to shower. I did not intend to move an inch. Nobody understood what I was going through, what it was like to be me, to be inside the prison of my head, to have my crappy life. They couldn't feel my pain. If they did, they'd realize I just wanted to be left alone.

I'd been in bed for over three weeks now, my mind engulfed with negative thoughts and catastrophic images that haunted my soul. I was in a downward mental and emotional spiral that I felt I couldn't control, and I wanted to die. Life was too hard. I also wanted to quit my job. I couldn't see the purpose in being there anymore. Oh sure, it paid the bills, but it wasn't fulfilling, and I couldn't find the motivation to deal with the deadlines, the responsibilities, having to get dressed every-day, put on make-up, talk to people . . . it was all too much hard work. What was the point? None of it made sense. *Why is the world punishing me? Why can't I just be like everyone else? What's wrong with me?* I sighed another deep sigh. *Why am I even here?*

I decided to quit my job. Besides, I was certain everyone at work knew I hadn't really been sick for the last three weeks. I convinced myself that they all considered me a horrible liar and loser and, let's face it, they were right. I could imagine them talking about me in the cafeteria, discussing how shocking it was that I hadn't shown up for work, chatting about how horrible I was . . . I shuddered with feelings of guilt. I felt guilty a lot lately. Guilty for being alive. Guilty for being on this planet. It felt overwhelming. I wanted to vomit. God, I was pathetic. *I hate myself. I hate being awake! Why can't I go back to sleep?!*

I continued thinking about work. I couldn't bear the thought of how everyone would look at me if I went back. I imagined they could see right into my pain, into all my dark secrets, making me feel exposed and vulnerable, as if I were being interrogated under a huge spotlight. It felt unsafe. There was no way I would go back. I couldn't deal with the shame — everyone thinking me a failure. I rolled over again. This time

I noticed my journal on my bedside table. It had a picture of a woman sitting on a chair with her head down, alone in a dimly lit room. To me, she looked suicidal. She looked like me. Instinctively, I reached my hand between the mattress and box spring to grab onto a half-gnawed pencil. With the little bit of energy I had left in me, I began to write: *"Inside the darkness of my mind there is nothing but pain and sadness . . . ."* The words started little by little to pour onto the page, first like tiny raindrops on a giant lily pad, then like a torrential downpour. Once the storm finished, I put my pencil down to admire my melancholy masterpiece. *Boooring!! Who would ever read this junk?* I wondered. *God, I'm so stupid! Why am I so dumb? What's wrong with me? Why can't I get my life together? How did I get this way?* It got me wondering . . .

I mean, my life isn't really *that* bad, is it? So okay, I had a challenging childhood, with its many ups and downs, but who hadn't? My parents separated during a time when I desperately needed them, and it was no secret the divorce was unpleasant. But in the greater scheme of things, if I wanted to, I could actually reflect back on my life and focus in on all the positives. If I *really* chose to want to, I could look back and actually feel a sense of gratitude for all that I'd been fortunate to experience. It wasn't easy to do, but I realized my life could have been very different. I could have been born an orphan, with no parents at all. I could have been born blind, deaf, or otherwise physically impaired in some way. I could have been born into a third world country, where food and water were a scarce blessing. But I wasn't. I was born healthy, into a family that loved me despite my beliefs at the time. I started to reflect back further over my life . . . I was a reasonably smart young lady — no Einstein, but I did well in school. I loved to dance, and despite my low self-esteem telling me otherwise, I had to admit I was pretty good at it. I recognized that when I set my mind to achieving something I wanted, I often got it. My parents loved me, despite my continued resistance and low self-worth. I could easily make friends and establish relationships, so that was a positive, and seeing all this got me to realize . . . I hadn't always been like this. Life hadn't always been depressing for me. I'd loved my life once.

When I reflected back on my childhood then, I recalled so many dreams about what my life was going to be like in the future. I was full of imagination, inspiration, love, trust, curiosity, and joy. Life was fun and enjoyable once! I recalled with some glimmer of hope how excited and inspired I used to be . . . how much I really loved life, loved nature, and loved people. There had been a time when I awoke each morning delighted to find a brand new day of possibility and opportunity before me. As I remembered that feeling of endless possibilities, I stopped for a moment and wondered, *Where did that little child of innocence go? Why did I end up here? How did I end up so depressed and alone?* I swallowed hard in a desperate attempt to push back the seemingly endless stream of tears that built up inside. A lump developed in my throat like a lemon seed stuck in a vodka straw. *What on earth happened to me? Why was this experience happening to me?*

I suddenly felt very restless. An old energy awoke within me, and I was caught in a spaghetti of mixed emotions, sadness, and anger, tangled with old familiar feelings of excitement, motivation, and wonder. My curiosity stirred, and I began wondering, *why is this happening to me?* I remember, growing up, that Mum suggested to me that everything in life happens for a reason. You just have to look for the blessings, the learnings, and opportunities inside everything that happens. Life isn't random. There are opportunities inside every experience, whether it be good or bad to rediscover ourselves; to peel back another onion layer; to go deeper; to become wiser; to evolve and become the very best that we can be.

I realized my depression was a gift! A blessing in disguise! I glanced down at my journal, immediately recalling all that I had written over the past few weeks. The words flooded my consciousness with a greater depth of understanding about who I really am, what I'm here to be on this planet! Small waves of excitement crept into my body. I tingled and vibrated as I allowed the truth of my depression to fill my understanding. *What if I need to experience my depression in order to find myself? What if I'd chosen to experience depression at some unconscious level for the purposes of finding my place in the world? What if I could use my depression as a propulsion system to launch me into the next phase of my life?*

My heart beat faster as a surge of unknown energy burst throughout my body. I felt immediately grateful for what I was going through, and I realized in that very second, I had free will over my life. My eyes slowly widened, and things became very clear. My life boiled down to a fork in the road, and there were two options, with one choice to make. I could choose the road of pain, disillusionment, and inevitable death, probably at my own hand. Or I could choose to be responsible for my life and take the path of liberation, appreciation, personal power, and joy! I leapt out of bed like a five year old who knows that Santa has just delivered that present she's been waiting an entire year for, and I stood tall in the center of my room, feeling incredibly alive. I felt so pumped up and energized that I threw apart the drapes in my room to be instantly drenched in the brightest spectrum of light you've ever seen! I stared out longingly into the day, drinking in as much of the moment as I could get. The sun, which seemingly had been mocking me only moments before, now looked totally different to me. It felt more warm, loving, and inviting. *Hmm, isn't that interesting,* I thought to myself. The world itself suddenly appeared a very different place. It was now a friendly world, full of love and possibility. With a sudden change of focus and appreciation for my experiences, the world had changed from a dark world full of situations I didn't want to face, to a world of endless possibility and freedom. But surely the entire world hadn't just changed in the last few minutes . . . I had! I had simply changed my perception about the world, and it started with a little gratitude. Right then, I experienced an epiphany. I could hardly believe I'd not seen all this before! Until now, I had not noticed all the endless possibilities that were available to me in any given moment. I did not realize my power of choice. In an instant it dawned on me . . . I was always in control of all the results produced in my life. If I wanted to produce different results, all I needed to do was to change my thinking, my perception and the meaning about my experiences! It was so obvious, I laughed out loud in delight! I had been letting my mind control me, rather than me managing and directing my mind. What clarity! What insight! What freedom!

With a force deep within me that is not easy to articulate, I gained a perfect sense of clarity about this world in which I occupy a space, and a connection to a force so powerful, so loving, and so perfect that I'll never again feel lost or depressed by life. I might have sad days, which are normal, but deep clinical depression will never again be a noose around my neck. I recognized life and my relationship to it in a way that was both freeing and empowering. It was as if a light bulb suddenly switched on inside me, and for the first time, I could see who I truly was — the creator of my destiny. And then a voice deep inside me said, "Michelle now is the time to get off your butt and *go live your life*!!"

So that's exactly what I did. I made an appointment with a local counselor to work through my depression and my unconscious blocks, and I got my butt out of the house and back into the world, a new world, ripe and ready for me to make of it whatever I wanted. That day I began the journey of unraveling my past and peeling back the layers of my unresourceful thinking and behaving that had kept me stuck for so long. That day I began to take an honest look at who I really was and what I really wanted in my life. And, let me tell you, having this awareness is by far the best feeling in the world!

Having gratitude not just for my depression, but for all the other perceived negative experiences in life motivated me to become an empowered person. It inspired me to become a coach, a writer, and a motivational speaker. I am so grateful to my depression because it now affords me the opportunity to help others find their place and power in the world. I love knowing that as a consequence of my experiences, I now get to share with other people how they, too, can easily overcome their personal struggles and live the lives they want to live. Thank God I had depression! I am so grateful for this gift.

Steps to Discovering the Blessings in Your Life

1. Journal your thoughts and feelings.
2. Reflect on your past and present situation. Seek out the positives inside what is happening that you may be perceiving as negative.
3. Recognize everything happens for a purpose always.
4. Express gratitude and appreciation for everything that's happened and is happening, even if you don't understand why.

❤   ❤   ❤

Michelle went from an unsatisfying career, depression, frustration, and thousands of dollars in debt, to a career and life she loves and is passionate about, and being thousands of dollars in the black. Michelle is a published author, business owner, and the creator of The Armstrong Method™. Michelle now teaches business professionals how they, too, can have the passionate life and career they love by learning to manage their mindset.

Her credentials include: Master Results Coach, Master Certification in Neuro-Linguistic Programming (NLP) and Hypnosis, Master NLP Trainer, Bachelors Degree in Metaphysical Sciences, Diploma in Counseling and Communications (Australian College of Applied Psychology), Diploma in Clinical Hypnotherapy, Certified Workplace Trainer IV, Master Certification in Neuro-Semantics and Meta-Time Line Therapy. To find out more about Michelle visit www.ArmstrongMethod.com.

Contact info:
Michelle Armstrong
MIND MANAGEMENT LLC
409 N. Pacific Coast Hwy #453
Redondo Beach, CA 90277
e-mail: Michelle@ArmstrongMethod.com
Web: www.ArmstrongMethod.com.

Thank God I Went Broke

MY INVESTMENT PORTFOLIO WENT FROM BOOM TO BUST

MYLES L. MATHIEU

*H*ow would you feel if you were well on your way to fulfilling your childhood dream of being as rich as Croesus ... and then you lost it all? From childhood finances interested me and the stock market intrigued me. I watched the evening news with my father, believing the nightly broadcasters covered the financial markets because that is where investors won or lost their fortunes. My family called me Alex P. Keaton (the nerdy, teenage businessman character played by Michael J. Fox, in the eighties comedy television show *Family Ties*).

Fast-forward about ten years. I graduated from a college in upstate New York with a major in Computer Science and a minor in Finance, after which a Fortune 500 company hired me. I wet my investment whistle by opening a 401(k) deferred retirement account with my new employer and investing in my company's stock. As time went on I purchased my first home and used some of my savings to open my first online brokerage account for stock option trading upon the advice of a friend. I knew of trading concepts such as leveragability, buying on margin, and short selling, but I didn't understand

them. (For you non-investors, these mechanisms are ways to purchase investments with money you don't have in hopes of increasing
your potential investment returns . . . and oh, by the way, these same
vehicles also increase your investment risks as well.)

In September of 1996, I purchased call options against a stock that
allowed me to control 3,000 shares of the stock at a cost of $6,750, less
commissions and fees. During this time the internet was erupting, the
dot-com era was in full force, and most technical stocks were setting
new highs each year. Well, six short months later, I sold those stock
options for over a 1,000% profit, which skyrocketed my liquid investment portfolio to over $75,000. I then proceeded to triple the size of my
portfolio to nearly $250,000 in just eighteen months.

Sounds good, doesn't it? But wait . . . there's a very bumpy road
before the happy ending. I must tell you, going to a job that you don't
really love while you're making $30,000 a month in the stock market
really takes the stress out of your day. When combining my retirement account with my investment account, I had nearly half a million
dollars in investments, and on my way to reaching my personal goal
of becoming a millionaire by the time I was thirty-five. I mistakenly
believed I was becoming wealthy in life; however, it wasn't until I faced
true trials and tribulations before I fully understood the real meaning
of wealth.

Just a mere seven months later, I lost my entire non-retirement
investment portfolio! Deeply depressed, I cried in the shower most
mornings. Since my self-worth depended on my investment portfolio
balance, I felt like an utter failure as a person . . . and as a son. "Why as
a son?" you ask. Well, in the midst of my newfound investment eupho-
ria, I shared my limited knowledge of stock option investing with my
parents and convinced them to turn their modest retirement account
and life insurance proceeds over to an unscrupulous investment advisor, who proceeded to lose their entire retirement portfolio. How would
you feel? If all this weren't enough, just a couple of years later, my
401(k) investment portfolio, which I had grown to $250,000 in under
ten years, fell to $17,000 as my company's pre-split stock price plum-
meted from over $300 a share to $1.10. My once positive net worth
was now negative. I was flat broke.

Looking back, I am sincerely grateful for my "perceived" problems, trials, and tribulations and view it as a true gift from God. Today, I am of the strong belief that the problems that we all face are specific to each one of us. God intentionally uses them to prove a point, to grow our character, and/or to obtain a result. Our most difficult events in life involve our dearest loves and result in exponential growth and rewards. This is certainly the case in my circumstance as my dearest love was the love of money. I possessed an inward focus that concentrated on making more money. I wrestled with feelings and beliefs of greed, scarcity, worry, and fear.

So, just how did my greatest perceived problem become my greatest gift? What did I do to make this transformation of understanding? First and foremost, thanks to my now-wife, Tracey, and a dear friend, Pastor Paul Piraino, I became a Christian and committed my life to Jesus Christ. I read God's word, praying, and focusing on the wisdom that God offers to each believer through our faith in him. God's word tells us in II Corinthians 5:17, "Therefore, if anyone is in Christ, he is a new creation; the old has gone, the new has come!" Christians believe that when we accept Jesus, we transform and begin to think like Jesus and, consequently, act like Jesus. Colossians 3:12-14 gives us a glimpse of what acting like Jesus means: "Therefore, as God's chosen people, holy and dearly loved, clothe yourselves with compassion, kindness, humility, gentleness, and patience. Bear with each other and forgive whatever grievances you may have against one another. Forgive as the Lord forgave you. And over all these virtues put on love, which binds them all together in perfect unity."

I'm also a student of the metaphysical teachings of Dr. John F. Demartini. Dr. Demartini teaches a technique called the *Demartini Method*®, a predetermined set of questions and actions that neutralizes your emotional charges and brings balance to your mind and body. In working through this method, I could see all of the "good" things that occurred or would occur by becoming broke. When I truly believed in my heart and not in my intellectual mind that becoming broke was a true gift, I had tears of gratitude and inspiration running down my face. At the point when I connected the event to my life's purpose, I reached complete acceptance, complete gratitude, and a complete wholeness for becoming broke.

Some experience this breakthrough event in an enlightened "ah-ha" moment that takes minutes; but for others it may take many years. For me, God gradually transformed me over a five-year period, replacing my greedy money qualities with contentment and gratitude for what I have. I now realize that there is abundance in the world for everyone, as opposed to my prior scarcity mentality. I replaced my fears and worries with positive affirmations, and a belief that I can attract anything I want into my life so long as I think, believe, and feel it to be true. Above all else, I believe that my greatest personal character change was a shift in my character from focusing on myself to serving others. My life is not about me, it is about God and serving others. Focusing on doing what I love to do and serving others, I've been able to create a compassionate purpose for my life. When I'm working on my life purpose, I feel the most fulfilled, content, and open to receive God's blessings.

After losing my investment portfolio, I determined not to make the same mistakes again, so I set out upon an intensive period of learning that included an in-depth multi-year period of studying stock option trading, technical analysis, money management principles, and the psychology of investing. Additionally, I formulated a personal prosperity plan for myself that charted a step-by-step process to get out of debt, restore my investment portfolio, and build a new business. Over the last three years, with the help of Dave Ramsey's Financial Peace University curriculum and my local church, I've been able to share my financial learning with others in my community. On a volunteer basis, to date I've impacted the lives of one hundred families. In aggregate, these families have experienced a financial turn-around of $719,307 in just ninety-one days by paying off $473,795 of debt and saving $245,512!

Over the course of just a few short years, God restored all of my prior financial losses and more. However, my newfound understanding of wealth is much broader than purely money. It encompasses all areas of my life — spiritual, financial, physical, relationship, and intellectual. If it weren't for the good fortune of losing my entire investment portfolio, I wouldn't be the person I am today. Thank God that I went broke because without this experience I might have never found my life's purpose of assisting others in achieving their financial aspirations to enable them to fulfill their dreams in life.

♥   ♥   ♥

Myles L. Mathieu is an investment advisor with Twin Tiers Investment Advisors, LLC in Corning, New York, who provides capital management services to high net worth clients whose capital assets exceed $500,000. You may reach him at 607-936-4217 to discuss how he can assist you in achieving your financial goals.

Thank God
I Had an Eating Disorder

PAULA D. ATKINSON

*I*n my thirty-one years on this planet, I've weighed 250 lbs., and I've weighed 80 lbs. Extremely obese as a child and teen, I almost died from starvation in college due to anorexia, bulimia, and addiction to exercise. I was the fat daughter of an alcoholic father and an extremely depressed mother. An only child and a lonely gal, I used food to numb out. I felt like Alice in Wonderland: I didn't fit in with my family at all, and they really didn't comprehend me. Curiosity and energy filled me. The people around me seemed resentful, annoyed, and almost fearful of my desire for knowledge and insatiable hunger for stimulation. I ate to not feel. I became obese to hide and to shelter them from my obviously unacceptable characteristics. By age sixteen I weighed 250 lbs.

One day, at the start of my junior year of high school, I snapped and made the decision to be anorexic. I was definitely not a victim of anorexia. I am a person who does what she sets out to do. Years prior I concluded that my fat body directly caused every problem in my life. Now I was going to change that so I could finally be perfect. For in my head, like any overweight person, I truly believed that being fat was my only problem. So I did it. I lost over 100 lbs. in eight months by over-exercising and starving. I obtained the results I thought I wanted — I was the Homecoming queen by my senior year, attended Homecoming with the quarterback of the football team, and I fell deeply in love with a guy I'd had a crush on since sixth grade. Wherever I turned, I received accolades and compliments for my "discipline" and my "hard work." No one knew that I had starved to get there. I lied to everyone all the time without a second thought.

It didn't take long to realize that I couldn't stop. I would not go back to being fat and I didn't know how to eat normally, but it would be a cold day in hell before I asked another person for help. I continued to starve and over-exercise my way through college. I lived on hard candy, milk, and tomato juice for months. I spent so much time on the step machine at my local gym that they asked me to leave. I never set foot in the dormitory mess hall. In my dorm room, with the door locked, I chewed up and spit out hundreds of dollars' worth of food. The chewing made my mind think I was eating and soothed my rumbling tummy for a short while. Late at night, when the dorm was quiet, I would sneak down to the garbage room to drop off grocery bags full of chewed-up food. When the gym forbade me to work out, I ran miles and miles each day on the streets. Living in San Francisco at the time, I would run up and down hills for hours and hours to burn off imaginary fat. I was completely out of control, crazy, depressed, and trapped in a hell I could have never anticipated. The disease that I invited into my body and mind took over, and there was no room for any remnants of the person I once had been. By age twenty-one, I had starved my body down to a deadly weight.

The day I arrived at the front door of a treatment center, I weighed 80 lbs. I could no longer digest solid foods — my stomach gave up, as it had been so long since I had chewed anything substantial. I stayed in the treatment center for a year while nursing my body back to a healthy weight. The re-feeding process was the most physically uncomfortable thing I have ever gone through, and I had to have more faith than I knew how to assemble. Every day the pendulum swung between great despair and even greater trust. The most valuable lesson throughout was this new concept for me — the idea of gratitude. I had never before been grateful — not once. I had never known humility, trust, or serenity. I had never said, "Thank you," and meant it — never.

That was ten years ago, and my life now isn't perfect. My food isn't perfect, my body is far from perfect, and my head still sometimes gets caught in the tornado of diet and calorie worries. My mind is like a radio stuck on an old station that I hate listening to, but I can't find the dial to turn it. But each day I feel thankful. Each and every day, I cultivate more to be grateful for. Just as I had never known gratitude before my painful journey with my body, today I never feel a sense of victimization. The idea of "why me?" has been totally lifted. The self-obsession and the focus on what's missing from you and from me is no longer a familiar place. It's not even somewhere I visit occasionally. Because of the painful journey I have walked in this body, I want nothing more than to be of service to those who still suffer. That is the absolute greatest gift of all.

Today I am a thirty-one year old healthy woman with big dreams and wild hopes and a wicked sense of humor. I'm obsessed with Hello Kitty and have a mouth like a sailor. I think my eyes are gorgeous and my laugh is awesome. Today I appreciate who I am. Everything good in my life is a direct result of the pain I've been through with my weight, my body, and my health.

I'm a yoga teacher, a freelance writer, an author, a speaker, a successful model, and an artist. I sponsor other girls and speak in high schools and junior highs and on college campuses about addiction to diets and compulsive eating. I am so grateful for the weight-body-food issues of my past. Today I am a healthy woman with a full and opulent life. I came to trust a while ago that gratitude is an instant and free pass to sanity and peace. After over twenty years of looking for an outside source of confidence and serenity, I now rely upon active gratitude as an immediate remedy for the bizarre idea that I'm not enough, or I don't have enough. In my case, the feelings and habitual thoughts of lack and insecurity played out in my life through body hatred, compulsive exercise, and food addiction.

One of my many dreams is to bring workshops to high schools and colleges for girls and young women. I have so much to reveal to them and such a burning wish to connect that it sometimes overwhelms me. I want them to love themselves, as I did not. I want them to hear and take in and believe that appreciation for the body we have is the only way we can battle the culture's messages telling us that our worth depends on our body's appearance and size. When I speak from a fearlessly authentic place to young women, I see their eyes sparkle. They give themselves permission to be as wise as they naturally are. I remind them to love themselves, and that their most important job is to take care of themselves. My gratitude for them and for where I am today is contagious; they feel it and radiate it back. Together, we can all muster up the faith to be thankful for what we have. Gratitude, in my experience, is the mightiest sword against suffering and the softest way to peace.

❤   ❤   ❤

Paula D. Atkinson is a registered yoga instructor at five hundred hours, a freelance writer, and a creativity coach. Her yoga practice started in northern California, where she remembers going to yoga classes with her mother when she was very young. Then she gave it up for a decade as she grappled with obesity and anorexia, compulsive exercise, and deep depression. She has been teaching full-time for seven years in Washington, DC. She now divides her time teaching yoga, speaking at sororities and high schools about her journey, and writing freelance. Paula also facilitates creativity focus groups in her home. Paula and her partner, Carlo, live in New York City, where Paula works toward a graduate degree from Columbia University so she can reach more people with her message of hope. Please check her out at www.pauladatkinson.com.

Thank God
I Lost My Mind

Brittany Lund

A gun was the most obvious choice. That would be my way out. I couldn't live like this anymore. I desired freedom from myself . . . freedom from this fog that seemed ever pervasive, ever present, ever terrorizing. This wasn't sanity. My very presence, my actions, my words all reinforced in me the realization that I had lost my memory — or, as some would be so bold to frame it, I had lost my mind. Hence this painful and well-thought-out conclusion: I wanted "off the ride."

But did I want to end a life with so much potential? Excuse the pun, but wouldn't that be a cheap shot? Sure, I was miserable and in pain, but shooting myself had too much cataclysmic terror associated with it. Then what about pills? That was a little slower, a little more pitiful . . . depression mixed in with a yearning to be noticed. A sick thought to many, but this was my reality, and to me these were the thoughts that truly mattered. The truth is, I did want to be noticed; however, I wanted to be noticed for who I used to be, not what I had become. Where did "me" go? What happened to "me"?

It seemed like I could reach out and nearly access me, like stretching out to grab something just out of touch, but when I would close my eyes and give that extra little stretch, I still fell short. Where was "me"?

I was lost in this dark little space that seemed to have kidnapped my entire brain. I couldn't remember my last sentence. I had a hard time remembering those unforgettable names, like my mom's middle name. I couldn't remember who my friends were. There are times when we face this question from more of an ethereal and introspective viewpoint, yet in my case, I really didn't know who my friends were. As for my career, I knew what I did: I was a news reporter and a talk show host, but I couldn't remember how I actually did it.

The walls were closing in all around me. Black walls, beyond which lay a grey hue that faded into oblivion. There in the depth of the black was the story of my perfectly planned fairy tale life — The life I knew I must have lived, the person I knew I was, and the story I knew I had been living. Yet it had all changed now because, I lived in another story. It felt like someone else's story.

The date was October 11, 2003, I think. To be perfectly honest, I don't remember the day that changed my life. I thought I would never forget that date, but forgetting things is all part of my journey. I know it was a Saturday. I returned a few days earlier from L.A., where I had met with several agents. My career as a TV host showed signs of taking off. I planned to work through the holidays and then head westward to begin my lifelong dream of living in L.A. and working in front of the camera. I could not have been more excited. I could smell the heady aroma of true possibility. I believed in me and knew my life was on the brink of changing drastically. I could feel it!

I left work in the late afternoon and headed home to prepare for a blind date set up by friends who felt it was a shame for me to be single. They said he was in that rarified, hard-to-find category that all us girls supposedly yearn for.

The weather forecasted rain, and indeed a torrential Florida downpour preceded my date. The doorbell rang promptly at 8 P.M. I remember the rain being heavy and warm, immediately soaking. We were in the car on our way to dine on Cuban food, a personal favorite. I remember the rain bouncing off the windshield with great force as I buckled my seatbelt. The last thing I remember was hanging up the phone and looking at the speedometer. Even the speed limit seemed too fast for these conditions. As we made our way at 50mph through a blanket of rain, it happened: The car hydroplaned on the pools of water dressing the highway and fishtailed and swerved. We were out of control!

The car slid across the rain-slicked grass meridian and into oncoming traffic. The first few cars reacted as best they could, some swerved off the road, and others narrowly avoid hitting us. But, the driver of a huge pickup truck, unable to avoid us, slammed head-on into my side of the car. At a 100 mph of combined impact, and with my seat belt still intact, the force of the collision launched my body over the airbag. I shattered the windshield with my head before recoiling back into my seat. I was unconscious for forty-five minutes, which was about the time it took the ambulance to navigate through the bad weather to reach me. Right then and there, my life transformed in more ways than I knew at the time. It seemed I had fallen like Alice in Wonderland, down the rabbit hole into an unfamiliar and unfriendly new world.

When I arrived at the hospital in Orlando, I drifted in and out of consciousness and could barely speak. My tongue felt huge, swollen, and too big for my mouth, which was dry. Yet there were few other noticeable physical effects. As they observed me, in a sign of things to come, it took the doctor five minutes to extract my mom's phone number from me. The doctor told my parents that it was a miracle I had survived, and miraculous that I was in such relatively good external physical condition. However, I would require constant supervision in the short term.

And there my important journey began . . . far from any fairy tale I had imagined. I faced a new reality of doctor's offices, waiting rooms, wish lists, and sympathy sighs. I didn't know it then, but anger, fear, pain, sadness, loneliness, and deep depression would soon follow.

For me, no singular thing in the world, no possession, no emotion, and no organ is as irreplaceable and central to life as the brain. Nothing! And when you lose it, when it's not working like it did the day before, the stakes become high. There is no limit to the money or time you would give as an offering to the gods of sanity, hoping to regain what you perceive as being lost. And so, although I appeared to have recovered physically, it was clear that I was in an altered cognitive reality. I could not access the pathway back to the "normal me." I co-habited with what I referred to as my "foggy brain." Pen and paper became my friends, as I had to write everything down. This wasn't amnesia; this was insanity! Life and my experiences had become an altered reality. I went from being social and outgoing to the bitter opposite: anti-social and introverted.

It seemed that a mirage, a sleight-of-hand, or magic trick would soon reveal itself. Never, ever could I imagine that I would be so unable to access large parts of who I was. I felt my past life just beyond my reach as I desperately tried to awaken from this nightmare. I was angry! Angry because at twenty-eight years of age, I had to quit my job and move back in with my parents. For the first three weeks at home, I required constant supervision because the doctors feared seizures. My life and this glorious climb of accomplishment all seemed for naught. My life had taken a drastic turn, and my TV career was no longer possible. Much of what I did on-camera was spontaneous and unscripted dialogue, at which I excelled. Now, with my post-concussive trauma and short-term, and possibly even long-term memory loss, my brain responded to the slightest amount of stress or pressure by going blank. So the idea of having to go "live" in 3-2-1 in front of the camera was out of the question. My dream was gone.

Depression was another side effect. However, I can now appreciate how the anger merely facilitated my pity and despair. Anger and frustration toward my situation fed my depression. I felt like I was trying to climb up and out of the steep, slippery slope of a dark cavern; I was on unstable footing and unable to see my way out. When I would forget the name of the person I was talking to or, worse yet, forget what we were talking about, I would often repeat to myself a little sing-song jingle I had created: "I am losing my mind, losing my mind, I am totally losing my mind," which I realize now was a self-fulfilling prophecy.

I share all of this and still I say, what makes me special? What makes me someone to feel sorry for? I had no broken bones, or scars across my face from the broken glass. Nothing visible to elicit sympathy. You might say, "So, big deal. You were in a car accident, and you lost your memory. Many people wish they could forget parts of growing up. Get over it!"

Then it hit me, like a new life at the end of a real-life gestation period: A grand epiphany occurred to me nine months later . . . ironically, while I was driving my car. Sitting at a traffic light, I felt I was observing myself as a distant third person. I could see all these negative thoughts corroding my body like acid coursing through my arteries and veins. After spending so much time wallowing in my own cesspool of loss, depression, and anger, I fully received that I am the miracle! My life is a miracle because I survived. That's when I got it. I damaged my brain and through that I truly have lost my mind! To me, every time I choose to stand separate from my true greatness, my mindful self, I am choosing separation and loss over abundance and truth.

A Course in Miracles says, "Healing is always certain . . . Yet what if the patient uses sickness as a way of life, believing healing is the way to death?" I stood in loss, lack, separation, and truly unconnected to my Source. Call it whatever works for you; for me, it is God. To be contemplating suicide, to be miserable, frustrated, angry, sad, and to be standing in a place of lack was truly destroying me. I conducted my own Kevorkian death wish by the thoughts I was thinking! I did damage my brain, and through that pain, I was operating outside of myself, without my presence of mind. Although it would take another two years before I would start to feel like myself again, my journey to healing began at that moment when I realized how much my own brain and my negative thoughts contributed to my state of despair.

Was I in a car accident where I suffered serious cognitive distortion and memory loss? Yes! Did doctors tell me that if I regained my cognitive ability I could anticipate being "average" at best? Yes! Did this car accident send me on a journey of pain and despair? Yes! Yet I came out the other side enhanced by love, understanding, and my now-unshakeable powerful outlook. I own the thoughts I think and the words I use to paint my reality. Am I able to use all of these supposedly negative events to enhance my life and make the world a better place? Absolutely!

Although my life did not change overnight, I now had a foundation from which to recover and reconfigure my personality and my passions from a place of abundance. I decided to release myself from the negative associations I felt surrounding me, such as people seeing my life and me as a pitiful story of despair resulting from a tragic car accident. This time, I decided that "getting off the ride" meant reconnecting with myself, and that was my gift to myself. I wanted to experience my outgoing personality and my sense of humor again. I wanted to feel those butterflies in my stomach from the joy I experienced in being so fulfilled in life.

I decided to create success experiences for myself in pursuit of regaining my confidence. Googling "educational travel experiences," I found a picture of a man rowing an outrigger canoe through a mangrove forest. On a far-off, distant island named Kosrae, Micronesia, I would find myself again. This trip was about a journey back to myself and an opportunity to realize another life goal: living among an indigenous culture and learning their native traditions and natural remedies. Because I believe in balanced giving, I offered my TV skills and volunteered my time, resources, and expertise to help a non-government organization (NGO) create a video about island conservation to obtain grant funds.

Kosrae changed my life. I fell in love with my life and myself again. I returned to writing and, for the first time in almost a year, I felt like my personality was returning. My awareness and inner spirit set me on this path, and the people of Kosrae — this remote "island of the sleeping lady" in the Pacific — embraced me so warmly that I awakened to my true self. My host family accepted me like one of their own, and I connected with the islanders more than most foreigners had ever done. My one American friend was shocked to see that my host family held a going-away party for me. He told me he had never seen such a turnout for a departing American.

Micronesia was just the beginning. I moved from the small island to the Big Apple. My first job proved to be too much of a step. I stayed awake at night wondering how to survive this job, as I could see my cognitive limitations presenting themselves. For the first time in my life, I was fired, fired for not being able to keep up with the pace. What a relief! Focusing beyond my pain of being fired and into my gratitude, I decided I would accomplish more by seeking ways to challenge my brain. So I made a bold leap into the unknown, it was time to face my fears and challenge myself by performing stand-up comedy. Ah, what a gift to challenge myself beyond my comfort zone.

Doing comedy forced me to see the world through different eyes. I saw everything in the form of a joke and a punch line. When I finally made it to the stage, I was terrified I might forget my jokes, but I made a conscious choice to own who I am and to see the humor in forgetting. It was there, amidst my opportunity to be fearful that I found myself on stage. I found my stride again, and the audience was my confirmation that I once again was comfortable in front of people. I was ready to live my dream again!

Later that year, I took a job at a production company. After dipping my toe in production and hosting once again, I knew I was living my passion. That experience motivated me to create my own company, Mindful Media Works, in the spring of 2007. Immediately I found possibility and opportunity dancing around me. Although I still encounter some trying moments, my mind continues to improve and impress me. I feel my brain and my mind, like a broken bone, have grown stronger because of the car accident. The bottom line? I wake up every morning knowing I live a life that powerfully impacts not only me but also those around me. For this I am infinitely blessed.

From my first-hand experience, I truly believe we all deplete and compromise our minds when we stand in a place of lack and loss. I believe our mind is that part of our essential being that connects us to the soul of who we are, to our true selves. Our access to the magician and alchemist resides in every one of us and enables us to get out there and choose to live a masterful life. To live this awareness I say, "Thank God I lost my mind!"

💜   💜   💜

Brittany Lund is a licensed and certified SACAT Strategic Attraction Life Coach. In addition to coaching and conducting empowerment workshops for women, The Law of Attraction has been Brittany J. Lund's personal mantra for the past sixteen years. She's achieved private audiences with numerous luminaries including Mother Teresa, the Dalai

Lama, and Desmond Tutu. She has worked for Marianne Williamson and is currently working with *The Secret's* Lisa Nichols and her "Motivating the Teen Spirit" program. She's had the privilege of interviewing such notable figures as Norman Lear, John Glenn, and numerous best-selling authors. In addition, Brittany interviewed a number of featured contributors to "*The Secret*": Rev. Michael Beckwith, James Ray, Marci Shimoff, and Jack Canfield.

Ms. Lund's company, Mindful Media Works, develops empowering media projects. She is also a published author and talk show host, with additional experience behind the camera. For more information, please contact Brittany at BrittanyLund.com.

Thank God
I Had Breast Cancer

ANNABELLE BONDAR

With all my heart, I loved my father. His wife (my stepmother), however, was the bane of my existence. Not until I found a lump in my breast and experienced the terror resulting from cancer did I finally find inner peace about my family-of-origin's dynamics. . . . I also found my vocational calling. So you see, my story, while it is a cancer journey, really is more about healing my entire life.

My story probably begins the night my uncle took me to my dying mother's hospital room, I was only seven years old. I remember giving her a kiss on the cheek and saying a final tearful goodbye. Although I was just a child, I knew my life would never be the same. After Mom's passing, my father became my "everything." I depended on him to make sense of this world — and to take care of me. Then it all changed. . . .

When the "intruder" arrived, I felt I was losing my last remaining parent — my daddy. I never much liked my stepmother, and we argued often. I resented my father telling me to "be the bigger person." Why did my father always take her side over mine? Why was she more special than me? Why did I have to be the tough, emotionless one?

Fast-forward to the present. Owing to my distrust of hospitals and doctors, I put off seeing the doctor for five years, but I couldn't put it off any longer — I found a lump. I grew increasingly frustrated and scared as I waited for answers. I lived a healthy lifestyle, worked out regularly and ate well. My children were my highest priority, and I considered myself a good mother. Why was this happening to me? I enjoyed my life, provided for my family, and lived as I thought my father would approve. When those bearers of bad news finally confirmed my diagnosis, I went into shock on many levels. I didn't want to burden my family, yet I didn't really have anyone to talk to. I worried, and worried, and worried some more. Would they be able to save my breast? Would I be able to enjoy a full life again? Would I get to see my children grow and prosper? Even after the surgery, even after they assured me they removed all the cancer, the chaos only seemed to grow more intense.

I became a castaway — completely isolated. I wasn't looking to cope; I was looking to unplug. I was angry at life and especially those who were trying to force healing upon me. For almost two full years, I did very little except care for my children. My cancer, surgery, and life became so emotionally unbearable that something just had to change . . . and thank God it did! They say it's always darkest before the dawn. This was definitely true for me. I remember the time as if it were yesterday. The first major shift occurred as I watched the other patients. I found my perspective while looking at others who were going through similar or even worse ordeals. I felt sorry for and yet turned off by all these sick people. I knew my situation could be much worse, yet I also knew I needed to seek alternative solutions to the surrounding misery.

One of the biggest realizations I learned through my cancer was to listen to my intuition. Find the "aha!" moments and honor them. My cancer seemed to be a magnet for "aha!" moments. (I even found my lump by intuitively checking myself.) One particular intuitive insight came while reading a small ad for a holistic cancer treatment center. With all the time I spent in hospitals, I normally would have avoided another doctor with great fervor, but this ad really called to me (powerful aha! moment) — and I made the appointment that changed the rest of my life.

Dr Hoffman's Centre for Integrative Medicine was different from anything I'd seen or experienced before. He focused on "the healing journey" — the complete healing of body, mind, and soul. Physically, I went through chelation therapy, mercury testing (previous root canal), and many other treatments not offered elsewhere. This clinic appealed to my integrated sensibility. I meditated, rediscovered journaling (a long-lost love from my childhood), and began to crystallize an inner spirituality vastly different from the one my father promoted. I found teachers and mentors who understood what I was going through! The real healing process began through deep introspection. I drowned in emotion after my original diagnosis. Over time I found strength in this person birthed through apparent tragedy. I began to appreciate my life . . . and eventually myself.

Dealing with the emotional work, not the physical became my biggest challenge. So much anger boiled to the surface, but strangely it wasn't toward my dreaded stepmother — but aimed at my beloved father. How could this be? I adored my father! "But my wicked. . . . " Luckily, this confusion and torment dissipated when I began working with Dr John Demartini. Dr Demartini's work and teachings focused on finding the balance, service, and appreciation in all things — including cancer and a seemingly evil stepmother. What I learned will inspire me until the day I pass from this earth. I came to truly understand two key principles that unlocked my family dynamic growing up. The first principle required me to find and own every trait I perceived in others. I had to own every trait I idolized in my father (strength, generosity) and every trait I despised in my stepmother (emotional basket case). I really struggled to own the weakness and selfishness I saw in my stepmother, yet I also began to see my "tormenter" and my past quite differently.

Scarier yet, was discovering the "Pit and Pedestal" principle, because it forced me to face my relationship with my father. You see, whomever you put on a pedestal you will eventually resent. If you have someone on a pedestal, by definition you must have someone else (stepmother, in my case) and yourself in the pit relative to them. Although I consciously adored my father, I unconsciously resented him for choosing his wife over me. Yet incredible healing sprang from truly understanding my family dynamic. I discovered that my strength, independence (not needing Daddy's approval), and tenaciousness — all traits I appreciate in myself — came directly from my "stressful" home dynamic. I saw how my family perfectly crafted my identity and my path, as well as the cancer that has become such a tremendous gift!

An interesting side note: Dr. Demartini taught me that breast cancer in the right breast meant issues with male dominance — another major aha! moment. I repressed standing up to the man on the pedestal in countless family disputes. Cancer was an expression of this repression. If the lump had been on the left side, according to Dr. Demartini, it would have indicated a similar issue with female dominance. I now value time and cherish every moment. I immerse myself in gratitude daily and truly honor my closest relationships. I've met so many wonderful people who really care about helping others — even those doctors I dreaded for so long. I forced myself to integrate all areas of my life and I've found abundance in every one of them.

Through my cancer, I learned to value my inner voice and inner spirituality. Although I lost a small piece of my breast, I now appreciate my body. I now understand and love my family in a way that would have been unthinkable otherwise. Thank God I had breast cancer!

Through intense study, journaling, physical therapy, and emotional work, a new woman emerged from my cancer cocoon. Through my healing journey, I unexpectedly found myself assisting other uncertain and unsure cancer patients. I knew the fear and turmoil they experienced. I also amassed a tremendous wealth of knowledge about cancer and healing as a whole. More than anything, I received the gift of service through my breast cancer!

I was so moved by my experiences that I published *Messages from the Heart: Learning to Love Cancer* in 2005. I also began my non-profit organization "It's Me Annabelle, Inc.", dedicated to raising awareness of complementary cancer treatment and optimum wellness. Through product sales, fundraising, "It's Me Annabelle, Inc." community events, and speaking engagements, I assist people (throughout Canada and

America) with their biggest challenges in life. Not in my wildest dreams would I have pictured such a valuable life for myself.

I am now wonderfully cancer-free — but more importantly, I replaced the tremendous gift of cancer with even greater gifts of gratitude and service. I am truly inspired every day to help people find the beauty in healing and the blessings of "illness." I am blessed to help folks find the hope that sometimes seems impossible to find in traditional medicine. Most importantly, I connect with people and let them know how special they are. If you or someone you love is dealing with the incredible challenge and gift of cancer, take the time to stop and listen to what life seems to be telling you. Pay attention to that intuitive voice. If you love yourself, commit to gratitude, and live life to the fullest. Wonderful things will happen!

Annabelle Bondar was born and raised in Calgary and now spends her time sharing her personal journey through lectures based on her book. Annabelle is the director of It's Me Annabelle, Inc., a not-for-profit organization dedicated to raising awareness of Complementary cancer care and hosting "It's Me" communities, which offer support and education to those with life-altering conditions.

Thank God
I Am a Single, Motherless Mom

ALANA PRATT

A decrepit, rotting witch, crazy gray hair astray, pointed her bony finger at me. "You weak waste of life!" Desperate, I pleaded my case. "But I have an infant. I can't sleep. My mom just died. I'm not working. I'm supporting my unemployed husband on her inheritance . . . and you want me to leave?" Hunched over, she turned away, chuckling, "Your son knows you're a wimp. A loser."

Infuriated, I felt a dormant power deep within me rise up, and I screamed, "Fine! I'll jump off the cliff! Not another day will pass letting my son see his mother void of Power and Grace!" The witch turned, cunningly smiled, and transformed before my eyes into Xena, Warrior Princess. "I was worried you'd never come around, sister. We've got work to do. Know I am a part of you. Kick him out. Now."

Talk about a powerful meditation . . . ! I barely slept that night, rigid and boiling, beside the man to whom I'd given away all my power. The next morning I fed my son, stormed downstairs, blared Gypsy Kings, and screamed at the top of my lungs, "You're going down. Get out now!" No more believing his accusations that I was crazy. No more paying his way. No more putting up with his manipulations, threats, pushing me, then calling the cops to say I attacked him. No more insanity. No more hiding my power. No more buying into this victim story that drained my energy, withholding joy, grace, and radiance from my son.

Why had I stayed so long? Why did I feel so powerless? My inner Warrior had only just begun to awaken when . . . Mom died.

I don't know how close you've been to someone dying of cancer. They stop eating, don't pee, don't talk, and they have bedsores and dry skin. By the end they don't even have an IV, just a sponge to wet their lips, and bags upon bags of morphine alongside morphine boosters for nightmarish pain attacks. I seemed to win the prize of always being there alone when crisis struck . . . upon her admittance, I breathed every single painful breath with her, cheek-to-cheek, holding her until the morphine kicked in.

Once I was alone with her when she bolted up, asking, "How do I die?"

I said, "Mom, I think the angels come when you're ready, and you go with them."

She said, "Well, let's make a plan. We have to figure it out. Where do we go?"

Then all of a sudden she was up, out of bed . . . pulling out the morphine IV and catheter — heading off to die. When I tried to hold her back, she screamed at me with this high-pitched, possessed voice, and then bit my hand . . . immediately piercing through the skin, messing with bones, veins, arteries . . . deep, and she wasn't letting go. I was screaming, she was screaming, nurses came running and calmed her down. Now I was evil. I was a spy sent to take her money and keep her from dying. Holy crap!

And no one was sympathetic. "Don't be upset. She didn't mean it." No shit, Sherlock, but it was a wee bit terrifying, and I could use a little empathy here.

I went down to the ER for a tetanus shot. "Yes, my dying mother bit me." How humiliating . . . how hysterically funny in hindsight . . .

how dearly I coveted my wound . . . how sad I was when the scabs fell away.

Alone in the room with her, I told her I no longer resisted her leaving, that I was sorry it took me a little while to accept it, that I loved her forever. I put in earplugs because her strained breath would stop for up to a minute at a time and start up again. Then at 5am on a beautiful, clear blue Sunday morning, the nurse gently woke me. Irritated and deaf I barked, "What?" taking out my earplugs.

Shit — she was gone. I had missed it. The big moment! Did she reach out, say something, smile? Did the light float up? I had missed it! Now on autopilot, I called my sister and aunt at home. "She's gone."

I was afraid to touch her at first. Then I breathed, smoothed her hair, touched her. She was already cool. I looked at her beautiful hands, her soft skin . . . my mom. Lying there. Dead. Clearly she wasn't there, really, just her body, but it was the body that gave birth to me, that held me . . . and that bit me.

Family arrived, and the nurse reappeared. Checkout is at nine. Will she be donating her organs? Whispering, we collected our things. (Why are we whispering? She's dead.) Then we were done. Everyone was fidgeting. I boldly gathered everyone at the end of her bed for a prayer. Then we left. We just left my mom's body there. Relief . . . grief . . . numbness.

We walked into the '70s-décor mortuary. Is it okay to cremate her in a plywood box? Do we want something snazzier? What style urn would we like? Would you like that shipped to LA? Anesthetized but functioning, we found the will, planned the funeral, called everyone, changed the answering machine message, and oh yes, drove to Alberta for my dear sister's wedding. We sisters drove alone in silence, then laughter, then streaming tears. We decided to pretend Mom was on vacation. My sis was courageous, bold, and vulnerable. Then we drove back to BC and pulled up to our dead mother's condo. We hosted a hundred people at a beautiful afternoon tea in our mother's honor at the Botanical Gardens. Over the next few weeks, we drank a lot, eating up all the food in her fridge and cupboards as we packed up her life and put her condo on the market.

Packing up was wild. She had little white mints in nearly all her pockets. In a Rice Krispies box she had kept every letter and card I'd ever sent her. She had more sex toys than I'm comfortable mentioning. (Go, Mom!) Oh, and I was pregnant. It had happened at the wedding, before the funeral. This little soul knew what it was doing and helped me to experience the richest joy and deepest sorrow all at once. I knew I had to work through my feelings so that I'd be clear and present when he was born. I held my belly, telling him that I was crying about my mom, not him, and to allow this energy to pass through us both and back to the earth. I hid alone to cry, feeling isolated in an unsupportive marriage. I even gave birth on my side, clinging to a girlfriend, my back to my husband.

After the grueling divorce, I was able to forgive him because I saw that I was being the victim, attracting someone to blame. I found myself again. Just like I helped my mom find herself in the last year of her life. We created a "room of her own," stringing Christmas lights as she nestled in to listen to healing meditation CDs. Mom and I had created a bright poster for the fridge titled "Priorities: music, travel, adventure, and laughter".

Now, for my healing. I forgave myself (multiple times daily, at first). I put affirmation sticky notes around the house, asked for help with financial issues, told the truth of how scared I was, got coaching on my career, dressed confidently, and exercised. I danced a few nights a week by candlelight, once my son was asleep for the night. I faced the truth of how needy I still felt, how I wanted a man to save me, an investment to sustain me, something on the outside to make the pain on the inside go away.

I started dating and vowed to tell the truth, be myself, explore my true sensual expression, and never settle again. Slowly, I began to live sensually, in the moment, savoring life more deeply and cherishing motherhood. I felt this unexplainable, unconditional love for my son that healed the loss of my mom, for I knew the depth to which she had

really loved me. My son and I would swirl our fingers through lus-
cious shaving cream on the bright red picnic table, just as my mom had
once done with me. However, with a boy, there was maybe a minute
of painting before my soapy toddler and I were in a full-fledged foam
fight. We artfully compared our sudsy Mohawks, rinsed off, and retired
for a restorative nap. His trumpeting voice would alert me that he was
ready to race into the afternoon so, crouching down on all fours, I
would enter the room clucking like a chicken. He'd laugh hysterically,
and so would I.

Maybe it was ushering in death and then giving birth, spreading
my legs for all to see, that began to dismantle my preoccupation with
what people thought of me. Until the death of my mom and birth
of my son, I sought approval for my every decision. Disapproval felt
like fingernails down a chalkboard. I remember the shame of being
turned away by my then-husband, too preoccupied to enjoy my surprise lunchtime strip tease. I remember women's glances of pity as I,
the poor girl who hadn't the pedigree to know any better, chatted and
tore open my power bar for a homeless, fingerless man.

So I shut down. Until I opened up — literally, through the cycle
of death and birth. I had been waiting for permission to stop flatlin-
ing through life. Single, motherless motherhood became my portal
to freedom. I hit rock bottom to be reborn, creative, and alive. I
finally think I'm pretty cool. Especially when my son plops into the
public fountain or sticks his head up my bridesmaid dress at a Catholic wedding, and all I do is breathe, correct, and continue. From
my new vantage point, it turns out dirt is decadent, mess is marvel-
ous, and gazing at tree trunks is grand. My creativity abounds as we
picnic in the backyard tree house, read under forts of blankets, nap
in tents in his room. My brain says I don't have the time or energy
for this silliness. But my heart whispers, "Nourish and liberate your
soul to the brim with sticky hands and make-believe."

This latitude has spilled over into juicy girlfriend time. Instead of
victim sessions over the phone, we have fun painting each other's toes
in the driveway at sunset and dining by candlelight on the shag rug
around the coffee table. Conversations are magical, laughter intoxi-
cating, and insights divinely inspired. I'm still pissy on my period,

embarrassed when my kid clobbers another kid, mad when drivers cut me off, lonely as I still miss my mom, and aching when I yearn for my soul mate . . . yet these moods pass more easily now because I see perception is my choice, my responsibility, and my birthright.

I love living sensually. I love feeling deeply. I love inhaling each moment knowing I can handle anything, and I love exhaling my full self-expression into an experience. I love being able to compassionately chuckle at myself, and I also love a really good cry. Bless single, motherless motherhood for being the catalyst to pour forth my wellspring of inspiration and teach me that I am a limitless vessel of love sourced from within.

Let's just hope my son forgets that I clucked like a chicken. Actually, let's hope not.

♥   ♥   ♥

Master interviewer Alana Pratt knows that taking care of ourselves isn't a luxury, it's a necessity. Host of the #1 rated radio show *Sensual Living,* found at alanapratt.com, and author of soon-to-be-released *Redefining Sensuality; Every Woman's Guide to a Soulful, Succulent & Savored Life,* Pratt is internationally featured on *LeezaLIVE, Hollywood Confidential,* and TLC's *That Ying Yang Thing. People Magazine* reported Pratt was the first person Leeza Gibbons called for guidance when she signed on with *Dancing with the Stars.* As an interviewer and writer, Pratt helps thousands of overwhelmed women find the key to juicy relationships and the access to the deeper, wiser, intuitive part of themselves. Filling up your tank first is not one more thing on your to-do list, it's about coming home, so sign up for six free weeks of support from Alana today!

Thank God
I Was Sent to Prison

KEITH MCEACHERN

*T*oday I am the marketing executive of a wonderful organization called FreeLife. Not that long ago, though, I was a convicted felon. My story is absolute proof that all obstacles are only temporary. Even having a prison record.

In my early years, following graduation from college, I knew that my goal was to work for myself, specifically in something that would have a residual benefit. Like many young college grads, I tried a number of things, and eventually I built up a successful burglar alarm business. The monitoring fees afforded me the residual income I desired, but ultimately, and for many reasons, we sold the business. I ended up with more money in my pocket than I knew what to do with. Then I made some bad decisions. I don't just mean kind of bad. I mean really bad. Some of you may be able to relate to this in small ways. Have you ever done something wrong and hoped no one would find out? Is there something in your past that would cause you extreme embarrassment if announced right now perhaps in this book or in the newspaper? If the answer to any of those questions is "yes," then you'll have some understanding of what I am about to tell you.

In 1983 I became involved with a group of people who smuggled marijuana into the United States. I didn't get into it for the drugs or even for the money. But like all great wrongs, I did it one small step at a time, for all the wrong reasons. For nearly three years, I participated in that illegal activity. Like the Biblical story of the prodigal son, I abandoned my lifelong principles, threw away my mother's hopes for me, and turned my back on God. In the story of The Prodigal Son, he awakened one day and "came to himself." I'm not sure exactly what that means, but for me it meant coming back to my true self. It meant coming home. It meant trying to find meaning and purpose in life. It meant another chance. It meant asking God to somehow, some way, forgive me. But it also meant burying that record of wrongdoing and wrong living, and "stuffing it into a closet" like the proverbial skeleton, locking it tight, and hoping it would never surface again.

I can't prove that prayer changes God's mind, but I'm sure it changes the hearts of humans. It did mine. I donated my time and my ill-gotten gains to a worthy charity. I couldn't get rid of my money fast enough. Slowly my life filled with light again. In 1989 I married my lovely wife, Pam, and I discovered the world of network marketing. I tried at least eight different companies, hoping to find one that would last long enough to create the residual income. I will be honest with you: I wanted to make lots of money — but this time I wanted to do it with my head held high.

In each company, I rose to the top only to watch the company disappear. When a company goes away, or breaks its promises, it doesn't just disappear. It takes with it your hopes and dreams. However, I just kept on believing something good would happen. I worked hard, and the closet door still locked tight on my sordid past. One day I enrolled Ray Faltinsky, a young college student, into one of the companies. We never did much in that company, but he impressed me, and I guess he felt kind of good about me, too. The company failed to prosper, but a real friendship grew between Ray and me. Then it happened. Seven years after I'd put my criminal career behind me and started a new life, working legitimately, married to my beautiful wife, and now with a young son, Lucas — that closet door swung wide open, and the skeleton came lunging out, grabbing me by the throat, screaming for the world to hear.

As I sat in my house, nestled in the quiet woods of Connecticut on Candlewood Lake, I could hear . . . no, I think I could feel . . . the vibration of my quiet neighborhood being violated by the onrush of a caravan of strangers' cars . . . strangers who meant me no good. I knew exactly what it was: the long arm of the law. I knew this was my day of reckoning. They intended to arrest me for my illegal activities dating back to 1983. All kinds of emotions filled me. Can you imagine if you were in my shoes, the shame, fear, and disbelief that after all these years you were going to be held accountable? But here's an emotion you might not imagine: relief. I felt relieved that now everyone knew. No more deception. No more lying. No more cover-ups.

I hired a lawyer, who bailed me out of jail and kept me out for as long as possible. I continued to try to hide the skeleton in my closet from some people. Shortly after that, I received another surprise — this time a good one. I got a phone call from my old friend Ray. He wanted to meet with me. He said he had finished law school, and he and his partner, Kevin Fournier, wanted a meeting. They were going to start their own company. I'll never forget the name of the Danbury, Connecticut restaurant where we met: Rosy Tomorrows!

In the arrest process, the federal government stripped us of every asset except our home. I never in my life wanted and needed anything more than a rosy tomorrow. As we met together, Ray and Kevin told me they hoped I would help them start the company. Over the next several weeks, we agreed that I would be the company's first distributor. What we didn't discuss — what Ray and Kevin knew nothing about — was my criminal past and forthcoming trial. But I planned to plead guilty, and I knew I had to come clean with Kevin and Ray. We met in another restaurant, and it sure didn't feel like any kind of "Rosy Tomorrow." I related the nature of my crimes, told them of the high likelihood that I would be imprisoned, and that my greatest fear was the heartbreak of leaving my wife and my precious son behind. We talked about how this would impact the launch of the company, FreeLife, and its network. I assumed I'd get walking papers. I assumed they would drop me like a hot potato.

The only thing I remember of that meal was the courage, the love, and the acceptance served up so abundantly by Kevin and Ray. Kevin, who was also blessed with a toddler son, embraced me and wept with me. He understood so clearly what separation from what you love most would mean. Kevin felt my heart, my pain. Both of them agreed that, though it might be a rough road, they made their choice and they would stand by me. I would continue to be their choice for their first distributor. These two young, inexperienced businessmen had everything at risk on the business table, but they stood their ground shoulder to shoulder with undeserving me. Ray went so far as to say that he wanted to come with me to face my sentencing. He said that, having observed me during my better-behaved years, he wanted to make a case before the judge that, in his opinion, my life should be given another chance and not destroyed. He wanted to let the judge know of the good I did in the past, and that, if I were free, I could and would do a lot more.

The hardest thing I ever had to do was to sit down with my family and share the likelihood of our family being torn apart. We sat down in a little circle Indian-style on the floor, legs crossed, and I told my son the error of my ways. I explained to him exactly what I'd done, that I knew that I made a bad decision to break the law. I told him I must face the judge and confess my guilt; and that I was going to pay the price by being put in a cage for a very long time. I let him know he would be a young man before I could be free to enjoy time together with him again — that he would grow up without a father.

Tears streamed down all of our faces. But my son drew himself to me, nose to nose, "We're crying, Dad, not because we're afraid, right? But because we're going to miss each other," and I said, "Yeah, that's right." At the end, I took him up to bed to say his prayers. But this night he said, "Let me say my prayers, Dad." He started, "Jesus, I pray to you every night and tell you I love you and I believe in your magic. I want you to make them let my daddy go, please let my dad come home soon." I came out of that room a man stooped and bent over with the weight of my earlier actions on my mind. If I'd known in my earlier life that God would so richly grace me in my later life with this son, I would never have been so self-absorbed and reckless.

The next morning I caught an early plane to go face a man who had a reputation as a "hanging judge." Friends bolstered my courage in court. True to his word, Ray showed up, as did a number of others from around the world, to give testimony regarding my character for the previous seven years. I knew from my lawyer that no matter what testimony they gave, what letters written, I would be sentenced to many, many years in prison. As I listened to these dear friends tell their stories of me to the judge, I was humbled. I felt like I was being eulogized at my funeral.

Listening impatiently, the judge strummed through a stack of reference letters from all over the world, written on my behalf. Then he directed everyone's attention to my dear wife, who sat quietly in the back with head bowed and hands clasped, praying. All the speakers were eloquent, but the person from whom the judge most wanted to hear was my wife, Pam.

With tremendous bearing, with head up and shoulders back, she approached the bench. The courtroom grew totally still. He asked her if she had something on her mind. She said, "I do!" She simply told him with the conviction of absolute truth in her voice that the man she was married to was not the same man with the criminal intent of a decade earlier. She said how rich in truth her life had become. She said other things that would only embarrass me to say now. In the seemingly interminable silence that followed, you could literally have heard a pin drop — and I actually heard people cry.

The judge stood sternly frozen, then looked me in the eye and asked me, "Do you have any idea how lucky you are, Mr. McEachern?" I responded, "Yes, sir." He looked down at a piece of paper upon which he had earlier penciled in the time in prison he was sure he would give me, prior to hearing the voices of my friends. Hesitatingly, he put his eraser to the paper and penciled in another number, announcing that I would serve only thirty months in federal prison! I thanked him. It even surprised my lawyer that it was so light a sentence. He'd never seen anything like that in that judge's courtroom. Further, the judge granted me twenty-four days to go home and put my affairs in order.

On the plane with Ray, I told him I knew my other MLM income would not hold up. I told him that with only twenty-four days of freedom, I needed to start recruiting for FreeLife. Ray said, "We're not ready; we have no products, we have no applications, we have no literature, our computers aren't hooked up, and none of this will happen for at least forty-five days, so I guess we'll have to call it a prelaunch." Ray was so gracious in assuring me that he wanted me to prosper.

I told Pam, "Look, we can cry all month over ourselves, but I have twenty-four days to build a business. I'm going to spend every hour of every day on the phone until I fall over in my chair." I took my list of names and a collection of business cards from all over the United States. I garnered names from all kinds of sources — everything you can think of, anybody who might listen to a business opportunity. I talked to people, asking for referrals, gathering even more names, and I made presentations to their best people for them. If they expressed a real interest, I felt morally obligated to tell them that I had been busted, what I had been busted for, and that I was going away to prison and wouldn't be able to help them under any circumstances. Recruiting can be challenging under the best of circumstances, but try doing it that way!

Life in prison was everything it was advertised to be. But I had time to exercise, to pray, to reflect, to read, and to talk with God. Early on, I prayed fervently that God would help me through those thirty months. At night until about 9 P.M., we had the freedom to walk around a track surrounded by a hillside that created a natural amphitheatre. There was a tall post with lights for surveillance at the opening to the grounds. As I walked around, I took great comfort in watching my shadow cast on the hill by the light on the post behind me. It helped me feel less alone. I prayed that, undeserving as I was, God would give me a sign that He was in this place with me. I came around again to the area of the light while making this plea, and instantly two shadows were cast on the hill. I cried.

Composing myself, I walked and watched as the two shadows disappeared into the darkness. I came around again to my shadow of

one and made my request to see it two again. This time, my doubting Thomas self surfaced, trying to assess exactly what was happening.
Looking around, I figured it out. There were two light bulbs on the
post, one good one and one bad one, and each time I made my request,
the intermittent bad connection was made good, and two light bulbs
instead of just one would cast two shadows walking on the hill. At first
I said, "Ah-ha — it was nothing — just electricity." Then I remembered
that I had only asked for a sign. I had gotten one. Suddenly I felt a
whole lot better about how my life was about to change.

I was eager to call my wife the next day and tell her how good her
life was going to be. She said, "You've lost your mind already. Have
you forgotten where you are? We're about to lose our house." I said,
"Just make up a list of everything you've ever wanted."

The warden had his own ideas of what made a good prison, and I
got a handle on what those ideas were. If the floors were clean and polished, he saw himself as running a good prison. I suggested to him that,
with his support, I could make even the huge telephone room, which
was a mess and an eyesore due to inmate abuse, a polished beauty to
behold. I told him that if he could rope it off for a few hours a day,
making it off bounds to other inmates, I'd make sure in effect that his
job as the greatest warden could be assured. I knew I desperately needed
to use the phone. By promising to get on my hands and knees and shine
the warden's phone room, as well as the shoes of some very connected
prisoners, I captured the right to be in the phone room alone. Every
day I scrubbed and polished on my hands and knees. From that prison
phone, I organized meetings, talked with Ray a few times a week, and
built my FreeLife business.

They released me after only twenty months and I returned home to
Pam and Lucas in Connecticut, to start my life again. I quickly moved
up in the FreeLife plan ladder. Pam and I received the last spots on the
eight-person President's Team Trip to Europe. On stage at the event,
Ray began his presentation of what he called the company's highest
award, and Pam and I wondered who would be the lucky distributor.
As we looked around the stage at the assembly of incredible talent,
thinking it must be one of them, we heard Ray say, "One thing for sure,
this year's winners will never forget where they've come from." At that

frozen moment, Pam and I could feel the eyes of everyone corporate, many with tears in their eyes, looking at us. You can't imagine how we felt as Ray called our names. We both broke into tears. We had gone from the bowels of hell to the pinnacle of success in the shortest time imaginable — thanks to God.

Pam took the microphone and praised Ray and Kevin, then expressed her love for me. And then it was my turn. After thanking Ray, Kevin, and Pam, I told people that I'd come from a dark hole of my own creation. I recounted how I had a "road to Damascus" type experience in my little hell, and just like St. Paul commanded on that road, I was moved to forget all that is past and chose to press on. You can be born again every day — you can reinvent yourself. FreeLife came out with a new video that year, entitled *Flight to Freedom*. Well, no one ever had a greater "flight to freedom" than I did. And no one had more wind under his wings than I did. I said, "It feels so good to be home."

If you've ever doubted, don't. If you've either given or accepted excuses, don't. Cherish your freedom. Make it count. Treasure your time. Don't squander it. If you've gone wrong, stand now with men and women who stand for what's right. Know the value of keeping commitments. There is no hurdle so great that you can't overcome it. Make faith a part of your life. If you have any kind of black hole in your life, any skeleton in your closet, work through it, and start over today. If you realize you are not doing all you can to be all you can, if you know you haven't maximized your potential, if you are not truly fulfilling your destiny, start over today. If you have a dream of what can be, let nothing get in your way. If you have that dream, thank God for it. And then go out and fulfill it . . . as I have.

Many of us live in "prison" all our lives — the prison of unfulfilled potential. Don't wall yourself in. Break free. Do it now.

❦   ❦   ❦

Except for one errant run down a misdirected path, all of Keith McEachern's professional life has been dedicated to both serving others and developing businesses with a model of strong residual income. Early on, he was a primary participant in creating a cutting-edge electronics and security company, protecting people's lives and property. A subsequent residual income was generated through the over six thousand home alarm subscribers paying monthly monitoring fees.

During the next phase of his career, Keith became the top earner and trainer in FreeLife International, a network marketing nutritional company. Beyond his own personal titles and achievements, he is most proud of having helped over 35,000 people earn monthly walk-away income, with several becoming millionaires. His email address is Keithmceachern@aol.com.

Thank God
I'm an Entrepreneur

CHRISTINE KLOSER

Growing up, I always felt like I was different. I didn't quite belong. Even though I excelled in competitive figure skating and was an accomplished dancer, I had an underlying feeling of not fitting into the mold of a typical New Englander. I rebelled against conformity and had an innate sense that there must be a different way of living than that which I saw in my suburban Connecticut town. Perhaps that explains why I felt sick to my stomach when, as a senior in college, I dressed in a gray suit and black pumps to go on job interviews. Nothing about the suit, the pumps, the interview, or the "box" felt right. For me, the thought of a regular job and nine-to-five hours was an unappealing proposition. I had no idea what I wanted to do, but I knew a J-O-B was not it. I hadn't heard of entrepreneurship as a career option, so I was completely unaware of the world (and experiences) that were possible for me.

Thanks to college "senior-itis," I decided to enroll a few good friends in a plan to move to sunny Southern California after we graduated. Nobody believed we would actually do it. After all, nobody from a conservative private Catholic college would think of packing up the car and moving 3,000 miles away with no job, no connections, no place to live, and just enough money to survive for a month or two. However, for someone with an untapped entrepreneurial spirit and eagerness to experience all that life had to offer, this was the only logical choice for me to make.

After waving goodbye to my shocked family and squeezing into a Volkswagen Fox with two friends, a suitcase, a map from AAA, and a cooler full of snacks, I was off for the journey of a lifetime . . . a journey I didn't anticipate when we pulled out of the driveway. As we entered the freeway, I felt a thrill at the anticipation of the unknown experiences and opportunities that lay ahead for me. Even though I was still unaware of my entrepreneurial possibilities, I remember feeling that I loved taking this risk and doing my "own thing" rather than what society expected of a recent college grad.

The following year was all about fun! Heck, what college graduate wouldn't thrive in a hip San Diego beach town with nightclubs on every corner and beautiful weather all year? When I needed money, I got a one-month temporary job at San Diego's number-one rock radio station. This temporary job led to a nine-month assignment there. It was good to know I could have fun and be an asset to a company. Then, still unaware of the option of entrepreneurship, I returned to Connecticut to get a "real" job as an account executive for Hartford's number-one radio station. I think society finally got its message through to me that I should get serious about my life. For two whole years, I pretended I liked the job . . . until I was fired. I guess my pretending hadn't fooled anyone. Looking back, being fired was the best thing that could have happened to me. This is when my true entrepreneurial journey finally began.

Packing up the car again, I headed west — this time to Los Angeles. Finally, in Los Angeles, at the age of twenty-four, my life came together. By the grace of God, I fell into a job as a personal trainer, and within twelve months of getting started in the field, I launched my own private personal training business. Clients found me; so I didn't need to advertise. I worked only twenty-five hours a week, enjoyed my clients, made great money, and loved my life. I found my groove as a free-spirited entrepreneur helping people be healthy and fit. What more could I ask for? Life was good! Life appeared to get better when

I had the opportunity to open my own private gym and yoga studio in an upscale location. After running that business for one year (working sixty hours per week and not having much fun), another opportunity surfaced: to take over a larger yoga studio. Naturally I said, "Yes!" And now my true entrepreneurial journey began.

Faced with $10,000 per month in overhead (not including my salary) and only $5,000 per month in revenue, I was in way over my head. Every other endeavor I'd embraced was easy, came naturally, and was fun . . . but not this one. I financed my payroll on personal credit cards; I figured out how to live on a poverty-level income; I was discouraged and isolated; I was on the verge of bankruptcy. I sat on my bed dialing the bankruptcy attorney on the phone, in tears, with my heart racing, and I felt like a complete failure, convinced I would never amount to anything in my life. It embarrassed and shamed me to make that phone call. It brought up a lot of fear, doubt, sadness, anger, frustration, and self-doubt. Maybe the entrepreneurial life wasn't right for me, after all. Maybe I just didn't have what it took to succeed.

Somewhere amidst the depth of my emotions, I knew this experience would either make me or break me. At the time I had this realization, I did not yet know about the multitudes of mega-successful entrepreneurs who also experienced failure. It was before I understood the Divine Perfection of my journey, and it was before I embraced challenges as opportunities for success. Thankfully, a few years earlier, I started a women's networking group to connect with other like-minded entrepreneurs in Los Angeles. In this time of darkness and despair about my business and finances, I drew upon the energy of the women in this group. In their faces I could see I wasn't a failure and could access the gratitude I felt for every moment of my experience through this challenge. Through their mirror, something changed in me, and gave me the courage to not file for bankruptcy and make a conscious choice to have this experience make me rather than break me.

Two of the most profound blessings of being an entrepreneur are the power of choice and the freedom to create work you love. The journey I've experienced since making the choice to succeed has been a continual source of fuel for me to discover and be more of who I am, for me to experience freedom. During the seven-year journey of owning and operating my women's networking group (NEW Entrepreneurs, Inc.), I was stretched, challenged, and I grew in ways I never imagined possible. I launched a successful seminar company, helped more than two hundred entrepreneurs become published authors through my publishing company, facilitated retreats, and hosted tele-summits in which I interviewed experts like Michael Gerber, author of *The E-Myth*, Neale Donald Walsch, author of *Conversations with God*, Seth Godin, "America's Greatest Marketer" and Dr. Joe Vitale from *The Secret*.

The deeper I engrossed myself in the entrepreneurial journey (and discovered how to succeed as a "conscious" business owner), the more I embraced my true gift as an entrepreneur. My gift was to coach other entrepreneurs in embracing their journey, turning failures into success, engaging the law of attraction, and manifesting their goals and dreams. People often tell me that my experience with the yoga studio as an owner and instructor helped me develop the unique gift of blending intangible/Universal principles with tangible business strategies. Now I coach my clients in creating business strategies, operations, marketing plans, and product/service development . . . and provide them with guided meditations and grounding exercises to tap into the Universal energy that abundantly supports them in manifesting their goals and dreams.

When I set forth on my first cross-country journey, I had no idea where I would be today. It's difficult to imagine what my life would be like if I weren't an entrepreneur. Being an entrepreneur identifies me nearly as much as my role as wife and mother. Entrepreneurship is at the core of who I am and my desire to be fully expressed as my Self in the world. I am who I am today because of every challenge, obstacle, success, failure, dream and goal I've experienced along my exciting journey. Thank God I'm an entrepreneur!

LET YOUR BUSINESS LEAD YOU
by Christine Kloser

Let your business lead you.
Let it guide you to those places in your heart you have yet to discover.

Let it call your soul to be fully expressed and engaged in the world.

Let it be the way for you to contribute your unique gifts to the world.

Let it be your tool for making the planet a better place.
Let it be your vehicle for leaving a legacy long after you are gone.
Let it be YOU . . . mind and body, heart and soul.

Christine Kloser is an inspirational business coach, engaging speaker, award-winning book publisher, and author of *The Freedom Formula: How to Put Soul in Your Business and Money in Your Bank.* Since 1991 she has been an entrepreneur, continually exploring new ways to integrate her spiritual understandings with strategic business tactics for herself and her clients. She provides lectures, training, coaching, and book publishing services to thousands of entrepreneurs worldwide. You can get a free copy of Christine's *Conscious Business Success Kit* by visiting http://www.loveyourlife.com today.

Join the *Thank God ?...* community online to share your story and chat with the authors at **www.thankgodi.com**

Thank God
I Died Giving Birth to Twins

CHARLOTTE G.

On July 4, 1989, I had the "pleasure" of experiencing an extremely traumatic and painful blessing! I was twenty-five, professionally successful, and had just purchased my first home. The future looked clear and promising, yet everything changed that Independence Day. . . .

During a neighborhood block party, I found myself engaged in a conversation with a large man who played on my sympathies. He told me that his estranged wife had taken his two young children away on Christmas Day. Depressed, he asked to show me the tree and presents still on display. Although somewhat inebriated, I never considered him a threat as I walked to his place. He kept talking about the family he wanted back . . . but then his demeanor unexpectedly and abruptly changed. He instantly became very angry . . . then he forced himself on me! I pleaded with him to stop. I wanted to get back to the party and my friends. His pent-up frustrations and anger exploded all over me. He hit me with his fist repeatedly as I again pleaded with him to stop. He ripped off all my clothes. In fear and in pain, I gave in to his anger because I wanted to live.

When he finished, he got into the shower. I crawled on the floor and quietly grabbed my torn clothing before running out the door. He literally chased after me with a towel around his waist, yelling, "Please, don't tell anyone . . . I'm sorry!" When I got home, a concerned friend who had noticed my disappearance was waiting. She consoled me and took me to the local police department to give my statement. The officer told me that my situation might be considered a date rape and that I should not press charges. "Just let it go. . . . The trial will be worse than the event itself." I continued with my life as if nothing had happened, convinced it was my fault.

I resumed my life as best I could. I threw myself into my work, which required a fair amount of traveling. While on a business trip several weeks later, I became dizzy, light-headed, and weak. Can you imagine how surprised, angry, and confused I felt when I found out I was pregnant with twins? How was this possible? I'd been told during a previous relationship that I would be unable to conceive due to cystic endometriosis. I worked so hard to succeed in a man's world. Now I found myself considering my options and beliefs. In the end, however, I decided this must be God's plan for me. Looking back, my decision really wasn't hard, but life's next curve ball was. With all the travel my job entailed, my company decided that a single mother was unfit for my line of work. I felt like my life was out of control.

My life has been an adventure almost from the beginning. I grew up an independent tomboy from an upper middle class family. While my twin sister played with dolls, I played Army, went camping, and rode dirt bikes with my older brother. Despite a challenging childhood with an abusive, alcoholic father, I became very self-sufficient. I joined the Navy out of high school to become successful. Unfortunately, a series of medical challenges not only ended my naval career but seemed to foreshadow the chaos to come. After the Navy, I entered the workforce as a hard-working woman trying to make it in a masculine paradigm. I did well with my training in electronics and maintenance repair. I made money and had fun. Before I knew it, I was a twenty-five-year-old, purchasing my first home.

Not only did my life change completely that July 4th, I ended up dying both figuratively and literally. My identity was stripped away by my attacker, my employer, and by motherhood itself. I didn't know what I was going to do or how I was going to feed my family, but I knew I would find a way to survive. Yet, I almost didn't survive at all.

I died giving birth to my boys! I was rushed into the surgical delivery room after both of my sons' heartbeats had stopped. I bled to death on the table, trying to deliver my son Christopher. As I rose out of my body above the surgical lights, I saw and heard everything, including my mother screaming, "Somebody do something! She's blue. She's my baby — please do something!" I watched from above as the doctor said, "We have to go c-section. We have no time to prep — we'll lose him!" I remember the horror on my mother's face as they pushed her out of the room while I was clinically deceased. I remember praying to God, "Whatever you do, please save my son." Suddenly, I was jolted back into my body. I sat up as the doctor started to cut me. I felt the knife. I looked at the doctor and said, "Please save my son!" before passing out.

I woke up in the recovery room and was told not to move or talk too much as I had lost over half my blood supply. I received blood transfusions, but all I wanted to know was if my boys were OK. They eventually wheeled me into the nursery, where I saw Christopher (5 lbs. 8 oz.) and Michael (6 lbs. 4 oz.) for the first time. Ten fingers, ten toes . . . they were perfect.

Over the years, I've learned the benefit of taking a step back. To fully understand the impact of my attack, I needed time and perspective to see the big picture. What would have happened if I decided to skip that party? When I think back on that fateful night, I can honestly say I would not trade it for the world. Through that potentially traumatizing experience, I received my reason for living! In many ways, my womanhood was never a clean subject. Although I liked boys, I always seemed to attract the losers. It would be fair to say I considered myself a broken woman before the attack. In that painful moment of necessary surrender, I received so much! I was validated as a woman. I was saved.

My two boys — my gifts from heaven — have given my life meaning and depth. Christopher and Michael not only became my best friends, but being their mother brought out in me both strength and compassion. I began to know and understand myself like never before. Although I'll always cherish the times spent together traveling or just hanging out with my boys, I'll also fondly remember the struggle to put it all together. I have always prided myself on being a fighter, and being a single mother was a monumental challenge. Whether working two jobs or persevering through one of many health issues throughout the years, I always found a way to get it done. No one can ever take this accomplishment away from me. I can honestly say I am proud of myself.

When I received the opportunity to share my story, I thought of family members, and other women especially, who get stuck by "traumatic" events. Looking back through all my experiences, I believe the key is to know that the blessings are there even if not apparent at the moment. I know they certainly were not clear initially for me. Many seemingly negative events occur that are meant to happen. These tragic events become the perfect catalysts for change and growth.

My conclusion? Life can be a bitch sometimes, but you've just got to keep on trucking. I've experienced hell on earth and even death itself, but I found a loving God through my experiences. I know if, today, I came across the man who forced himself on me, I would actually thank him. I am so grateful for him!

♥   ♥   ♥

Charlotte G. left a job with seven years vested in civil service in order to move to a new area, believing she would thus improve the quality of life for her sons. An on-the-job injury led to two surgeries that put her out of work for seven months. Only her determination to be there for her sons kept her hanging on. She believes she doesn't have much time left on earth but wants to leave her sons in the best possible position that she can. She says, "They have been my blessing. I love them with all that I am. They're my world; they are why I exist. They've made my life worth every bit of living. I love my sons. They've made my every downfall and disappointment in life my most rewarding because they were there."

Thank God
I Lost My Babies

DENISE LAURIA VENITELLI, LCSW

ou're pregnant!" The words rang in my ears, filling me with excitement, disbelief, even panic. Just three months before, struggling with infertility, I underwent surgery to remedy reproductive abnormalities that my doctors could trace all the way back to when I was in my own mother's womb.

The hormone drug DES, given to my mother by her doctor while she was pregnant with me, had a profound effect on my life. It was supposed to make me a stronger, healthier baby. The doctor gave my mother pills and injections to hold her pregnancy to full term. After nine months, I was born on Christmas Eve, Mommy and Daddy's 5½-pound miracle baby, Grandma and Grandpa's little princess. But the DES treatments my mother underwent would pose terrible and long-lasting consequences that would follow me for the rest of my life, especially when it became my turn to become a mom.

So here I was, thirty years old, having struggled with infertility and finally pregnant; the words of my doctor colliding with the disbelief that had long accompanied me through my attempts to have a child. I just didn't think I would ever be able to conceive, never mind carry a baby to term, because of the extensive uterine anomalies I had developed from being DES-exposed in my mother's uterus. Fears of miscarriage would never be far away. Nor would they be unfounded. To my horror and crushing heartbreak, at twenty-five weeks, through forty-one hours of labor, my beautiful baby, my daughter, was born gray and congested with a fatal infection. With tears streaming down my face, I held her in my arms. I counted each of her tiny fingers and toes. I wondered what color her eyes would have been, what her laugh would sound like, how she would have looked when she noticed me. I knew I would never see her open her beautiful eyes, nor see her tiny lips curl into a smile, or hear her call me "Mama." The phantom cries of my little girl, Alexandra Elizabeth, haunted me as I ached to hold her one last time before they took her away.

Her dying left me sick — emotionally, physically, and spiritually — a lonely pain I could not salve. I wanted only to die. But in the depth of that pain, feeling very afraid and very alone, I touched bottom. I resolved to pick myself up, to carry on, move forward on a still rocky path, where the loss would echo and haunt me and shake me to my core. Late one night, just months after my daughter died at birth, I was preparing an application for graduate school. I thought I heard — swore I heard — the cries of a baby, through the music of Vivaldi coming from the stereo. I froze, then quickly turned, glancing around the room. My eyes fell upon the dog's bed, where my Doberman puppy, Dino, lay asleep in the very place my daughter's crib should have been. Dissolving into tears, I walked over and fell to the floor beside my puppy's bed. Taking the blue-fawn Doberman in my arms, I rocked him as the tears drenched my cheeks.

Such was my personal pain. For many days, months, even years, my hope and desire to give birth only grew. This longing led me to undergo multiple surgeries to make it happen. The many doctors I consulted all agreed that I could indeed become pregnant again. However, carrying a baby to term was always another question, a complication that would leave me feeling stripped of my biological right to motherhood. After a tremendous amount of soul-searching, emotional, physical, and spiritual healing, we came to the decision to build our family through adoption. I was riddled with anxiety, fear, excitement, and joy at the thought of having our very own baby. By this time, my desperation for motherhood was more important to me than giving birth. I knew I had a tremendous amount of love to offer a child and that I would be a great mother. And yet, at that point, I did not quite fathom how adoption would help me to feel whole again.

When my strawberry-blond, hazel-eyed baby boy was placed in my arms, I knew from that moment that he was my baby. As I held him up, looking deeply into his eyes, the words rang from my lips: "I am your mommy. You are a beautiful gift from God. Welcome to your brand new life." My son, Dimitri, born in Bucharest, Romania, in August 1995, was very small, malnourished, frail, extremely ill, and developmentally delayed. As I held him, fear enveloped me, yet a deep sense of peace overtook me. I knew in that moment I had the tools to help this child, my baby, have the best possible life. My baby. The words sang through my mind like the sweetest melody. I was so overjoyed!

Over the next few years, I dedicated my time and attention to being a devoted mother, loving wife, and companion. I pledged to help others troubled by infertility. I completed a Masters program in social work while working at an infertility/reproductive medicine clinic. Still I wrestled with my unfulfilled desire to give birth. We tried yet again. The infertility treatments, joy of conceiving, and heartache of miscarrying would visit us again. "You are pregnant!" Those familiar words rang in my ears again. Only this time I was pregnant with triplets. On New Year's Day, after a rocky pregnancy, miscarrying one of the triplets and being on complete bed rest, my twin daughters were born. After thirty-six hours of labor, at twenty-three weeks' gestation, another crushing blow: My twin daughters, Athena Lourdes and Jacqueline Gerard, would die shortly after their birth. With an ironic twist, the words Happy New Year blared through my head simultaneously as the nurses called for help. I was hemorrhaging, and my blood pressure was crashing!

The crisis left me petrified that my son would again be motherless. All I could remember was screaming out, "Save me, my son needs me!" Those were the last words I remembered as they rushed me to the operating room for emergency surgery to save my own life. I was so grateful to be alive. Tears of gratitude filled my eyes, knowing that my son would never again be left without a mother.

For many months afterward, I sought to rebuild myself physically, emotionally, and spiritually. I knew my son needed me. Through multiple surgeries, difficulty walking, tremendous physical and emotional pain, and almost losing my eyesight, I concentrated on the joy my precious son had brought to me (his sweet and gentle smile, his cute laugh, and his adorable personality). Every day I focused on him, thankful that I have him in my life. Many people would say to me that he was a very lucky little boy to be adopted by us because we saved his life when we brought him from Romania. "No," I would say, "I'm the lucky one because he saved my life."

Through my son, I've learned many things about myself, about him, about life, and about humanity. I found the greatest love, admiration, and respect, not only for his birth mother, but for all birth mothers separated from their children. I cannot think of a greater gift of love that someone can give another than the gift of life. After realizing that I had all that it took internally to create what I needed externally, the strength of my intellect and my creativity flowed. This has helped me tremendously to be the mom, the teacher, the healer, the humanitarian and visionary I am today. With an open heart, I have taken the culmination of all of my experiences and have been able to channel it into my work as a therapist and teacher.

For me, the words "God doesn't give you more then you can handle" have profound meaning. When I first heard those words, they were not a source of comfort to me — knowing how strong I was, I feared those words. Now I truly understand what those words mean, and I am blessed to be able to share what I have learned with my son, my family, my friends, my students, and the families I work with. I have seen a huge transformation in my own life and the lives of many. For that my heart is overwhelmed with an abundance of love, health, and gratitude. I am in awe of my "miracle child," who is incredibly gifted and talented. He too is a teacher, a humanitarian, a visionary, and a tremendous healer.

Every day he inspires me to live life to the fullest and be the best that I can be. I couldn't have given birth to a more incredible or more wonderful child. I am truly blessed for all of my experiences that brought me to him and him to me. When he was twelve years old, he said to me, "Mommy, I always knew you were coming for me. I didn't know how, but I knew, I just knew. I was waiting for you to come!"

♥   ♥   ♥

Denise Lauria Venitelli, LCSW, a visionary and humanitarian, is a licensed clinical social worker, child advocate, and adjunct college professor. A graduate of Rutgers University with an M.S.W. and a B.A. in early childhood education and psychology, Ms. Venitelli provides individual and family therapy, specializing in integrating a multi-dimensional approach utilizing different holistic modalities.

Her professional career centers on work with children and families, specializing in adoption-related issues, early childhood trauma and abuse, issues pertaining to abandonment and attachment. She has experience working with children with learning differences: gifted with ADHD, those on the autistic spectrum, and those with sensory integration difficulties. Previously, Ms. Venitelli facilitated groups and workshops for those facing the challenges of infertility and third-party reproduction and has extensive research experience in the field of reproductive endocrinology/infertility. She can be reached via email at DVenitelliLCSW@aol.com.

Thank God
I Had Cancer

Your Soul Will Guide
if You Are Ready to Listen

Cassandra Gatzow

It was about 3:00 P.M. on September 15, 2006 when I got the call. I was in the midst of my working day, about to walk into one of my accounts. I worked as a salon consultant for a beauty distribution company at the time. About a month and a half earlier, I'd had a wink from God take place in my life. While doing a late spring-cleaning, I somehow decided my birth control pills had expired. The date read May 2007, and it was only May 2006, but for some reason I thought we were in 2007. So I grabbed the pills and tossed them in the trash. About a month later, as my pack was ending, I looked at the date again and realized what I had done. So I scheduled an appointment with my gynecologist for July and went on with my business.

My GYN found some abnormal cells, which resulted in more tests, more appointments. This in turn led up to the phone call. I sat in the accountant's parking lot when the call came in: My gynecologist had my biopsy results. Being twenty-two at the time and never having been sick a day in my life, I could not even fathom what she said next. First asking if I was in a place to talk, she told me that I had full-blown cancer developing in me. She said there was nothing more she could do, and I needed to contact a specialist. After giving me his name and number, she wished me good luck. I sat in my car and just about lost feeling in every inch of my body.

That night and the days to follow were a blur. I had to tell my family and my friends. I had to notify my work and make an appointment to see this doctor. Three days later, I sat in his office and awaited my future. He told me that I had cervical cancer, rather large, and that it had invaded both sides. I had only one option — undergo a hysterectomy in nine days. Then based on the results of that, I might proceed into treatment.

Many members of my family have been lost to cancer, so the very word created a large, open wound within my family and me. One of my grandmothers is a survivor of seven years, but the other four members of my family were not so lucky. I remember being twelve and standing by my other grandmother's hospital bed just moments before she passed. She was in such horrible pain, and we could do nothing. I could feel the wound start to bleed in all of us as the process began.

Those nine days seemed to go by slowly, and my heart broke every time I had a moment with a loved one. The hardest conversation I had was with my sixteen-year-old brother. My heart split right open when tears filled his eyes and he asked me if I was going to die. I grabbed him and told him I was going to be just fine — we had to take it one day at a time. That is what I continued to tell myself as the days passed. It took me a week to tell the man I loved. The strong woman I once knew was scattered and scared to death.

The day of my surgery was an interesting one. I had to be at the hospital at 9:00 A.M. for surgery at 11:00 A.M. My boyfriend, David, and I arrived at the hospital, with him as sick as can be. He was shaking and throwing up. I had no idea what was wrong with him. The whole thing going on with him did take my mind off me. It allowed me to go into caring mode. He was quickly sent to emergency and away from me. A few moments later, they wheeled me into the elevator on a gurney, toward the preparation room. While we were in the elevator, I told my mother not to worry . . . I would be just fine. She was overwhelmed with tears. I can't explain the peace that came over

me that morning, or the peace that has stayed with me since. It was
as if angels' wings were holding me.

I awoke from surgery to find a tube in my nose and several beeping
machines surrounding me. I was freezing cold and couldn't stop shaking. Shortly after, they wheeled me up to my room, where my sweet
mother and family waited for me. David was nowhere to be found. I
got a phone call from him about an hour later, saying, "Honey, I was
right beside you in the recovery room. I had my appendix removed!"
There he was, a floor under me, with the same tummy scars as me.

I remained in the hospital for a week due to the intensity of the surgery. The healing process would be a long one, with more to it than I
thought. Having David in the hospital with me those first three days was
wonderful. I was so heartbroken about what I had been through and what
was going to happen next. His smile gave me hope. It's interesting how the
Universe works. The people who have surrounded me since the beginning
are truly earth angels. Three weeks passed, and I was back in my doctor's
office awaiting the news. I was ready to move past this event and get on
with my emotional and physical healing. I had to deal with not being able
to bear children and the feeling that I had been robbed of my innocence. I
was only twenty-two, and what work I had ahead of me!

Well, it wasn't quite over yet. My doctor informed me that the
cancer had spread to the outside tissues, and the only way to ensure
that it was gone was with chemotherapy and radiation. At the moment
those two words were spoken, I once again lost all feeling in my being.
My doctor told me that I was very special and was going to make it
through. "Well, okay then," I said, "but I must go back to work so
I can feel normal in some way." He referred me to a chemotherapy
specialist and a radiation center.

I returned to work, and about a week later I went in to see the
specialist about starting treatment. They performed various scans and
tests, and I was ready to get started in a week. In the process of waiting,
I continued working while experiencing the most incredible pain in my
side. When I returned to start treatment and informed them of this pain,
I had no clue what was in store for me. I was soon told, "Your tumor
has returned." In the six weeks since surgery, my tumor had returned
and was hitting some nerves on my side. So what now?

I started treatment and put on some heavy-duty pain pills that I could not tolerate. Once again I was not able to work and could barely even sleep. I looked in the mirror and had no idea who stood there. My soul burned through my eyes, and I knew it was not ready to go. I lasted three days on the pills and decided I would rather be in pain. I had chemo once a week for six weeks, while the radiation was daily. After my first treatment, I was hospitalized and told that I had one bad kidney. My ability to continue with the chemo depended on how my kidneys reacted to the treatments. Every treatment was closely monitored.

There were times that I would lie on my bathroom floor and pray to leave my body. I've never felt such emotional and physical pain before. I couldn't sleep, I couldn't eat, and I couldn't care for myself. There were times that I was so weak I could barely brush my hair or shower. At the time I was living alone and my mother moved in to care for me. With her help, along with David, and my dear friend Laurie, I made it through all of my treatments.

What I thought was the end of the treatments, I learned was only the middle. I had yet to undergo two internal implants and another five-week course of external radiation.

Back to the hospital daily, and two more times being put under for the implants. I cannot find the words to explain how out of control I felt. I had to hand over my body to a medical staff. I had to open up and allow others to care for me. Both are things I had never had to do before. The process of being treated for cancer is an emotional and physical challenge. There were pieces of it that led me to want to leave my body. It truly was as though my soul led me and my body was being dragged along throughout this process. One day as I walked on the beach outside my home, there was this energy and strength that rose out of the center of my being. It was as if I had awakened from a deep sleep. I realized how blessed I was to have this experience so young. My soul was speaking to me in a way that I could not understand until I was ready to listen.

Throughout my treatments, I changed my thoughts and actions. I would dress up to go into my implant surgery and bake for the staff that cared for me the next couple of days. I decided to celebrate my life and become grateful for this experience. I would spend many days and nights alone, looking at my life — looking at who I was and who I wanted to be. I looked at who surrounded me and how beautiful the moments were that we spent together. My heart began to open, and I started to ask what I needed to learn.

This event came into my life to change my direction. It came to teach me something, and all the elements of it were designed especially for me. It was then that my spirit started to sing. I started to nurture myself. During this process I lost twenty-five pounds . . . they flew right off me. I had also lost all my strength and confidence. It was that day on the beach that I decided to consciously pick up the pieces of Cassandra and put them back together again. In doing this, I was given the opportunity to look at them like I had never seen them before. Every day, my eyes filled with tears of gratitude for every moment and every breath. I started to walk more and laugh more. I started to work out with a group of cancer survivors and patients. I found the "Thank God I . . . " project and began to live from my heart and step back to see what a beautiful life I had.

I am writing my story because cancer has changed my life. It has allowed me to go after my dreams, to live from my heart, and to truly be free. I thank God for my cancer and for allowing me to reach a place in myself that I don't think would have been possible without this experience. I am now twenty-three and feel that I have stepped into my skin proudly. I have felt an inner peace that many don't find until later in life. I am truly grateful for all my earth angels and want to thank them for sharing with me this wonderful journey.

It is in the moments of complete chaos that the most beautiful clarity comes to us. It is in becoming grateful for everything and loving every piece of it that you start to hear the truth. It is in that piece of frozen time that you can look back and see who you are. In the midst of this illness, which I was convinced would remove me from my physical body, I have come to embrace my body and feel comfort in it like never before. Learning to be grateful for this illness as it was happening to me, through every stage, has truly transformed me.

This "Thank God I . . . " project has inspired me because it helped me remember to be grateful throughout my illness. It reminded me that

I am here to heal others and to share what I have learned. As I am coming to a close of this process called "Cancer," I see how it was exactly what I needed to become Cassandra. It has allowed me to love every inch of myself, and in doing that I can love every inch of you. I can appreciate and know that we all have our journeys and processes, but all serve and come for a reason. I thank God for my Cancer and for the opportunity to step into my new skin, skin that I wear proudly and cannot wait to share with you!

Peace and many blessings to each and every one of you.

Cassandra Ann Gatzow blessed this earth in her physical form by sharing wisdom that was well beyond her twenty-three precious years. Our angel's beautiful old soul touched numerous lives through her generous spirit of love, grace, and gratitude. Cassandra inspired us all to cherish every day by not taking anything for granted, and her message of compassion, joy, courage, and kindness remains reflected in all that she influenced. After a year-long fight with cervical cancer, Cassandra transitioned to continue her work in her spiritual form for God, humanity, and nature that extends well beyond this realm of life. Through Cassandra's sincere consciousness of "One Love," we can all feel her presence, shine her light, and make every day special and meaningful. Live for Today! (Spoken for Cassandra through David Baumann.)

Thank God
I Had a Miscarriage

DR. SARAH FARRANT

t 3:00 P.M., I ran out of the toilet cubicle, tears rolling down my eyes. Panic overcame me when Randall wasn't where I had left him waiting. Searching for Randall among the crowd of people in the Borders bookstore, I eventually found him in the CD section. I ran toward him and collapsed into his arms, burying my head in his chest.

"What's the matter?" he asked as he tried to lift up my head to look into my eyes. I couldn't face him. I kept snuggled in his chest and arms while staring at the ground.

"There's blood on my underpants!" I sobbed, allowing the tears to flow. "It . . . it . . . it won't stop!" Randall bundled me up like a celebrity trying to escape the paparazzi, and I slowly climbed into the back of our car and laid down, hoping that would help to stop the bleeding. Randall hurried to the driver's side, and we took off. We could go only as fast as the snowfall would allow.

"It would be good to get an adjustment, Sare," he said, trying to find me in his rear vision mirror.

"Yes," I agreed. Anything to stop the blood loss, I thought. "Can you take me to Marie and Tammy's?"

We didn't speak again until we arrived at our friends' house. The only exchange between us was an energy of love. We both knew what was happening. The ride seemed to take forever. The Bellagio penthouse suite in Las Vegas where we had made love seemed light years away from where I was now. I felt my thoughts focus on the power of what I'd created. I understood now how powerful my thoughts are in creating the scenarios I wish to see. The snow fell, the windshield wipers ticked like metronomes. I shut my eyes and replayed the pregnancy from conception to present. I felt a blood clot leave my body.

I couldn't help but think about my daily mantra, "It's okay to die." Guilt paralyzed my body as I lay in the back seat of the car, remembering the words I had chosen to speak to our baby. I pictured the breakfast table where I sat and spoke while Randall showered. I'd been concerned with the loss parenting would bring — sleep, movies, flying, cultural experiences, five-star restaurants, and freedom. I failed to entertain the possible gain of having children and being a parent. However, I kept my greatest fear under lock and key.

Why wasn't the exhaustion, fatigue, and nausea changing? I would ask myself. I am almost three months; people say it changes about now. Perhaps this blood loss is the physiological dip where the placenta takes over the production of the hormones to give life to the conceptus, and the corpus luteum is no longer required. Yes, that's what it is. I felt more blood flow from my body. In the back seat of the car, my two greatest fears, birth and trust, confronted me. They were the two reasons why I avoided pregnancy for the twelve years of our relationship. Although at the time I was studying chiropractic and the profession's remarkable philosophy, I doubted the reality of an innate (inborn, internal) intelligence — that the body that forms, grows, and nurtures the baby also has the intelligence to birth the baby. I understood the philosophy at an intellectual level, but right now, I was being given an opportunity to experience this understanding at a practical level. I curled into a fetal position on the back seat of the car, my hands over my head, and let out a deep primal scream as I realized my fears were fast approaching.

"No . . . !" I yelled. The contraction of my abdomen forced more blood from my body.

As we arrived at our friends' house, I felt weak and limp. I was stunned. Randall helped me out of the car, tears rolling down his cheeks. Still no words were spoken, just love. What I wanted all along was now being given to me. Present at our friends' house was the lecturer who filled in for the pediatrics class at college. She's a midwife and a chiropractor, and the synchronicity was astounding. I shared with them the events thus far. They just listened, letting me talk. We weren't there for long — I felt tired and wanted to be home in our bed. As we left they wished us luck. When I walked down the stairs of their apartment, I felt blood gush from my body.

We arrived home, and I went straight to our bed. I slept for what seemed like an eternity. I awoke in a daze, wondering if I had been dreaming or if in fact this was real. I got up and went to the toilet. When I urinated, I didn't feel any blood loss from my vagina. I had a moment of reprieve. It was 8:00 P.M., and I had been bleeding well over five hours. This isn't spotting, I told myself. This is a miscarriage: birth and death. I curled again on our bed and let out a huge scream. "Why? Why? Why?" I yelled as a heavier flow of blood left my body. I knew why; I knew what I created. I knew I made this happen.

A couple of hours later, the contractions began. No longer just blood flow; it was now time to focus, to breathe; a time to go further within and trust that my body knew what to do. I had to get out of my own way. The contractions intensified, and I felt the need to go to the toilet — to squat and to push. As I made my way to the bathroom, I felt my sensitivity increase. I didn't want to be touched. My heart rate quickened, and my skin dripped perspiration; I couldn't stop the diarrhea. I sat on the toilet and placed my left hand at the level of my uterus, an almost symbolic way of trying to touch our child, to nurture and to help it through its new journey. My right hand gripped on the rim of the bath. As the contractions intensified, I felt I wanted to escape my body. My breathing was fast and high-pitched, not deep like I had experienced with a friend who had recently given birth. What's wrong? I asked myself. Why is this so painful — physically, chemically, and emotionally?

The contractions came closer together, and I reached a crescendo. I vomited all over the bathroom floor and then felt the urge to push. After a few pushes I felt a conceptus pass, and then another one — my first indication that I was carrying twins, and finally the placenta. I buried my head in my hands, bowed my head to the floor, and felt so guilty and ashamed at the thought of killing our children. I shook uncontrollably. Randall wiped the vomit from my face, my hair, and my hands, and with loving tears in his eyes, he ever so gently picked me up off the toilet seat, and carried me back to the bedroom. As we came out of our tiny bathroom, I heard the flush of the toilet. "No . . . !" I yelled as I collapsed on the bed, mortified.

Over the next months, I felt challenged by my hormones. My progesterone had plummeted post-birth, and I was angry, confused, and trapped — feelings I hadn't experienced at this intensity before. Randall noticed the difference in me and decided to take me away to a small town called Galena to a beautiful bed & breakfast, where I could escape the phone and the knocks on the door. Much to my surprise, I took with me some beautiful watercolor paints and a deck of self-healing cards. I wanted to draw, paint, and communicate with our children. During our stay, I was reminded of the birth by each blood clot that still passed through my body, although they were much less frequent. I sat at the window looking out over a field. The weather was cold, and Randall lit the fire. I pulled three cards, one for me and one for each of our children. I asked what I needed to know. My card said:

> "All is well in my world: everything is working out for my highest good. Out of this situation only good will come. I am safe."

Then I pulled two cards — ironically one was male and one was female. The male card said:

> "Life is simple and easy; all that I need to know at any given moment is revealed to me. I trust myself and I trust in life. All is well."

The female card read:

"I am beautiful, and everybody loves me. I radiate acceptance, and I am deeply loved by others. Love surrounds me and protects me".

I looked at these cards with an uncanny feeling. At this point, I understood two pertinent epiphanies. One, that nothing is ever missing in our life. We have everything we need; however, it just might be in a form we have not yet recognized or experienced. Second, the world exists in balance. Here I am holding our two children: one a male and one a female, having just experienced birth and death with them, the perfect balance. Both of them were teaching me to trust, to feel safe.

I went on to sketch the information I received. Upon completion of the drawing and painting, I realized that we indeed hadn't lost our children. I saw that they were in fact still with us; they had just changed form. They were now a beautiful painting, which would hang brightly in our children's rooms in the years to come.

The day after I finished painting, and experienced those epiphanies, the blood flow stopped. No longer did I need to experience the loss, it no longer served me. I had our children with us; they were now in a picture form.

Upon our return to Davenport, I felt a little shaky at getting back into the swing of life. My hormones were still up and down, and I was tired. The midwife and college lecturer, the lady at our friends' house that eventful day, approached me to ask if I would be interested in speaking to the pediatrics class to share my story. I immediately said yes. Despite the ordeal Randall and I had lived through in losing our children, I always felt my life would unfold on the stage, sharing with people the amazing power of the innate intelligence that lives inside us. And here I was being given an opportunity to start it off, to share this vision.

Over the next eighteen months, I shared the story of my newfound trust in the body with hundreds of students who were eager to hear and learn about the wisdom of the body. In each audience, listeners responded with gratitude because that I gave a voice to the innate understanding of the body, which knows what to do every time, all the time. Repeatedly, people would come up to me afterward to share with me the current form of their baby. I lived in awe of the power of the truth I learned to share and felt humbled at the joy people experienced. When the audience realized this universal truth, they experienced a huge relief and an understanding that nothing is ever missing; it just changes form. I was privileged to see listeners able to reconnect with their own "little ones," and to recognize the gift that had brought them to this point.

A few months into the next college trimester, I realized I was pushing myself too much, and I said to Randall, "I'm not coping. I need to get away." We decided we would go to Mexico. He booked the tickets, and within a week, we were there. We went to Adventura Palace, an adults-only resort, staying there for a week. Here I got space, sleep, cultural experiences, sun, and five-star restaurants — things I thought I'd miss when I became a parent. It was here that I was truly able to distance from the event, and in taking this distance, I was able to gain clarity and see another perspective on what had taken place. I saw the gifts in all that had transpired.

Thank God I had a miscarriage. Both the miscarriage experience and our children increased my trust that the body knows what to do every time in any circumstance. I didn't go off to the hospital to have a D & C. I didn't call a doctor to find out if everything had passed and to find out if I was okay. I didn't want anything external interrupting my flow, the gift our "little ones" had given me — the ultimate gift of trust. I learned first-hand to get the educated mind out of the way because it only interferes with what the innate already knows. This deep trust and respect for the body's innate knowing enabled me to go on to have three remarkable home births, by choice, all of them unassisted. Each was a beautiful dance; I didn't feel the pain that many people report. Each one gave me a gift of looking within myself. Our first son enabled me to look at my chemical reality, our second son my emotional reality, and our most recent addition, a little girl who entered the world via a breech home birth only thirteen months ago, reframed my physical reality.

All of our children awakened channels in me that had been dormant. After the birth of our second child, I received volumes of information as to how my life was to unfold. I asked the universe when I laid down to rest one day, "How can I continue to serve and adjust people chiropractically from home?" I awoke with my mind overflowing with instructions! Within the information, I received my inspiration. This was what I wrote: "to share vitalistic philosophy with the world and how it relates to health for the purpose of changing the health consciousness of individuals, families, communities, cities, states, nations, and the world; to inspire a desire in others to do their life differently; to ask different questions." I then wrote the word BOOK. Write a book.

As a result of my experience with our twins and our subsequent home births, my first book explains the innate intelligence we live with on a daily basis. The book is titled *The Vital Truth: Accessing the Possibilities of Unlimited Health*. I understand from my miscarriage experience that I'm here to share the understanding of vitalism and chiropractic, and how they relate to pregnancy, birth, and health. It's my inspiration to educate people on vitalism and the chiropractic philosophical understanding of how the body works, in relation to both itself and the universe. I am inspired to further educate people, from a vitalistic and chiropractic perspective, on the physical, chemical, and emotional changes that may occur as we bring forth new life. My vision is to open people's eyes to the power of innate intelligence. *The Vital Truth: Accessing the Possibilities of Unlimited Health* is making it possible for individuals to integrate into their life this unique understanding of health, the human body, and its expression. Lives are being changed. This in turn is changing the health consciousness of the communities, cities, states, nations and the world.

The death and birth of our twins enabled me to awaken the trust inside, to be humbled by the sheer genius of the body we live in. Their death and birth enabled me to ask different questions and to be awakened to new answers. Their death and birth were pivotal in bringing me to where I am today. I have the beauty now of adjusting people mentally via my book rather than physically. Nothing's ever missing; it just changes form.

♥   ♥   ♥

Dr. Sarah Farrant, chiropractor, mother, author, and international speaker, says, "I understand from my miscarriage experience that I am here to share the understanding of vitalism and chiropractic and how they relate to health, pregnancy, birth, and post-birth." She's recently established the Global Pregnancy Centre, which will be the largest educational online community where people learn about the power of their body from a vitalistic perspective. Her book, *The Vital Truth: Accessing the Possibilities of Unlimited Health*, explains in greater detail the nature of our innate (internal, inborn) intelligence as it relates to health. The book is helping individuals integrate this unique understanding of health, the human body, and its expression into their lives. This in turn is having profound effects on communities, cities, states, nations and the world. You can reach Dr. Farrant at info@drsarahfarrant.com. Her websites are www.drsarahfarrant.com and www.globalpregnancycenter.com.

Thank God
My Friend Was Sexually Abused by Her Grandfather

Elizabeth Pasquale, LMT, CST

We were walking downtown together, toward the big gray cloud. The cloud's edges covered the entire financial district, and the toxins reached out over all of Manhattan, Brooklyn, and Queens. It was the cloud from the collapse of the World Trade Center towers, the day after the planes hit. We wanted to volunteer, to help in any way. We were both massage therapists, and we thought we could be helpful. For the purpose of this story, let's call my friend "Alice."

I'll admit that we were scared. Though we wanted to help, we joked about being turned away, not making it to the center of the nightmare. It took some guts to walk straight into that cloud. If we hadn't happened to meet as we both exited the subway at 14th Street, either one of us might have turned back. We gave each other courage. As it turned out, a group of rescuers in a van picked us up and gave us a ride right to Ground Zero.

We worked side by side for about a week, working through the nights. We had massage tables set up in a dusty school building in the midst of the wreckage, and as the rescue workers collapsed from fatigue and trauma, we fed them, massaged them, listened to their stories, dried their tears, and sent them to the showers and then back out again to dig.

That was 2001. This is 2007. I hadn't seen her since, until last weekend. We both attended the *Demartini Breakthrough Experience®* in New York City. During and after the class, she told me her story. Like so many New Yorkers, and probably people all over the country, after 9/11, Alice was traumatized. What she didn't realize until later was that the 9/11 group trauma we went through stirred up personal traumas. After 9/11, those personal traumas exploded forth for those trying to keep them buried. Others sought the most expert of therapists, to carefully dismantle these traumas. When Alice began to "remember" things, she sought out one of those expert therapists, one who was also an energy healer. Alice saw things in her head, as people do when remembering. But these things were shocking to her. She asked herself, "How can I remember things that never happened?"

Alice saw pictures in her head that were clear as any memory she'd ever had. She saw herself as an infant in a crib. She saw her grandfather come over to the crib and pick her up. Grandfather held her upside-down against his chest. He unbuttoned his shirt. His chest was hairy. He unbuttoned his fly. He stroked her. He held her head against his penis . . . and let her suck on him. She remembered Grandmother coming in, and Grandfather hurriedly putting her back in the crib. To make a bad situation worse, in his haste he didn't bother to right her. He just held her upside-down by her feet, took the one or two steps from the side of the bed, where he was sitting with her. Nervous and fearing discovery, he lifted her into the crib, misjudged the height of the crib railing, and banged her head against it.

This didn't come to her all at once. She got fragments of it. She fought against it. How could she have a memory of something that never happened? Her grandfather never abused her. The therapist disagreed. Alice had all the classic signs of child sexual abuse; unexplained depression, low self-esteem, an inability to love, feelings of not deserving of love, a kind of numbness when it came to love, and inability to enjoy sex. She had married twice, and both marriages failed.

She was baffled. How could she know if it had really happened? Grandfather died more than twenty years earlier, as had Grandmother. She didn't want to bring it up to her family. She decided not to concern herself about whether it was real or not but to treat it as if it had been a real event. The funny thing about our bodies, whatever we can vividly imagine, our bodies will treat as real. When scientists studied Olympic athletes, they asked them to imagine their events. With the athletes hooked up to electrodes, the scientists could see that the athletes' muscles were firing in imagination identically to the way they would fire during the actual event. Whether the event actually happened or not, Alice suffered from infant sexual abuse, it was real to her. She went through years of therapy dealing with it, and she thought she had come to a place of acceptance. Then it came up at the *Demartini Breakthrough Experience®*.

In the *Demartini Method®*, you complete pages of questions. Then you pick a person that angered, hurt, or disappointed you. You examine the incident and the person's actions in detail. You list the traits you liked about the person, and the traits you disliked. How did you benefit from those seemingly bad things that happened? How did you suffer from the good things?

It's a methodical process, and the class went about it with some complaining. Alice did her process on the relationship with her boyfriend, which had broken up earlier that same week. She saw all the good things that had come from the relationship, all the good things in the man. She came to the point of gratitude; tears of gratitude filled her eyes. She felt so peaceful about the man and the break-up . . . when, suddenly, there was Grandfather again.

John said that when you come to a place of peace and gratitude, you make a quantum leap from where you were in anger and disappointment to this new level of finding balance and gratitude. Alice asked a question: "Then why did it trigger in me this memory of my grandfather abusing me when I was a baby? I'm not even sure it is a memory or that it really happened."

"That's because you have reached a new level, and with the new level there is a new challenge," John explained. "Think about it. What benefits did you get from this abuse?"

"Well," Alice said, "I'm now a therapist, and I treat many women who were abused. I'm able to understand and help them."

"See," said John, "there was a benefit. You might not have been such a good therapist for them if that hadn't happened to you. You might not have become a therapist at all! You need to do the process on your grandfather."

After the class, Alice and I teamed up to continue studying John's method. About a week later, she had completed the *Demartini Method*® and "collapsed" her grandfather. (John calls it a collapse when you see through all the events you have built up into this story, this fantasy, and come to a new insight, a more whole truth.) Alice told me she went through the process, and found the many benefits of the trauma. She credited it for turning her towards becoming an excellent therapist. She pursued a path of learning, largely because of her yearning to find answers to a question she couldn't even formulate. She even felt that the birth of her child was in some way a result of this event. In fact, she felt that her whole being, the type of person she'd become, her work, her strength and determination, were all a direct result of this event.

She could imagine sitting with Grandfather and thanking him. She'd imagined sitting with him several times before, but never had she thanked him. Before this, he appeared remote, confused, taciturn, and unremorseful. Now he was warm. She now understood why he had never apologized. She understood why she repeatedly attracted disempowered financially insecure men. She realized that it was her way of keeping control. Grandfather at that time was the financial benefactor for the family. Her parents lived in his house while they saved for their own. She came into adulthood with this childhood fear of men controlling her. So, she drew disempowered men to her. She had one impoverished boyfriend and husband after another. Now it's no longer necessary. Alice can attract a man who can match her with his strength. She can be safe even if the man is powerful and financially strong. Life looks different to her after this *Breakthrough Experience*®.

Challenging experiences shape us in a multitude of ways. Suppression of the event stunts our growth. Accept it with gratitude and we grow. I've heard of infant memory before. People ask, "Is it real?" That's a trick question. It takes us out of the process. A better question is, "What if it is real? What then? What is it telling me?" Ask that and proceed from there.

Enjoy your life lessons!

♥   ♥   ♥

Elizabeth Pasquale, LMT, CST is the director of Well On The Way®, a holistic treatment center in Westchester County, New York. She specializes in trauma therapy, treating adults as well as children. Elizabeth is also widely known for her personal coaching and group trainings, her Gratitude Magnifier System, and entrepreneur development. For more information visit www.wellontheway.org, or call 914-762-4693 to share your own struggles, ask key questions, and talk about solutions free of charge.

Thank God
I Lost My Home and My Love
. . . and Ended Up a Winner

BRUCE HOFFMAN

I once owned a magnificent home in the Noordhoek Valley, outside of Cape Town, South Africa. It was a large, sprawling home on an acre and a half of land, perched on the hillside overlooking miles and miles of white, sandy beaches and excellent surf. (Riding the waves was a huge part of my lifestyle.) After impulsively selling the house, I experienced deep regret and a sense of futility, shame, loss, and self-reproach that no amount of cognitive rationalizing could shift . . . that is, until I saw things differently. This is my story of the illusion of gain and loss that exists in the relative world, and how a simple shift from a local to a cosmological point of view changed everything.

I attended medical school at the University of Cape from 1977 through 1981. For most of those years, I lived up in the mountains around the Noordhoek Valley, on the outskirts of Cape Town. I used to hitchhike into medical school. When not studying, I surfed on the beach breaks surrounding the idyllic valley. My home was an abandoned church, with a cross embedded in the main wall. There I looked after my dogs, my chickens, and my pet goat, Big Lil. One of my dogs, Zana, was not quite trainable. He fought with all the other dogs, and he ran away on a regular basis. He often came down with tick bite fever, lying on the floor with a white tongue and panting in a search for more air. I would take him to the vet, who gave him injections, within a few days of which he recovered.

I loved his presence and took him to the university with me. He loved to sit in my car. I'd roll down the window, and he would jump in and out, as he wanted. At lunch, I would come down and sit with him, and we would look out over the hospital graveyard and just be together. I loved being in Noordhoek with my chickens, my dog, and the shower at the bottom of the garden. Staying up late at night, I'd huddle over my gas lantern, read, and write long poetic pieces that emulated my heroes, Allen Ginsberg and Jack Kerouac. I wanted to pull down the curtain on my daily life and sing in exaltation to the life of poetry I was not living. In a half-altered state from drinking wine, I'd write to women I'd met who eluded me and taunted me with their beauty and unattainability, sirens beckoning from the gloom. I would also reluctantly study for my medical school exams, wishing all the while to answer only to the ecstatic poetic voices that I heard in my head.

The Noordhoek valley held us all together in its big mystery. Hippies, artists, farmers, schizophrenics, cows, surfers, dogs, and medical students — we all circled each other and looked to each other for support during our more vulnerable moments. My view from my small cottage swept over the Noordhoek beach and valley. To the right and perched on the cliff above the surf, was a long, sprawling ranch-type home belonging to a reclusive gay misanthrope. As a student, I visited his home once. A friend of mine rented a room there. The house was spectacular, with its incredible view of a seven-mile beach and the Slangkop lighthouse in the distance. In the evening, the sun dropped past the horizon, and the whole valley lit up in smoky splendor. I could not imagine living in such a spectacular home — it was beyond my student dreams.

After graduating from medical school, I left the Noordhoek Valley and moved to Canada. I adjusted to life on the Canadian prairies, with their vast plains of wheat fields and their grain silos. I learned the art and craft of family medicine, taking it all quite seriously, and I accumulated a little money. Uneasily I adjusted to the father/husband archetypes. I dreamt of the sea every night and longed for the day I could move back to South Africa.

One winter, a number of years after I left the Noordhoek Valley for Canada, I visited Cape Town and surfed off the Noordhoek beach. I passed the driveway to the ranch-type home and noticed a cardboard sign hammered onto a tree with one nail. It said "Auction tomorrow morning, 9:00 A.M." I had nothing to lose and thought it worthwhile to show up. The auction took about three minutes. I found myself bidding at a ridiculously low figure of 80,000 Rand. I expected the price to reach R300,000. Another person bid R90,000 and I went to R100,000. I heard the auctioneer announce, "The home is sold to the surfer gentleman over there." I signed the papers and went into the back garden to contemplate my unexpected fate. This was quite surreal. I had not planned this at all.

The home was large, sprawling on over an acre and a half, perched on a hillside overlooking a vast expanse of clean white sand. My favorite surf spot was visible from every room in the house. I could wake up in the morning and scan the swells, tune into the wind directions and the nuances of the changing seasons. Behind the house were huge obelisk-like granite rocks. I would sit on these rocks for hours on end, listening to the noises, dog barks, and children's voices from the valley below. In the dusk and dawn moments of the changing light, I would vibrate at a slow harmonic, not believing my luck. I wanted to be buried on this land. I wanted generations of my family to know this grounding.

For the first five years, I didn't live in the house. My good friend Bobby took up residence there, and my family and I would visit once a year and have large Christmas gatherings of the bloodlines, celebrating life and each other. Every morning, I would wake up and walk around the property, pulling out wayward weeds and watering the endless gardens. When it was hot at night, I would cool off in the swimming pool and delight in the comforts of the still night. I could not believe my luck and how good it made me feel.

Meanwhile, life happened: Back in Canada, I went through a divorce, and my family split up. I attempted to put my life together as a single person, but anxiety and stress got the better of me. I fell apart. My psychiatrist said, "Either we admit you to the hospital, or you go back to South Africa for a break." One day, after a year of trying to start again, I put my pen down on my desk at work. At the time, I was running the most successful integrative medical clinic in the city and had a long waiting list of people wanting to move beyond the drug and surgery solutions to their issues. My resolve was final. I booked a flight and flew back to my Noordhoek home the next day.

Walking up the driveway, I felt the burden of the divorce lift. I sat for days in the lounge with the vast windows looking over the endless beach and waves, and I knew this was where I could put my life back together again. It was an incredible experience: allowing the sea and the waves to soothe me. Instead of returning to Calgary after three weeks as I planned, I let my staff, ex-wife, and children know that I was never coming back. I walked away from it all. It was a reckless, irresponsible thing to do, but I couldn't bear the thought of facing all the stress again. My physiology had given in, and my mind had followed. I was home with the earth, the sea, and the sky, my ego crushed but my sense of soul returning. I walked away from my practice making hundreds of thousands of dollars a year, my loyal and devoted staff, my incredible patients, my kids, my debts, and my life, as I knew it. Within weeks, the healing power of the view from the front lounge over the vast expanse of beach had moved me past my shrunken self.

Pablo Neruda ("Absense and Presence"):

> I need the sea because it teaches me
> I don't know if I learn music or awareness
> If it's a single wave or its vast existence,
> or only its harsh voice or its shining one,
> a suggestion of fishes and ships.
> The fact is that until I fall asleep,
> In some magnetic way I move in
> The university of the waves

I don't know what it was, but my bones seemed to rearrange themselves, and my mind woke back up to itself. I sensed a self-returning.
Within weeks, I recovered sufficiently to be open to a new love. She
walked up the same driveway to interview for a house-sitting job, and I
was smitten. It was love at first sight. But she was twenty years younger
than I was, and I felt out of my depth. Nonetheless, we became engaged
and lived out our destiny with color within the walls of the house. We
spoke of past loves, talked over wine, shared pasta in garlic sauce, and
planned our fate. At times, friends would visit. We would stand on the
porch and hold each other lightly, not quite sure of how best to reckon
with the fragile night air . . . always with the sea wind on our faces and
the moon on the roof.

After two years, at her insistence, we moved back to Canada. I
wanted to sort out the mess I had left behind and see my children; she
wanted to travel and see the world. After two years surrounded by this
magnificent home and my being in love with this mystery being, we
packed up and left the home, securing renters for the time being. Back
in Canada, she became homesick and longed for her youthful lifestyle. I
struggled to meet her needs, but it was no use. After one year, I drove her
to the airport, and we said our goodbyes. I had never felt so inconsolable.
But it was done, and we slipped away from each other for good. There is
no greater despondent feeling than knowing you are revisiting old behaviors and old circumstances, just in a recycled form. I struggled to find a
way to be in the world again.

By then I was having trouble with the renters, who never paid
their bills. The garden was overrun with weeds, the wood rotted on the
window frames, and the rental agency was unreliable. I could not find
anyone to help me get through this tough patch. Trying to manage the
problems from Canada without an intermediary proved insurmountable. It was at this time that a Shaman trickster came to live in my
basement. I met him at a country fair, sitting surrounded by his tarot
cards. He convinced me of his ability to help me heal my broken heart.
It was decided one night that I could not realize my destiny if I held
onto the past, and I needed to release my attachments to South Africa
and the home. That meant selling. It seemed like a good idea, especially
with the stress from managing the affairs from long distance. The house

went on sale and sold for R1.4 million — a profit of more than ten times what I paid for it. I took the money and, in the year 2000, rode the tech boom . . . for two weeks. I bought Intel, Microsoft, Cisco . . . the entire disastrous package. Within six months, my home and the money I had received for it disappeared. My fiancée and I split, my home sold, and my money lost. I had no idea what to do with my life. I just knew that I did not feel very well. I revisited that dark place that was becoming familiar. There seemed no way I could reinvent myself and recreate some of the joy and meaning that the home and the relationship had given me. I was deeply depressed and feeling hopeless.

Neruda ("Absense and Presence"):

> *There is no space wider than that of grief*
> *There is no universe like that which bleeds.*

I plunged into therapy, visited as many healers as I could, went on a trip to Mexico with Deepak Chopra and his group, and visited gurus in India. I sat in Ramana Maharishi's cave on Mt. Arunachala, and felt the aloneness and silence. I consulted with psychics and clairvoyants, and sat quietly in the suburbs collapsed in on myself . . . with no sense of recovery. I could not contemplate a life without love. I rationalized that by associating with the famous and visiting with saints who knew, I would see past the folly of the emotional self and glimpse the unseeing seer beyond. It was not to be. I remained distraught and empty.

One day, I came across a seminar flyer on my desk. I attended and was exposed to the work of John Demartini. I went to Houston, met him, and studied further. His work follows one central principle from which many other insights arise. There is a divine, hidden order, and everything that occurs in your life serves a purpose. This is a Platonic concept, discussed and written about by Emerson and Leibniz, and recently resurrected by James Hillman and others. Your biography is dictated by your Daemon, your Soul, so to speak, and you are called from above, by your Daemon, to live the life you were destined to fulfill. Every event in your biography serves that intent, if you train your mind to investigate the law. The other insight was that nothing is missing from your life.

Whatever you think you have lost is present in a new form, which you just have not seen or appreciated. The significance of Demartini's work is that his is the only cognitively applicable system that integrates the shadow without going through a long analysis. It's also the most direct method of seeing the Buddha Mind, your original face.

Demartini himself had systematically set out to examine many different branches of knowledge and, in so doing, discover some of the universal laws underlying the commonality of them all. I studied psychology, biology, astronomy, finances, health, and healing under him and received a vast education in many different branches of knowledge. In so doing, I relaxed my attachment to my fiancée and my ex-wife and moved on with my life. I placed myself with the impermanence of a changing universe, contemplated my insignificance against the drama of black holes and supernovas, and discovered the evidence for the insignificance of my ego self, against the backdrop of the infinite. It was somewhat overwhelming. But what a relief!

I began a successful practice and found renewed vigor and a sense of purpose in integrative medical practice. I felt resurrected and enlivened and connected once again to something other than my misery. I finally came to live in the world, without shame or despair. And my loves were present in so many new forms: companions, patients, cats, and the waitress at the bistro on the corner. I was missing nothing. Except . . . one issue kept nagging at me. I could not see the benefits of selling my home. I still regretted the decision and longed to return and undo what appeared to be a most foolish and rash decision. No matter how hard I tried, I kept coming up with the same recurring thought: What a ridiculous, impulsive decision I had made. The issue weighed heavily on me . . . and I carried that weight around with me, wherever I went. My heart had rested in the indigenous gardens; the bedrooms where I had lain haunted me with their views of the beaches and sea; now there was only the empty house with the winter northeastern winds.

Needing to resolve my longing, I attended a seminar and worked on the issue. In the seminar, they asked, "What is it about the home that you miss so much?" I thought about it for some time, and then proceeded to describe the view from the living room: the lighthouse in the distance, the waves, the solitariness, and fragrance of the wide, open, oceanic spaces. This prompted another question: "What is the form of your new view?" I thought for a moment and then fell into a deep, transcendent expanse of awareness. I knew I had replaced a geographical view with a cosmological one. I needed to leave behind the physical place in order to be exposed to the cosmology that had become my life's work. The entire melding of my medical training, my eastern religious and Ayurvedic exposure, my exposure to integrative medicine and psychological principles, my immersion in depth psychology, and discovering some of the basic laws of the universe would not have been possible if I had stayed in my home, looking out over the pristine Noordhoek beaches.

In that moment of realization, my yearning stopped and my mind fell apart. This moment can be described as a satori, or non-locality, or Buddha Mind. In that moment, all clinging, all sense of loss, all doubt about my actions entirely disappeared, replaced with the deepest sense of ecstatic awareness at the perfect unfolding of my life's journey. When asked about the drawbacks of the old view and the benefits of the new view, I instantly realized the hidden order in my perceived sense of loss. In that moment, all striving disappeared, and so did all need to influence the outcome of any further experience.

I saw the order and was graced.

Neruda ("The First Sea"):

The prison of the forests
Opened a green door,
Letting in the wave in all its thunder,
And, with the shock of the sea, my life widened out into space.

❤   ❤   ❤

As one of North America's leading integrative doctors, Dr. Bruce Hoffman has studied most of the major disciplines in the broad scope of integrative medicine. In addition to his clinical training, Dr. Hoffman has studied with many of the leading mind-body and spiritual healers, including Deepak Chopra, Paul Lowe, Osho, and Ramesh Balsekar. He was founder of the Centre for Preventative Medicine (Calgary, 1994) and is currently medical director of The Hoffman Centre for Integrative Medicine. His groundbreaking *7 Steps to Health and Transformation*™ model for healing offers an inspiring vision of health, healing, and self-actualization.

Thank God
My Son Died

CHRIS ADAMS

*I*imagine that many readers will be shocked and offended by the title of this story. But it takes a new perspective and understanding of what gratitude is, and isn't, to understand how gratitude can be mined, and found, within even what appears to be the most horrific of losses. I invite you to join me on that journey.

On the morning of September 3, 1999, I came downstairs to the kitchen to make coffee. I looked into the living room for my son, who had spent the night, to see if I needed to wake him to get ready for work. He was partially lying on the couch, his head on the floor, blue.

In that moment, every cell in my being changed, as it had done only once before: when I gave birth. I ran into the living room and carefully put his head back up on the couch. His beautiful turquoise eyes were open, fixed, staring not at me. He was gone. I knew he was, and yet I still tried to revive him while calling 911, begging for help. I lay down next to him, arms around him, for what I knew to be the last time. As I lay there, I recalled all the times, as a little boy, that he had asked to me lie down with him until he fell asleep.

I couldn't accept it and was unable to imagine having the ability to ever do so. I had to be with him. I couldn't live without him, so I died too. Now we can be together. I struggled to hold on as I felt myself teetering on the edge of an abyss that I knew falling into would be permanent — a one-way trip. The pain was terrifying. How to live through this? How to live through the next moment? Then another? I stood up and consciously tried to expand my being enough to have the ability to handle what faced me. He was never again coming home. I would never hear his voice or see him bursting through the door. Never again would he drive me crazy with another wild and hare-brained scheme. No more watching, in fascination, his growth. No grandchildren. The future erased. No hope. I would never again be addressed as "Mom." My entire identity was "Jesse's mom," so now who am I? Was I still a mother, or instantaneously not?

I went into shock to avoid going over the edge, but I remained there, dizzy, weaving. My new identity became My Loss. I descended further. I had to call his father and destroy him with this news. I had to choose a casket for my boy as I had once chosen a bassinet. I had to plan a funeral. I wore his shirt so I could smell him. Down, down I went as I entered the land of "what if?" and "if only." I examined everything I'd ever said or done as a mother and judged it all to be wrong. Fish sticks, Catholic school, braces . . . wrong. It must be so, I reasoned, or else why and how could he have allowed this to happen? I decided he must have hated me; therefore, I must deserve to be hated. I'll take over and hate myself.

Scores of friends and family members descended on me, holding me up, conspiring to keep me alive. Please don't, I thought. Let me go with my boy. Everyone knew Jesse was my life and was afraid I would no longer have reason to live. I couldn't work, drive, or eat. I frequently tripped over nothing, falling to the ground on sidewalks, in parking lots, and in stores. The weight was too much. I kept getting up, staggering on. I didn't look directly into the mirror for a year, didn't want to make eye contact. Many times, one part of my mind would take note of the irrational thinking going on in another part, yet the irrational part continued to assert itself in an attempt to dominate.

As instinct took over, I realized that I had a strong will to live, and I fought back. I refused to participate in any activity I thought Jesse should be doing, or would enjoy doing. I avoided anything that reminded me of him, which was everything. The world became unsafe; a dangerous minefield full of triggers: memories, songs, notes, photos, all hidden within the mundane landscape. I feared this world and withdrew from it. I wouldn't move forward because that would mean leaving him behind. Eventually, thoughts of him were so agonizing, I stopped having them in self-defense. I was doing hard time now, a life sentence without possibility of parole. Marking time, crossing off the days, waiting to die, wanting to.

Gifts and Gratitude

Slowly, slowly, I emerged from the fog of warped thinking. And as my thinking righted itself, new realizations replaced old assumptions. My vision cleared, perspective changed, and something new emerged as I shifted my focus. Despair over the time we no longer had together was replaced with gratitude and appreciation for the time we did have together. Thank God I had the chance to be Jesse's mom for twenty-one years. I am so grateful to have had the honor and the privilege of being mother to such an extraordinary human being. I had never, until now, acknowledged or even taken note of the incredible gift given to me, the twenty-one years my son and I had together. As soon as this perceptual shift occurred, I was flooded with thoughts, visions, memories of joy and exhilaration I had experienced being Jesse's mother, and a deep and moving sense of gratitude for all of it.

For our entire twenty-one years together, the sight, sound, and mere thought of him filled me with joy. But since I could no longer see or hear him physically, should I deny myself the joy that thoughts and memories of him brought? I realized that since I had forced myself to stop thinking about Jesse altogether, I shut him out of my heart, and in doing so, had shut out any joy that thoughts of him would bring. My negative focus allowed only pain, increased the pain, by turning my back on anything joyful. Does his physical absence now mean I should deny everything he was and all that we had? Because the story had changed direction, should I deny the story?

Jesse launched himself into this world with a voracious appetite for life and a daredevil style of expression. I stayed on red alert, trying to keep him out of harm's way. Raising him evoked inner resources I wasn't aware I had. He challenged me every moment and forced me to grow enormously just to keep up. He brought out the most in me, raised me so that I could raise him. He taught me unconditional love. He made me strong enough to handle his passing. He was, and is, my greatest gift, my hero.

As he threw himself at the world, he became involved in drugs and eventually became addicted. This put him on a road of heartache, pain, disappointment, and despair. He fought this battle with such courage, bravery, and hope. His heart, and mine, broke, as it became clear that he was not able to shake this monster. Gratitude is not exhilaration, joy, ecstasy. It is more a sense of peaceful understanding and grace. Thankfulness comes from viewing the big picture.

Clearly, had Jesse not passed away, he would have continued to struggle and suffer unbearably, and things would have continued to deteriorate. Eventually, his beautiful and gentle spirit would be corrupted and harmed by this horrific disease, and he would end up passing anyway. There are no accidents in the Universe; or if you prefer, God doesn't make mistakes. Jesse's passing was an act of mercy. He was spared further agony, struggle, despair, and left here with his beautiful soul . . . beautiful. He's around me all the time, making his presence apparent in his usual outrageous ways. As a parent, given my choices of having Jesse physically present, in pain and suffering, or having him pass out of the physical world into safety and love, I have to choose the latter. And so I say, with all my heart, Thank God my son died and was spared from further torture. I know he's safe now. I know I'll see him again. And for this, I am profoundly grateful.

There is much more to our story than loss and grief. It is, after all, a great love story — my boy and I.

❤   ❤   ❤

Rev. Chris Adams lives in Maryland and is an ordained non-denominational minister. She has a B.A degree from American University and graduated from the Baltimore Spiritual Science Center after completing the intensive five-year course of study in the areas of Metaphysics, Philosophy, Religion, and other esoteric subjects. She spends most of her time performing weddings and baby blessings. She is the daughter of the late Don Adams, best known as the star of the sixties sitcom, *Get Smart*.

Thank God
I Had a Miscarriage

IRENE NICHOLS

I was only twenty-two. I found myself slammed across the room, and as I hit the wall, I felt a pain I had never known before. It was surreal, like this couldn't be happening to me. As my head crashed, the next thing I heard was my two-year-old son screaming, "Daddy, nooooo!" The horrible pain ripped through my groin and I saw blood going down my leg as I ran to the bathroom. There, on the cold tiled floor, a huge blood clot fell out, attached to some misshapen little ball. I gathered it up with a towel and flushed it down the toilet. I'd had no idea I was pregnant; this was the embryo.

My husband, in need of a heroin fix, banged on the door, as the withdrawal stage escalated his violence. He wanted me to take the baby to a couple of drug stores, pinch him upon walking in so he would cry, and then beg the pharmacist for paregoric, an opiate used in the '60s for teething. Addicts boil down a few bottles for one opium fix. He was clueless to what just occurred, and when I came out and told him, he was genuinely sorry, but his dire need overshadowed the emotional need for condolence, compassion, apology, and reflection.

Terrified of the consequences if I didn't acquiesce, I entered the
Miami drugstore with my son, who was happy, smiling, and looking
adorable. Another mother stopped to chat, holding a little girl, and we
acknowledged how beautiful they both were. I could not bring myself
to hurt my son in any way, and instead called the Narcotics detectives,
explaining what my husband wanted me to do, and waited until they
arrived and escorted me home. I was hoping they would talk some
sense into my husband, but they arrested him, extraditing him back to
New York, where, unbeknownst to me, a warrant for his arrest was
waiting. They sentenced him to five years.

The writing was on the wall for a total change, including divorce,
single motherhood, a career, and cash flow issues. While most girls
my age were planning a holiday cruise, I was arranging babysitting
schedules. Thank God for family, as I had my mother, siblings, nieces,
and nephews nearby. I needed to know what to feed this child so he
would not continue to get sick and consequently cause me to lose work
and pay. That need led me to meet two famous holistic pioneers of the
Natural Hygiene movement, who guided me into becoming a holistic
nutritionist. Later, I opened a diet center, helping thousands of clients
lose weight and eat healthy, organic food. I was way ahead of the times
in offering yoga, vegetarianism, and whole foods in my program.

After a client spent a year diligently losing a hundred pounds, only to
have the inner saboteur allow them to gain back thirty of those pounds, I
knew something was missing in my education and expertise. I became a
hypnotherapist to fully understand the difference between the conscious
mind making intelligent decisions and the subconscious mind sabotag-
ing those decisions. Consequently, I was more successful but still noticed
those clients who transferred their mental disconnections into physical
diseases and ailments, so I became a healer as well. I learned EFT (Emotional Freedom Technique) and became a Reiki master. I thought that
would surely do the job. Then a Unity chaplain suggested the crown
jewel of becoming a minister in order to offer the connecting link to
Spirit and God. I became a Universal Brotherhood Reverend, teaching
and coaching lifestyle and spiritual development, lecturing at hospitals
and colleges to students interested in all the subjects I have mastered,
bringing metaphysics, God, and meaning to their lives.

As a hypnotherapist, you are required to be re-certified every year. Thousands of us meet at the International Hypnosis Convention held in Boston and go to classes with people from all over the world. A couple of years ago, I met Isobel, a beautiful Scottish woman with an English accent, living and working in Dubai. We shared an instant chemistry and mindset, ending up in similar classes. We became part of a group that included two psychics, and both of us had readings, apart from one another. We were astonished to hear we'd had three lives together as mother and daughter and contrastingly reversed roles. Two psychics reported the same information separately, explaining our instant familiarity. The connection further deepened upon learning that, along with hypnosis, Isobel was involved with nutrition, healing, and spiritual development, on the other side of the world, with primarily Muslim women. When the convention ended, we cried together, not wanting to part, but loving our newfound friendship and connection.

I came home to Miami and called my own noted, published, and acclaimed psychic. I brought Isobel's pictures to my session and asked, "Tell me about her." He said, "She is what we call a double daughter. You were very young when you had a miscarriage, right? Not only have you had other lives together both as mother and daughter, but when you miscarried, Isobel was the intended soul of that daughter, had it lived to full term. Her soul went back into the non-physical and made a decision to re-emerge, knowing it would not be your daughter in this lifetime but would somehow find you, re-unite, and possibly work together."

Wow and double wow. All my life, palmists and psychics who read me said, "You have two children, one boy one girl." I would say, "No, only a son." They all saw a daughter living on this planet, and I just chalked it up to incompetence and clouded vision. Obviously, they were tuning in to Isobel's energy and my palm, which has the lines of two children.

So, I have come full circle, and have my long-lost, beloved little girl back. She is two and a half years younger than my son is, and I have shown her pictures to him. Everyone has the same remark, that we actually have a similar look. Who knows what would have happened to that little girl had I carried her to full term. Given the circumstances,

I might have had to give her up. I am amazed at how the Universe arranged the people, place, and things for Isobel to come from the other side of the globe in order to re-unite with me and have the deliciousness of her soul back in my life again. I teach the Law of Attraction and Universal Laws, but I am still in awe of the magic, and now I am planning to go to Dubai and give my workshop on Deliberately Creating Your Destiny to Isobel's clients and spend time with my daughter. Thank You, God!

♥   ♥   ♥

Irene Faith Nichols is a certified holistic practitioner, hypnotist, Reiki healer, lecturer, and minister, teaching spiritual development in workshops and colleges in Miami, where she maintains her practice. For the past ten years, she's been a member of the Unity Church choir. She visits her New York roots every few months to hug those grandchildren . . . and is working on a children's book.

Thank God
I Have Cancer

THE CANCER ANSWER

KAI JACOBSON

hank God I have cancer. When you get the worst fear out of the way, there is nothing left to lose. What remains is following your bliss. I've often heard it said, "The greatest fear is the fear of death itself." In May of 1996, my beloved wife felt a small lump the size of a big piece of sand under my right nipple. "You know, men can get breast cancer too," she said. Beth was very intuitive, so I took her words to heart. I scheduled a doctor's visit the next day, and two weeks later, I was going in for a biopsy.

"Breast cancer," the surgeon pronounced. With these two words, I could literally feel my heart leaping out of my chest. The blood drained from my face. I felt as if I were in an Egyptian tomb, with a death curse cast upon me. I was about as far from feeling gratitude as one can get. Nowhere in my being was I thanking God. On the contrary, I was thinking, Why me? How could God abandon me like this? I have two young daughters, Ea and Sita, completely dependent on me. How could this be happening? It just isn't fair.

Not wanting to give my power away to anyone, especially the doctors, I jumped into finding out what was happening in my body. I went down to Barnes & Noble and bought every book on breast cancer I could find. The Internet was still rather new in those days, but I did as many searches as I could. For almost six months, I immersed myself in learning everything I could about cancer. A month after the biopsy, I elected to have surgery and cut out the bad cells, but I decided to pass on the radiation and chemotherapy until I learned more. Both seemed rather toxic. Where was that beautiful forgotten motto of the medical profession, "First, do no harm"?

Breast cancer is relatively rare for men, accounting for about two percent of the cases of breast cancer today — two out of each hundred cases. Statistically it is more deadly in men, primarily due to common late detection as well as far less buffering tissue in men's breasts before the cancer can reach the lymph nodes. I did not like the idea of radiation or chemotherapy, and the more I read, the more I learned about some very good alternatives, especially with early detection. In my investigation, I came across two ideas that profoundly changed my life.

In a book called *A Turning Point*, by Dr. Larry LeShan, I learned that the attitude of the cancer patient has a profound effect on the patient's chance of survival. Those who tend to feel like a victim and who blame the world, God, or a particular person for their situation, tend to have much lower survival rates. Patients who ask the question, "How did I create my cancer?", don't blame others, and take charge of their own healing, have much higher rates of survival statistically. Patients who embrace an attitude of gratitude and ask not only the question, "How did I create my cancer?" but also feel grateful and embrace cancer as a teacher, looking for what they can learn rather than blaming, have the highest survival rate of all.

This revolutionary way of thinking did not come easily for me, and I had to fake it until I made it, but over time, it truly became my attitude. Many people have seen the movie *The Secret*. It puts forth the powerful truth of the Law of Attraction. How and what we think becomes true in time. It's really that simple. Staying in a place of true and honest gratitude is the key. A wonderful story that Larry tells in *A Turning Point* is about a woman with terminal cancer, who had only a few months to live. Larry asked her the simple question, "If you could do anything you wanted with these last few months, what would you do?" She told Larry that she always wanted to travel around the world and see everything. She had kids when she was young and never had the chance. Larry knew she was not wealthy. He called some friends and found her a job on a cruise ship, working in the gift shop. She was ecstatic! Every month Larry received a postcard from some different port in a new country. This went on for many months, which stretched into many years. She became far too busy having fun, following her bliss, to bother with the serious business of dying. Joseph Campbell said it best, when asked what his most profound discovery in all his studies was. He replied, "Following your bliss."

The second life-changing idea I discovered was put forth by a famous turn-of-the-century German doctor, Günther Enderlein. Doctor Enderlein believed the key to fighting cancer, as well as many other systemic ailments, lay simply in changing the pH of the body, making it more alkalized. He described the pleomorphic life cycles of endobionts that rapidly grow in an acidic biological terrain. By alkalizing the patient's body, much of this could be reversed. I bought the best Zeiss dark field microscope I could and flew down to Scottsdale, Arizona, where I took a weeklong class with Dr. Maria Blecker, a direct student of Dr. Günther Enderlein and foremost expert on the subject. The class, composed mostly of MDs, was taught in German. Luckily, for me, they had a fabulous interpreter, Dr. Dietrich Klinghardt, who truly could communicate the intricacies of the subject matter.

I spent the next four years looking at my own blood on a regular basis and had the opportunity to work with and view the blood of over 4,000 people dealing with cancer. Having cancer personally led me into a deep personal investigation that spanned many years.

One realization I came to because of that investigation was that I had been the kind of person who carried all the responsibilities of the world on his own shoulders. I had to do it all and carry the load. Talk about "stinky thinking"! This is a cancer way of thinking: "I can bear it all."

Cancer is a kind of rotting process. Eventually, one implodes if one's thinking does not change to support life and vitality. Heart attacks and embolisms are more like an explosion in the body. The correlating personality tendencies are anger, yelling, blaming others, and a hot temper. Cancer victims tend to be more quiet, subdued, and pale/yellow in color, while heart attack people tend to be redder in color. These are generalizations and not always true, but they are more often true than not. The pathways these two diseases take are largely determined by our genetics; which pathway we find ourselves on is easily seen by looking at our family history. How fast we travel down the path is largely up to us. The truth is that 85% of the population will die from either cancer or a heart attack. It is becoming more and more apparent that things are accelerating. What our grandparents died of seems to be appearing in our parents ten years earlier . . . and now, in our peer generation, ten years earlier than in our parents' generation.

The way I see it, our bodies are like worlds. You may think you are solid and know who you are. But, in reality you and I are both made up of billions of living microbes that symbiotically live in unison with us: such as yeast, bacteria, and molds, just to name a few. We are just like the Earth. When the Earth is viewed from outer space, it appears to be the big, beautiful blue sphere, but when you get down here on the ground, there are billions of living creatures symbiotically living here: dogs, cats, people, trees, and sweet potatoes . . . and the list goes on.

When we feed sugar and starch to yeast, molds, and bacteria, they love to eat it and multiply exponentially. Their metabolic waste is vinegar . . . acid. And the more we feed sugar and starch to the yeast, molds, and bacteria that co-inhabit our bodies, the faster they multiply and the faster they excrete acid. This is how our diet causes us to become acidic. The more the yeast, molds, and bacteria take over, the more acidic we become, and the more acidic we become, the faster we compost. It's that simple. The pathway that the composting takes is largely up to our genes. How fast we go, and how acidic we become, is up to us. Stress creates acid too.

The key to reducing acidity in the body is changing our thinking, and our diet, water, and exercise habits.

Thinking

Go down to your favorite bookstore and buy three or four books today on gratitude thinking. Get a copy of the movie *The Secret* and watch it four times. Immerse yourself in stories of thankfulness. Read one every night just before you go to sleep. Start watching movies that make you feel grateful. Better yet, watch movies that make you laugh — really laugh, from the belly.

There are many stories of people who cured terminal cancer just by watching funny movies for hours and hours every day. What I know personally is that I realized if I did not change my way of thinking, my cancer was going to consume me. The way I figured it, I had in part, allowed cancer to take root in my body because of the way I had been thinking. I had to change that around 180 degrees, and fast. So, I got pen and paper and started making marks. Every time I had a victim thought, a martyr thought, I made a mark on my piece of paper. I had a lot of marks the first day.

The idea was not to judge anything (or I would just have to make another mark for being critical!). The idea was simply to bring aware-ness and witness to the way I was thinking, moment to moment. Over a week, the marks each day got fewer and fewer of their own accord. I did this long enough that I was now making very few marks on the paper each day. I even started to sing in the shower again.

Thank God for singing and the great acoustics in shower stalls, but most of all for the loud sound of water falling and the joy of being free to let go.

Diet

Eating foods that alkalize your body is essential. I do not believe in getting fanatical; rather, increase your awareness of alkalizing foods. Eating all things green is a good rule of thumb. All sugars create acidity. Starches turn to sugars in the digestion process and are best avoided or reduced. The best alkalizing grains are quinoa, millet, and buckwheat. Fruit juices are super acidifying. Do not eat late at night, and eat as

much of fresh, alive, organically grown foods as you can. Thank God
I love salad!

Water

There is a great book called *You're Not Sick, You're Thirsty*. Water is
life itself. Most people drink far too little water every day, and our cells
are vastly dehydrated. It's easy to forget to drink an abundance of water
each day. Drinking restructured, alkaline, and highly charged negative
O.R.P. water can be a significant benefit to your health.

Remember . . . water is life!

Exercise

The best exercise is the one you will do. If you love to dance, dance. If
you love yoga, do yoga. If you love sports, do sports. If you love running, run. If you love hiking, hike. Just make sure you exercise at least
one hour every day. The more aerobic the better. The more fun, the
better.

Getting your lymphatic system pumping good and strong is critical for cancer survivors. The circulatory system's pump is your heart,
which moves your blood throughout your body. This brings oxygen
and nutrients to every cell in it. The lymphatic system is like the garbage
collector; it gathers all the wastes from each cell and starts the process
of removing them from the body on a cellular level. The lymphatic
system does not have a pump to move things around and relies entirely
on the natural movements of our bodies.

Fill a bottle halfway up with water. Hold it with one hand and slap
it down into the open palm of your other hand. The percussive action
will cause the water to lap up the sides. This is exactly what causes
your lymph to move. If you do not move much, your lymph does not
move much. If the lymph does not move much, the garbage stays in. If
the garbage stays in for a few months, it starts to stink and rot. That's
exactly what starts to happen in your own body.

Jumping jacks on a small trampoline is the very best exercise you
can do for many cancers, as the motion super-stimulates the pumping

action of the lymph. Jumping jacks are fun to do on the mini-trampo-line . . . especially to your favorite music. Thank God for iPods!

It's been eleven years since I first discovered my breast cancer. So many amazing things have happened during these years. My girls have grown up to be fabulous young women. My older girl is getting married this fall to a wonderful man with a big heart. My younger one travels around the world, and I have been invited to join her in Bali for a few weeks.

I have been to India for two extended personal journeys. Made a lot of money, spent a lot of money. Shared a lot of money. Found amazing new friends everywhere. I've received the blessing of living on the beach in Maui for the past three years. I met my beloved here on Maui, and we are starting to create a life together.

Cancer never really goes away. It's something we cancer survivors learn to live with. Just like a beautiful garden with some weeds, it takes a little tending. What a gift it is living with cancer and learning something new each day.

Thank God for this living breath!

Kai Jacobson, the father of two beautiful daughters, currently lives on the beautiful island of Maui in the small beach town of Paia. He has been an influential life and health coach for over twenty-five years. He is involved in importing high-quality alkalizing water systems from Asia. In 1998, he co-formulated a unique and potent blend of super greens called "Green Alchemy" that is highly acclaimed by medical professionals around the world. He has also worked with Life Force International for over ten years in helping educate health-conscious people about the importance of sea vegetation trace minerals and whole food nutrition.

Thank God
My Mother Died

CHRISTINA PERRY

What do you mean, Mama is with God? Why can't she come back?" my sister asked. I can still see my father sitting on the sofa, leaning forward with his forearms resting on his knees and his hands clasped together as if the unfolding of his hands would create an unraveling stream of emotion. He delivered news to his three young children, ages six, five, and two, that he never thought possible as tears coursed down his cheek. My mother, only twenty-seven, died of severe brain damage due to a freak car accident after falling asleep at the wheel and then running head-on into a tree.

I had just turned five in early September, and on the morning of October 1, 1969, the course of my life changed forever. "Why did she have to go away, and why did she leave me?" I thought more times than you could imagine. Through the years, my father remarried several times, so for me there was always a fear of abandonment from the "mothers" who were in and out of my life. Since my mama died and left me, it only made sense that everyone else was going to do the same. Mama left me, my first step mom left, the second one left, the third one left. . . . Who else was going to leave me? As soon as I began to love someone, they left.

The following years, as a teenager and young adult, I made a series of unwise decisions based on my pain from abandonment. All I ever wanted was someone to love me for who I was, and I wanted to be good enough so no one would leave me. I did everything you could imagine to find love . . . or what my idea of love was at the time. When I was twenty-five, I met a man whom I fell deeply in love with, and we became engaged. I wanted to share all my life with him. I soon learned that sharing your past could be devastating. He left me standing at the altar — once again, abandoned.

Well, after that, I decided that no one was going to leave me again. Within five months, I married . . . although not to the guy who'd abandoned me. Instead, I married someone else, someone I thought would never do that to me. At age twenty-eight, I gave birth to my beautiful daughter, but within three years, I was divorced. For many reasons, my husband and I abandoned each other.

Through the years, hardly a day goes by that I don't think of my mother and how I wish she were here with me. All I want to do is crawl in her lap and have her tell me everything will be okay. I was so angry with her for leaving me, I felt all alone. As the next few years passed, I continued in the same direction as always, trying to find someone to love me. I'm not speaking only of female-and-male relationships — I was searching for acceptance in friendships, working relationships, and family relationships. I always wanted be a part of something. It's just that relationships with men seemed to be the most haunting.

Everything changed after an extremely volatile relationship . . . one I should have never been involved in, except that I wanted to feel loved. I feared not only for my life but also for the life of my daughter as well. Was all of this happening because my mother died? If she were still alive, would I be making decisions like this? Why couldn't I make the right decisions? I had to get away from this relationship! I had to get away from my own life! I had to figure out what to do. I needed help!

I met with counselors, who helped me to understand a little more of this abandonment issue and why I didn't have to feel the way I did. But it wasn't until reading a variety of books that I truly felt helped. I have always known that God was here with me. Most of the time, I just ignored what He had to say. I read about the soul, energy, and quantum physics, along with an array of books by well-known philosophers. But it wasn't until I read *One Last Time*, written by John Edwards, that my life got ready to take another turn!

John Edwards has the ability to connect with people who have passed on and helps those still here visit with those they have lost. After reading this wonderful book, I became aware that I might also have the ability to connect with people who have passed. This wasn't something I was ready to accept! Quite frankly, it scared me to death. I would have to sleep with the light on at night to feel safe. All I wanted to do was to connect with my mother. So I would look for signs . . . anything that would give me hope that she was with me. Well, it finally happened!

I dreamt one night that I was having a conversation with John Edwards. He was very clear to me. It was as though I were awake and talking with him. He sat at the edge of my bed. I could also see my mother standing behind him, although she was very faint. Still, despite the fact that she wasn't as clear as John was, I knew it was Mom. He proceeded to tell me that everything was going to be okay and that my mother had always been with me, watching over me. My mother was in the background, agreeing with John. "If this is true," I exclaimed, "then give me proof! I have to have proof!" At that very moment, my alarm sounded, and I leaned over to turn it off when I noticed the time. It was 6:29! I began to cry! "Thank you! Thank you! Thank you, God!" To me, 6:29 represented my mother's birthday: June 29th. This was a definite sign to me that I wasn't dreaming . . . this was real.

I realized from that moment that my mother had never left me. I couldn't see her, but she had always been there. The following days were almost like a rebirth. My outlook on life was somehow different. I realized my self-worth and the fact that I was deserving of all great things to come. I realized that if we are willing to be thankful for all that is involved in this incredible journey of life, we can be inspired within ourselves. I believe that if we truly learn from each encounter through this journey, our chances for true inspiration are much brighter!

You have to be able to like what you see in the mirror. Love what is in your soul, and do not pretend to be something you are not. If we believe we have reached our journey's goal in life at any time, we will stop the continual path of growth. Without encouraging mental, emotional, and spiritual growth, we stop living.

I also learned the difference between being alone and being lonely. I learned that being alone, not in a relationship, was perfectly fine. I learned that we are all lonely at times. It is the ones who can't be alone — the ones who have to have someone with them — who are the ones in relationships for the wrong reasons. I realized that I wanted to get the most out of life, and that life was too short to settle for mediocrity. Because I had been a single mother for seven and a half years, I realized through my experiences that children do not come into this world asking to be a child of divorce. I knew I wanted to find someone who had similar qualities to those I had. And I did just that! I married the man of my dreams in March of 2003. For the first time in my life, I made decisions regarding my relationships without the fear of abandonment being an issue. If you asked my husband, Todd, if he would have ever thought when he first met me that I would have this story to tell, he would say, "Impossible." But he, too, realizes that the loss of my mother and my being thankful for these experiences have made me the person I am today.

I am now the mother of three beautiful children, Alexandra (from my first marriage), Christopher (from Todd's first marriage), and Parker from our last marriage! In four years of marriage, we have gone through Todd having a kidney transplant, Christopher diagnosed with Asperger and ADHD, having a new baby at age forty, and my oldest child wanting to live with her father for a year. My husband and I become closer everyday. Had my mother not died and left me, would I have made it through all this? Would I know the meaning of unconditional love? Would I have the ability to connect with other people the way I do? Make a difference in people's life the way I do? The answer is emphatically no!

My mother gave me a gift! God gave me a gift . . . the gift of taking my mother! Romans 8:28 says: "And we know that God causes all things to work together for good to those who love God, to those who are called according to His purpose." It took me almost thirty-seven years to figure that out!

Although my family has faced many challenges in the past few years, my personal growth has continued to soar. I awaken each day with a new beginning and realize that without all experiences, (both bad and good), we would not be who we are today. And with this growth, I am accomplishing things I never thought possible. The difference now is that I know I can accomplish anything my heart truly desires.

In my current career as a network marketer, motivational speaker, and trainer, I help others in many ways. Not only am I helping people with their financial goals, but also I am helping them with their physical health. Even more importantly, I am able to help people with their emotional health. There is nothing more gratifying than being able to help someone understand some of the "whys" in their life. Every day I encounter new people. My gratitude toward my life experiences has given me the ability to understand people immediately. Whether on the phone or in person, I am able to connect with them. My heart and ears are open to hear what they say and what they don't say.

I would have never been able to do this without my gratitude to God for taking my mother away from me at such a young age. I want to say to each reader of this amazing series, "Be thankful to God for all of your life's experiences. The good ones are easy, but the negatives are the ones that will change your life! With loving gratitude, you can soar to all levels in life. Don't ever let anyone tell you different, and never, never let anyone steal your dreams!"

❤   ❤   ❤

In her current career as a network marketer, motivational speaker, international trainer, and author, Christina Perry helps people improve financially and improve physically. But more importantly, she is able to help people with their emotional health. "There is nothing more gratifying than being able to help someone understand some of the whys in their life." Christina holds a Bachelor's degree from the College of Charleston and currently resides in Jamestown, North Carolina with her very supportive husband, Todd, and three children, Alexandra (Christina's first marriage), Christopher (Todd's first marriage), and little Parker Perry, who brought them all together. She invites you to visit her website at www.ChristinaPerry.com.

Thank God
... *for Every Moment in My Life*

JANET ATTWOOD

*M*any people have seen me on television or heard me on the radio. People regularly seek my advice on how to determine their passions in life. The most remarkable thing is I can relate to almost anyone I meet, no matter their situation. After all, I was brought up in an alcoholic family, spent a part of my life strung out on LSD, lived with the president of the Oakland Hells Angels, was physically abused, and faced a whole list of challenges that most people would never think you could experience in one lifetime.

Life is a journey for all of us. When I look back on all of my life experiences, the painful ones were the huge blessings. Because of all those experiences, I can connect with almost anyone, in any circumstance. Those tough times in my life have created a compassion many people never get to experience.

Often in life, we don't change until our lives become so painful we have no choice. I remember living in a house filled with heroin addicts in Haight-Ashbury in San Francisco. In a moment of clarity, I glanced around the room at all of my so-called "friends" and recognized the all-time low my life had fallen to. In total shock and desperation, I prayed that I wouldn't continue down the path that clearly was leading me to the same hell these perceived "friends" already occupied. This rock-bottom time in my life became one of my launching points, which eventually led me onto the path of discovering a spiritual perspective and a rainbow of hope that would change my life.

Finally saying good-bye to drugs, I learned the Transcendental Meditation® technique and worked for two years as a meditation teacher in Palo Alto, California. Living at the local TM center, I was happy teaching meditation, but unfortunately, the pay was not very good, and I ended up sleeping on the floor, hopping over a fence every morning to "borrow" the swimming pool shower in the apartments across the street!

Money was scarce, but then again, money was always scarce for me. Thankfully, I had friends who helped me along my path, but in a very unexpected way. . . .

Hearing that I was sleeping on the TM Center floor, a few wealthy friends pulled some strings to get me a job in their company as a recruiter. "You'll make millions of dollars, Janet!" they all told me. Unfortunately, I never stopped to consider if I even had the talents this job called for. More importantly, I never asked myself, "Will I love it? Is this my passion?" Despite my best efforts and encouragement from my friends, I failed at this job terribly. Day after day, I'd go in to work and I'd hear the bell ring each time one of my colleagues made a placement. A month went by, and I had not landed a single commission. Desperation set in. I had to do something different — and fast!

Fortunately, my life completely changed in a most remarkable way. While meditating one night after work at the TM Center, I came across an ad for a seminar called "Yes to Success." Something inside told me this seminar was very important for me, so I went with that feeling and called in sick. Teaching meditation, I had finally learned to trust my intuition — and what did I have to lose? Everything changed for me the day I experienced Debra Poneman, the seminar leader, standing in front of me, totally on fire. I will forever be grateful for this day as it truly gave my life the direction I needed. As I watched Debra completely transform the room of participants, I wanted nothing less than to motivate and uplift others as she was doing.

"What You Love and God's Will for
You Are One and the Same"

— JANET BRAY ATTWOOD AND CHRIS ATTWOOD

As Debra talked, I realized that she was doing what I would love to do — motivate, inspire, and encourage others to live their greatness through sharing transformational knowledge. Debra told us that one hundred of the most successful people in America all had one thing in common: When asked to write down the five things that were most important to them, they all had achieved those five things. As Debra talked about dressing for success, I couldn't stop thinking about that study. "If the most successful people created five things that are most important to them, then the first step for me to enjoy success must be to clarify the five things that are most important to me."

It was in that moment The Passion Test® was born. I realized that the times I "failed," were the times I chased external rewards, money, and approval from others; and failed to listen to my inner calling. You see, the gift that turned my life around was the gift of apparent failure. Out of sheer desperation sprang a simple truth: Dedicate yourself to what matters most to you, and it will lead you to ever-increasing fulfillment.

The Most Commonly Shared Trait Among the One Hundred
Most Successful People Is their Commitment to their Passion

Even after I learned this key principle of success, and created the process that today we call The Passion Test®, I hadn't learned the secret that guarantees a passionate life. As a result, I spent many years distracted by my own, or others, lack of clarity often getting off the path of my passions.

Finally, when I partnered with Mark Victor Hansen and Robert Allen to create the Enlightened Millionaire program, I realized the key principle that I'd been missing. My business partner, Chris Attwood, and I call this principle "the secret that will guarantee you a passionate life", because when you do this consistently, you will live a passionate, turned-on life:

Whenever You Are Faced with a Choice, a Decision, or
an Opportunity, Choose in Favor of Your Passions.

When I look back at my life, there are so many reasons to be
grateful. . . .

- I discovered wonderful mentors, just at the time I needed them
  most.
- My challenges allowed me to help and support people at every
  level of society, in every stage of growth.
- I created a simple yet powerful tool in The Passion Test® that
  has helped thousands of people around the world change the
  course of their life to experience a level of joy and fulfillment
  that had been desperately missing.

Intention — Attention — No Tension

All of us create our lives from our intentions and from where we place
our attention. Most people create their lives unconsciously. Their intentions are a function of the often-misguided beliefs and concepts they've
had since childhood.

What you put your attention on grows stronger in your life. With
clear intentions, you are able to give attention to the things that matter
most to you. Taking action and choosing consistently in favor of your
passions moves your life in a direction that brings more and more joy
and fulfillment. One of the key principles of living a passionate life is
staying open. Do all that you can think to do, then let go. This is the
principle of "no tension."

So, what do you intend for your life? Can you think of a better way to
live than to wake up every day and love what you spend your time doing
. . . and being paid well to do it? I am grateful for the impact The Passion
Test® has had on so many people. If you're ready to get clear and focused
on living the life you always wanted, remember these key points:

1) Failure is an illusion. What appears to be failure is the guidance
   we're receiving to take a different direction

2) What you love and God's will for you are one and the same. Trust that the things you love and care most about are leading you to fulfill your purpose in life.

3) Intention — Attention — No Tension. Consistently choose in favor of your passions, and then let go. Allow miracles to manifest in your life.

❤   ❤   ❤

To find out more about Janet Attwood and The Passion Test®, go to: www.janetattwood.com or www.thepassiontest.com To contact Janet Attwood: janet@janetattwood.com.

Thank God
I Met the Debt Collector

SHAWN WIEDERIN

*M*oney was tight for our family back in the '80s. My dad's income barely supported us. There were four of us boys and one little sister. At that time, I couldn't figure out why we struggled so much. I didn't have the knowledge necessary to understand.

My first exposure to earning my own money was at the age of ten, when I got a paper route. At first, I earned $40 per week; after six years, I was making $100 a week. This was a lot of money for a sixteen-year-old boy with no clue about money's value. I didn't know how to handle or appreciate it, or the other tangible and intangible items in my life. Over the course of this first job, I made well over $20,000. By the time I moved on to other opportunities, I had less than $500 in my savings account. As I look back at that time of my life, I am not surprised that I spent almost every dime of my earnings.

My financial situation improved dramatically in 1991, when I got a summer internship as an information consultant at a local cereal plant. Most other companies didn't pay interns, but this company paid me $2,500 per month. By the end of my internship, once again

I had little to show, as I continued to be a "money-blowing" fool. Then in the fall of 1991, I got my first real full-time job, at a "Big 8" accounting firm, where I spent three successful years. It was during the fall of 1992 that I first learned of home-based business opportunities. The concept of residual income and pyramids would forever change my financial life.

During the mid-to-late 1990s, running this home-based business put me in credit card debt and tore down the equity in my first house. I chased a dream of financial freedom and the rich lifestyle, but I didn't possess the right mindset, gratitude, or commitment to succeed with the management of my finances. I also lacked the ability to foster proper communication between my wife and myself, which left everyone in the dark regarding our family's finances. I attempted to reduce our debt, including transferring the debt from credit card to credit card, and penny-pinching to turn around our finances. My finances, however, didn't improve one bit.

It wasn't until 2001 that I finally realized things needed to change immediately. My wife presented me with legal papers, which arrived from a local debt collection agency. I was being sued for a debt that I was in complete denial about. I thought this event was no big deal, and I told my wife that I would discover where the debt collection agency had gone wrong. I ignored the whole thing, when I should have been grateful for its occurring. Three months later, I personally met the same debt collector. This day changed my life forever and was the turning point in my expression of love and gratitude toward all aspects of my life.

I was playing with my kids outside when a man walked up to me and handed me a judgment from a major credit card company. At first, I told myself that I would be able to handle and resolve this situation without having to pay a dime, as I considered it a "newfound" debt. Then finally, I made a commitment to my family and myself that everything regarding my money and finances had to be changed now. My mindset, and my love and gratitude toward the universe needed an immediate makeover. I had to accept the financial wrongdoings of the past and the requirements to improve my life, and my financial future.

Several years prior to meeting the debt collector, I met an individual (now a mentor) who truly understood gratitude, love, and prosperity consciousness. He taught me several concepts and techniques for improving my mindset, learning how to love, and why it's important to be grateful for everything that you possess and everything that occurs in your life. He also taught me about the law of attraction and the law of equality. The law of attraction states that you attract the physical reality of your thoughts and the law of equality states that you will experience positive and negative experiences in physical reality that are equal in quantity and quality.

For many years, I followed his teachings, but I fell short by not being consistent with his recommendations. My progression toward true gratefulness and love for all in my life was not happening because I lacked implementation and understanding. The day I met the debt collector was the day that I truly became grateful for experiencing something that many people would perceive as a tragedy in their lives. How could I truly be grateful and blessed to meet an individual who had just delivered to me a judgment against me for a very large sum of money?

This experience allowed me to open my heart, my mind to the state of prosperity consciousness. Through consistent and focused thoughts and actions, I realized that my personal and financial life must focus on what I wanted to create of my life, and not on the penny-pinching mentality, I had previously possessed. The practice of being consistent and grateful for all realities in my life was the turning point in my transformation. Some transformations were monetary; other changes were non-monetary. In the past, I measured success based on financial numbers and results. This experience showed me that the non-monetary changes are a necessary precursor to the receiving of monetary rewards. I now expect both negative and positive financial events; the difference is that I now focus my energy, actions, and thoughts on the development of what I want to create as it occurs in my life.

I also have a better relationship open communication with my wife and with my children about life and money. I am no longer afraid to be open about my current financial state, and I'm more able to teach them about prosperity consciousness, love, and gratitude for what we currently possess or may/may not possess in the near future. In the past, I tithed on a very limited basis, and I tithed with hesitation. Now I tithe on a more regular basis, and I do not question why I am giving, nor do I question the thoughts or intentions of the recipient to whom I am giving. These actions have allowed me to bring more prosperity and financial improvements into my life.

The non-monetary changes in my life allowed me to experience monetary rewards that I now expect to become reality. My transformation to a more balanced and grateful person included an increase in my income by 70% and increased my net worth two and a half times. This is a substantial increase over a very short period. The improvement in our increased income also allowed us to control and reduce the money going out. We eliminated the short-term debt obligations presented by the debt collector within four years of this blessed meeting. We also increased our retirement savings by one-and-a-half times over that timeframe. The most important monetary benefit manifested was the ongoing financial opportunities and loving people presented to my family.

These rewards in our life would not have become a reality without the personal meeting with the debt collector. I am truly grateful for how the debt collector helped to transform my life.

❤   ❤   ❤

Shawn Wiederin is an entrepreneur, inventor, and author, whose primary mission in life is to help others make their lives and ideas a financial success. Shawn has been granted four patents in the areas of information technology and business process improvement and currently has four additional U.S. — and international-based patents pending. He is the author of the book *What Mom and Dad Should Have Taught Me About Money* and is the creator of the website http://www.onemillionbooksandbucks.com, which has the two-fold goal of selling 1,000,000 books and paying the leading affiliate up to $1,000,000 in commissions.

Thank God
My Husband Left Me Pregnant and an Employee Molested My Children

DR. SHAKTI DEVI KAHEALANI
KAWAIOLAMANALOA SATCHITANANDA

*H*e was my soul mate of many lifetimes, whom I loved more than life itself. We were the perfect couple, equally matched in personality and intelligence. He was a Beverly Hills attorney, and I was a Beverly Hills dentist. We were both good looking, and each had a child from a previous marriage, a year apart in age. We loved God and together studied *The Secret, the Law of Attraction, and the Truth.* Our whole relationship was built around longing to know the truth and walking the spiritual path. Our life was truly a divine celebration where the devoted met their divine destiny.

On a romantic Caribbean cruise, he asked the question, "What are you doing for the rest of your life?" After a silence, he continued, "Well?"

I said, "Well, what?"

"Well, will you marry me?"

My heart throbbed as I said, "Yes."

Another surprise came when he replied "Good, it's set for tomorrow at 2:30 P.M.." I was speechless, and the walk down to the restaurant was like walking in a perfect dream. Along the way, he invited everyone we met on the ship to attend the wedding.

We went shopping for my dress and ring in Curaçao, and my fiancé wore the ship captain's uniform. He was majestic in all white with stunning gold braids. Everything fell into its perfect place, and as I looked out at the ocean, I felt the very presence of the Divine. I intuitively knew that God had truly answered my heart's desire.

We became the perfect church couple, Doctor and Attorney. We were blessed with another beautiful baby girl, who was the sweet fruit of our ecstatic love for God and our love for each other. We learned the Law of Attraction well and manifested abundantly. Everything our hands and hearts touched turned to gold. Both of our professional practices thrived as we continued our study to become spiritual practitioners and ministers. We could "speak the word" and make it happen. God was truly giving us everything!

We felt unstoppable! In a matter of months, he had won three quarter-million-dollar settlements in a row. We had both worked incredibly hard, and as a reward, we decided to go to Hawaii. We stayed at the five-star Hale Kulani and made passionate love for three days. On the fourth day, I laughingly told my husband, "Baby, we'd better go to the beach and get a tan, or nobody is going to believe that we came to Hawaii!" He laughed and agreed. Once down at the beach, my husband wanted us to go into the aqua water together. I had no objection, it was so beautiful, but I also wanted a couple of minutes to lie in the warm sand and commune with God . . . to thank the Universe for giving us such an amazing opportunity. "Baby, give me five minutes," I told him.

All of a sudden, without warning or pause, my husband angrily blew up in my face! Hostility and rage seethed from within him. He screamed at me. I tried to calm him down, but he didn't want to hear it. I offered to go into the water with him, but that would no longer please him. I pleaded with him, I cried, but nothing could reach him through his rage and the barrage of painful accusations he threw at me.

Back at the hotel room, I called my spiritual practitioner for counseling. I tried to talk with my husband. Nothing worked. He refused to speak to me for the next six days. How did this happen? This couldn't possibly be the result of asking for five minutes of personal time! The shock of the entire event had left me in a daze, and I had no idea how to fix it. At that time, I didn't have enough self-love and took this very personally. I had him on a pedestal. He was my hero, my soul mate, my confidante, and as a result, his actions hurt me more deeply than I can express.

When we got back home, I found out that I had conceived a child during those romantic three days of perfection. That week my husband left me. I was emotionally devastated. The next nine months were a nightmare — as painful as our loving romance had been sweet. My husband's anger continued to mushroom, and his intense rage directed at me. He accused me of being the cause of everything that went wrong in his life. After some extensive counseling, our minister advised me to prepare to be a single woman again. I never knew such pain existed. I had a baby in my womb, I was breast-feeding another, and my teenage daughter, who was accustomed to seeing her powerful mother take on the world, was terrified as our lives buckled beneath us.

Not long after my baby was born, I received a phone call from a friend that made things a bit clearer. My classy, gorgeous, brilliant husband, who had brought me back to God, was in a really bad place. Although I had a better idea of what had happened to my marriage, life didn't get much easier. I decided to take maternity leave from my practice in order to breast feed my new baby and emotionally heal from all that had happened. I hired an accountant to watch over my practice and another dentist to see my patients. Before the smoke even had a chance to clear, a new employee chose to embezzle my dental practice, and my insurance policy reneged on payment, forcing me to leave my home with my babies in my arms.

The biggest blow came when I found out that my daughters, the true loves of my life, were being molested by the employee I had hired. I felt like I had been assaulted in the most violent way. My life slipped through my fingers, and now my precious babies had suffered something I couldn't even imagine. I fired the employee and hired a new woman, who we all adored. But this new woman started an affair with the maintenance man, letting him into our home, where another molestation happened all over again. This time I was dumbfounded, and frightened. How many times could this happen to us? Two years later, a different employee stopped showing up for work. My boyfriend at the time volunteered to watch the girls while I went to the office. His own son had been molested and murdered a year before, making me think he could identify with our fragile situation. I was wrong. Out of the pain of losing his own son, he molested my daughters. I couldn't understand it. How had my life come to this place of such utter turmoil and pain? And more importantly, how could I change it?

This takes me to the next part of my gratitude story. . . . I was driving down a beautiful tree-lined street one day after work, anxiously contemplating the painful challenges in my life, when all of a sudden something quite extraordinary happened! A Voice spoke very clearly inside me. It was authoritative and powerful, asking, "Do you be-lieve in Me?" I knew deep inside that God was speaking to me, so I replied with a sheepish "Yes". But . . . what about my husband, my children, my office? Why would these things happen to me if God were truly on my side? I would eventually come to find out that God does not hear the "buts" in our lives. It is not in him to dwell upon our imperfections, or our lack of devotion. All God heard from me that day was the "Yes," and with that, he replied, "Then know that everything is all right!" It was so powerful that I later shared it with my church counselor. This was God's divine intervention, in which He was establishing divine protection over my life.

From that moment on, I began to have some of the most powerful, tangible, direct spiritual experiences with the Divine. It was a courtship with the irresistible, loving kindness of God, the bliss and mercy of God, the divine guidance, and the presence of an all-powerful God everywhere. God began to instruct me one-on-one, heart-to-heart. He granted me understanding of my life and taught me that I was the common denominator in all of my painful situations: with my husband, the embezzlements, the molesters, my office, everything. He taught me that all of my life challenges actually existed within me, being a direct result of my choices, my attitude, my thoughts, and my harmonic vibration. I had a corresponding wound, a projection, and program that had attracted each of those circumstances. There was no longer any place for blame, because when you point one finger, three point back at you.

When you look at the three pointing back at you, you then have the ability to make corrections within, thereby becoming aligned with the Divine and the teachings of truth.

He taught me to take full "response-ability" for the entire creation of my life. He taught me that in some way, I had something to do with all that had happened. Now, that is real power . . . the ability to respond and not internally react to anything outside of yourself. Never giving your power away by seeing yourself as a victim, and learning to live in a constant state of love, aloha, and inner contentment — this is the peace that passeth all understanding! I began to feel some mastery over my life again. I had done all of this profound inner healing work with God, and things were falling back into place for my daughters and me.

However, my true test came a couple of years later. A friend invited my daughters and me up to swim in his pool. The girls were having fun playing with two young boys from next door. I needed to run an errand, and the kids were having such a good time that they wanted to stay and swim. Our friend agreed to watch the kids while I ran home. Just as I was leaving, the boys' father showed up and went out to the Jacuzzi. The man and I were introduced, and I dashed off to run my errand. I was gone less than an hour. When I returned, my daughter explained that something had happened to her. I knew the test when I heard it. Because of my internal healing process and spiritual growth, I felt completely buffered and protected. I had no knee-jerk reaction of victim consciousness. My mind didn't run away with reactionary programs of the past. I had no self-righteous judgments or condemnations. My mind was in silence, and the peace that passeth all understanding. I humbly asked, "Okay, God, it has happened again. What am I to do?" From that buffered state of calmness, I heard the divine guidance of God. He told me exactly what to do.

I went next door to speak with the father. I looked him directly in the eyes, and I saw God there. I intuitively knew that he and I were one without separation. I knew that my Lord lived inside of his heart and mine. He was God's child just as I was. I understood that he was acting under the influence of wounds and mentally addictive programs; he was acting through his own pain, and as a result had slipped and made a "not good choice." I had to realize that even I sometimes fall under the hypnotic influence of subconscious wounds and mental programs, and that all of us make "not good choices" in different areas. Speaking to him with love, I told him that his action was incorrect and had consequences. I asked, as I was divinely guided to ask, for him to pay for a full year of therapy for my daughter, as well as a year of therapy and Alcoholics Anonymous for himself, a win-win "soul-ution."

Because of my connection with the oneness of God, and my ability to speak to him with peace and love in my heart, he had no defense. He surrendered into tears and made a commitment to his healing. I also noticed that because I was in that state of oneness and true awareness, I was in the most beneficial healing consciousness possible for my daughter. I was fully present with her and for her. I wasn't adding my own wounds, resistance, judgments, and projections into the situation. Because of this, I could really hear her and help her heal. My daughter later told me a story about what she had experienced, saying, "Mommy, my Great Me told me that this was going to happen, but my Little Me didn't know what it was talking about, so I dropped my guard, and then the man came . . . ." When I heard this, I knew that there were no accidents in life and that God had taught my daughter a valuable lesson that most of us never learn . . . to never mentally override your inner guidance. The experience was a profound and spiritual one, a healing for us all. Deep within, I knew that I had finally passed the test of inner mastery and would never have to look into the face of another molester again.

Baba Muktananda once said, "Anything that occurs in your life that turns you within, seeking God, is Great Fortune!" In this case, my life was filled with Great Fortune! I was taught to spiritually see the higher, deeper truths of life and find the answers about true healing. I learned that honor, love, compassion, and knowing that we are one are the true secrets to life. There is never anyone outside of ourselves to blame, only a situation that can be transformed into greater love. I have come to understand that there is nothing to fear, nothing to resist, nothing to judge, nothing to become at odds against. There is only something to be true to, something to trust, the divine love and subtle sacred secrets of aloha within the heart. My daughters and I were so blessed that we were able to walk together, awaken together, and learn that we are spiritual beings here for a human experience, not human beings here for a spiritual experience. I thank God for the many painful situations that I experienced that gave me the motivation to change, to grow, and to apply the conscious wisdom that I learned along the way. During my life, it might be said that I've encountered disproportionate odds and tragedies. But I say thank God that my husband and soul mate left me pregnant. Thank God my children were molested. Thank God my dental practice was embezzled. Thank God I was abused. Thank God I was diagnosed with Lupus, praying to live through Christmas. Thank God I lost everything and had to leave my home. Thank God I was knocked to my knees, lost my faith, and prayed for reconnection. Thank God, thank God, thank God!

I have been enriched by every seemingly negative circumstance in my life. Because my daughters and I have learned the inner mastery and wealth of such powerful transforming lessons in life, we each revel daily in constant gratitude for the sacred relationship we enjoy with God, and the love that flows from within. It has empowered us as women to walk in beauty and grace, with fearless, peaceful, contented hearts. We are committed to manifesting our highest visions, and know our abilities to conquer crisis, overcome challenges, and change by conscious choice! We are so grateful for our entire walk, and pray that our experience will allow us to empower all those wanting to successfully navigate up the mountain of life! We love to share the wisdom of the walk. Aloha ia o'koa pa'ulo. "When we meet in love . . . we shall be whole!" Thank you, God!

♥   ♥   ♥

Dr. Kahealani Satchitananda is the founding CEO and spiritual director of High Visions of Satchitananda, a counseling, coaching, and consulting company for individuals and businesses wanting to "live their best life,". She is a founding member of Agape International Spiritual Center and one of the pioneers in Holistic Dentistry and Yogic Psychology. Dr. Satchitananda and her daughters, J'aime M. Sisson and Sisily C. Sisson, perform Hawaiian weddings, vow renewals, rites of passage, and blessings, accept keynote speaking engagements, and offer counseling and Living Life in Paradise Retreats and 7-Day Sacred Ceremony Transformational Cruises in the Hawaiian Islands. The dynamic trio also facilitates a Course in Conscious Enlightenment 2012, a personal plan for transformation, and sacred relationships trainings. Dr. Satchitananda is a Hawaiian Ho'oponopono practitioner. She is accepting new clients and offers phone sessions and teleconferences for clients around the world. For more information, please visit: http://www.myspace.com/livinglifeinparadise and HighVisions@aol.com.

Thank God
My Boyfriends Dumped Me

MULTI-COLORED HEARTBREAK

ERIS HUEMER

indsight is 20/20. When you're so close to an event in your life, it can be hard to see the reason to feel gratitude for it . . . at least, at the time. And it can also be uncomfortable at times to look back. But if you can, and you do, you will finally be able to open the gifts that have already been presented to you.

I have been through many break-ups. I have felt manipulated, cheated, angry, cajoled, victimized, and shattered. I have screamed and cried repeatedly: Why didn't my relationships work? Why didn't the men love me enough? Why did a guy pick someone else over me? Why wasn't I enough? Why me? Why, why, why, why, why? I saw myself as a victim.

When each of my boyfriends broke up with me, the pain felt insurmountable. I couldn't sleep, my heart pounded with fear, I lost weight . . . I was depressed. I would put all of my focus on him — why he had left, and what he did to me. The more I did that, the more dramatic my experience felt. I was more comfortable being driven by intense emotions. I attracted people who supported my victimhood. They would agree, "He's such a jerk, I can't believe he did that to you. You deserve better than him . . . ."

The first break-up I ever experienced, even before a succession of boyfriends dumped me, happened when my dad left my mom for another woman. He also left my sister and me. How could the man who was my Number One, the one I looked up to the most, walk out on me like that? I remember the exact moment, watching him pack his bags and then drive away. I was devastated. At this point in my life, I couldn't imagine the effect it would have on me and my future relationships. Here I was, just a teen, becoming aware of boys and dating. But I spent the next fifteen years trying to replace him with a prince who would rescue me and remain with me happily ever after. Instead I got a multitude of men, whom I categorize by colors for their different personalities.

Mr. Orange was just cool. He was charming, just like my father. (They all were.) He was a crush. The relationship, although seemingly real, was in all truth a figment of my imagination. I wrote him love letters and built a fantasy world in which he was my Prince Charming. Could he be the one? Then my supposed best friend called to tell me that Mr. Orange had just asked her to homecoming. I felt rejected. Was this how my mom had felt? Why did my dad choose the other woman over my mother? Why would Mr. Orange choose the other woman over me? But the debacle, I realized, had a good side: I could now relate to how my mom felt when my dad left her. I was no longer resentful toward her. Thank God . . . .

Shortly after that, I met Mr. Green. Thank God Mr. Orange had chosen someone else, leaving me available! Would he be the one? Mr. Green and I fell deeply in and out of love for the next five years. He showed me how I wanted a man to love me. He was honest, faithful, affectionate, hard working, and followed through. No, it was not always La-La Land. There were times when he drank, and that changed him. He would disappear, and his alter ego, whom I named Bob, would take his place. Bob and I would fight constantly. The verbal abuse was traumatizing. I remembered that I hated it when my parents drank and fought. Yet here I was in the same relationship. Still, in my need for love, I wondered, Is he the one? Can I overlook Bob? I wasn't sure.

There was something in me telling me to go, while another part of me was telling me to stay. I couldn't decide.

And then. . . . I had an opportunity to move 3,000 miles away to follow my dream. Mr. Green wanted us to marry and he would go with me. The love-addicted part of me wanted him to come, of course. I would be crazy to say no. Yet the realist in me knew that there were things that I still needed to do . . . on my own. Even though I knew I would miss Mr. Green, I wouldn't miss Bob. He made me feel like I couldn't do things on my own, that I was nothing without him, and nobody would ever love me like he did. I didn't realize at the time that his manipulation would empower me to make the most agonizing decision of my life. I chose to go. Thank God . . . .

Next was Mr. Black. I loved his spontaneity and intellect. He was rebellious without a cause. He gave me books such as *Conversations with God, The Celestine Prophecies, The Alchemist,* and *The Artist's Way.* These books were guides that showed me the pathway to my spiritual journey. He encouraged me to buy a journal and begin writing. I never stopped. I became inspired. Was he the one? It was the best of times and the worst of times. Mr. Black also had a shadow side, made up of bipolar tendencies, verbal abusiveness, lies, and alcohol and drug abuse. He talked down to me, lied, and threatened to hit me if I didn't shut up, and he didn't commit because he secretly had others (or maybe that's just the baggage of my childhood). All of these behaviors were caused by the fact that he was a seeker looking for answers that he didn't want to accept.

I talked myself into staying because I learned so much. But he soon left me for one of his others. Once again, I felt what my mother must have felt. But this time I realized that my mother was a much happier woman without my dad. She no longer had to live in fear, belittlement, and doubt. She had found her independence by starting a business of her own. Through Mr. Black's unanswered search for knowledge, I found and followed my spiritual path that led me to where I am today. Thank God . . . .

Then there was Mr. Blue. I liked his stability. He was a businessman. Was he the one? He was eighteen years my senior, had an expensive car, took me to nice restaurants, had a sensitive side, was a good friend, and gave me a job. However, he was my boss, so he kept our relationship secret for eighteen months, which ate away at me. He didn't want people to think I had the job because we were together. I didn't care that much about the job; I wanted him to want to be with me. I wanted him to want everyone to know it. I felt like I was living a lie. Each day I awoke wondering, is this the day that we would no longer have to hide the truth? He just couldn't admit, and wouldn't commit, to the reality of our relationship. When I couldn't take it anymore. I quit my job, and "we" were suddenly over. I no longer lived in a secret, but most of what I have learned about business and success I learned from him. Thank God . . . .

Through that job I met Mr. Yellow. He was incredibly artistic, talented, and free. One look at him and my knees buckled. Was he the one? We had so much fun together. We went on long nature hikes, he taught me about organic food, and brought me to my first yoga class. I believed we were soul mates. He wrote me songs about love and promised that we would be together forever. I was envisioning marriage, kids, and a white picket fence. He taught me how to find my inner voice and not only speak it but put it on paper. But this La-La Land was not meant to last. He broke up with me . . . over the phone and without warning. He said he needed space, a chance to find himself. I was devastated. I was convinced that he was my soul mate, my life partner. I didn't understand why he left, so I began writing about it in my journal, and out came a first draft of a self-help book with remedies on how to heal your broken heart. Thank God . . . .

Then there was Mr. Gray. I wasn't convinced that he was the one, but he said he was. I chose to play along and believe him, and it worked. My biological clock started to go tick-tock. Mr. Gray was a recovering addict and had embraced spirituality. I enjoyed the fact that we could talk for hours and hours about common ideologies and beliefs. He was rebuilding his life, and I thought he was including me in that process. It felt like we were starting over together. "This is it," I said. "Yes, I want to get married." I told him he was the one. He said he wasn't. He needed a ninety-day break to think it over. He never got back to me with an answer. He was the one, all right. The one who could focus only on himself. Thank God . . . .

I was exhausted. What was going on? How many more break-ups was I going to have to endure? Then someone suggested to me that I write a gratitude list, a list of at least ten things that I was grateful for, and that I include my ex. I listened. I began to find my gratitude. Gratitude was my catalyst to change. I saw the gifts that my father had given me by leaving. Not only was it good for my mom, who grew and became more inspired day after day, but if not for him, I wouldn't be where I am. That experience guided me to be a strong woman, support myself financially, commit to following my dreams, not allow people to walk all over me, find my voice, get a great education, travel the world, have a close relationship with my mother, and it guided me into making something of myself.

I learned that I could heal myself through acceptance and gratitude. When I learned that I could take responsibility to heal my "broken heart," I set an intention to do anything in my power to do so. It was up to me what I was going to do from that moment forward. I was inspired by the internal work. A light bulb went on within me, and I decided to stand on my own two feet and stop living in fear and being a victim of my circumstances. In fact, my heart being broken was itself an illusion. It was actually an experience that I attracted into my life so that I could learn more about myself to bring me to where I am today.

Every single person whom I attracted into my life was a mirror reflection of me. I chose them to awaken hidden, denied, and unconscious truths of myself that I did not love. Someone else is not responsible for my happiness, nor are they responsible for my unhappiness. I became more conscious, which felt rewarding. I felt empowered. I became confident and secure. My friendships became more solid and deeper than ever before, my work relationships were stronger, and I became closer to my parents and sister. I liked the woman I was becoming.

Thank God for my father leaving, which allowed me to become me.

Thank God for Mr. Orange picking her over me. Because of him I got to meet my next.

Thank God for Mr. Green's alter ego, Bob. Because of him I got to go out on my own and follow my dreams.

Thank God for Mr. Black leaving me for another woman. Because of him I started on my journey of self-discovery.

Thank God Mr. Blue chose to keep us a secret. Without knowing him I wouldn't have started my own career.

Thank God for Mr. Yellow breaking up with me. Without him I would never have started writing my book.

Thank God for Mr. Gray and his ninety days. Without him I would have never become a counselor and coach.

All the men were gifts in my path, and my experiences with them strengthened my light within. They shared similarities and differences and mirrored them back to me, so that I could become more conscious and aware. Once I owned these qualities within myself, I could find love and gratitude. They all filled the colors of my rainbow and still do to this day. Thank God for all my ex-boyfriends because without them I would never have been able to discover myself, help others heal their broken hearts, and finish my book, *Break-up Emergency*. Thank God for all of them because I realize that it take two to make a relationship, and that I am the one.

💜   💜   💜

Eris Huemer, life coach, author, and speaker, holds a master's degree in counseling psychology from Pacifica Graduate Institute; received her co-active coaching training from the Coaches Training Institute; and obtained her undergraduate degree in broadcast journalism from Florida State University. She has an active coaching and counseling business in Los Angeles. Eris is the author of the book *Break-Up Emergency, A Guide to Transform your Break UP into a Break THROUGH*. She is the relationship specialist who puts the REAL back into REALationship. Her unique take on the ups and downs and ins and outs of relationships helps guide people toward making lasting changes. She can be reached at Eris@LoveEris.com. Her website is http://www.loveeris.com/.

Thank God
I was Fat, Tired, Broke, and Beyond Hope

SANDY ELSBERG

*D*esperation. Do you know how it smells, tastes, feels? I do. Hope. Do you know the reality of hope? I know that, now, too. And what it can bring.

I believe that one of the keys to success in life is hope. It is powerful and healing, it is liberating and generous, but most of all, it is love. It is the drive for excellence that so many of us have lost or simply forgotten, buried under years of broken dreams and disappointment.

In 1989, I was completely broke and eight months pregnant with my second child. I had just gathered up my last shred of dignity and stormed out of a California Welfare office, with no plan. I was 250 pounds overweight, $250,000 in debt. I had just been turned away by my obstetrician because of unpaid bills. I didn't know what I would do or where I would get the strength to carry on. In that moment, for me, hope was just a fleeting memory.

Two hundred and fifty pounds overweight and $250,000 in personal debt. I felt suffocated, crushed in a vise of two hundred fifty, the two largest failures of my life pushing in on me from either side until

I could no longer breathe. It felt inescapable — a yoke of biblical pro-
portions — and I wondered why God had allowed it to happen to me.
I had a five-year-old daughter, a baby on the way, a husband who was
too sick to get out of bed, let alone work, and no one to turn to in my
hour of need. What had I done to deserve this? I looked through coat
pockets and piggy banks for loose change so that I could have enough
money to buy milk, eggs, and bread to feed my family. What horrible
sin had I committed, that my punishment was to be forced to sell my
furniture to pay the rent, and to watch my family sinking slowly into a
pit of desperation from which I could see no escape?

I felt weak and useless, powerless to effect the course of my own
life. Everywhere I turned, there was more evidence of the futility of even
trying. Turning on the radio, I heard "Why am I so soft in the middle;
why is my life so hard . . . ?" Paul Simon serving as a messenger, outlin-
ing my problem so perfectly. "I need a shot at redemption. Don't want
to end up a cartoon in a cartoon graveyard." I knew exactly where I did
not want to be and saw my life speeding right toward it. Going through
life with the goal of survival rather than excellence, buying generic
toilet paper instead of tissues, still living hand to mouth and in the
grip of terror that I would run out of things to sell for the rent, power,
and water. Pumping gas $2 at a time into a broken-down Volkswagen
camper van with no heat or air conditioner, no radio or cassette deck;
wearing a down coat while driving in the winter to keep warm; and
in the summer, keeping a cooler on the front seat to keep my makeup
from melting and to hold a cool washcloth to wipe the sweat from my
skin. With no music, the only thing I heard during the hours in that car
was the voice inside my head, my own personal demon, telling me that
my situation was beyond hope, that I was a failure, that I would let my
children down. I was systematically draining myself of every last drop
of possibility, and I didn't know how to stop.

I felt caught in a bear trap in the darkest woods. My life was closing in around me, crushing me. There was no light, no warmth, and no
sound — and if there had been, I probably would have been afraid of
it. There was only the certainty of loss and failure, and the desperation
of the truly desolate. I would have gnawed my own leg off to get free
of the trap.

That night, someone told me about a network marketing company that sold a product every woman wanted. She applied the product on my nails, and I was impressed — but I didn't have the money to sign up or buy the start-up kit, so that was that. A voice inside my head said, "If you don't ask, the answer is always no." I thought of the baby that I carried, and for her I swallowed my pride. I called my mother-in-law and pleaded for the $2000 to pay my doctor the balance of the bill, so I could have my baby delivered by her naturally. I begged her to give me two months to pay her back because I was going to sell a product that would give me enough money to reconcile the loan by the time she came to visit us to see her second granddaughter.

Out of debt with my doctor but still unable to buy into the company, I lucked out: My sponsor took pity on me and fronted me one hundred units of the product. I got to work, determined to keep my word. Just weeks from the delivery of my baby, I waddled onto airplanes, amidst choruses of disapproval from the flight attendants. "We can't let you fly, ma'am. You're nine months pregnant."

"What are you talking about?" I joked, refusing to be led off the aircraft, but not wanting to cause a scene. "I've got quintuplets here. I'm only in month five." They caved under the sheer force of my will. They put Post-It® notes on my belly with messages like "extra wide load" and "enter at your own risk," once I made it clear that I was in my seat and not leaving until I reached my destination. I kept them laughing the whole flight, so they wouldn't get me in trouble at the other end, and I sold every one of them a kit.

For the next three weeks, until the day I gave birth, I worked the business with everything in me. The results were nothing short of spectacular: My team sold $97,000 worth of product; my check from the company was $6,969.39, for less than a month's work. On top of all that, I earned an additional $5000 in retail profits.

This tale of rags to riches reverberated through the industry overnight. The story of incredible success in such a short time, and coming from such desperation, became a song of hope. For every mom struggling to provide for her children, for every woman searching for a way out, for every homemaker looking under the cushions of her sofa for milk money, this one testimony became an inspiration and the proof of the possibility of transformation. Shortly after this success, I went to a new company, knowing that I could be successful by losing the weight (110 pounds), and went on to make millions in an industry where a fat, tired, and broke housewife was able to make as much money as the CEO of a Fortune 500 company. This touchstone of success was like opening a floodgate. I became a teacher, mentor, coach, author, lecturer, motivational speaker, a role model for my two girls, and a role model for the industry.

When the promise of wealth and happiness seemed impossible, the thought of living in a world where I always knew exactly where my children's next meal was coming from was enough to get me to take one last chance on myself. Slowly, the doubt was pushed aside by successes, small at first, but still bringing me out of the darkness, inch by inch. The voices inside my head, telling me I would always be a failure, were proven wrong, and suddenly I saw the choices I had in my life, and the path to conquer fear.

Like a prayer, hope is luminous and limitless. But ultimately, the Lord helps those who help themselves, and that means moving beyond hope and into action. Hope is like a little girl trying to start a campfire, drawing the light of the sun through a magnifying glass, making sure the first small spark hits the carefully placed dry grass. But that spark has to be fed. It needs kindling, then some sticks, and finally the logs to create that monumental blaze. In the same way, the spark of hope in the human heart must also be fed, and what feeds hope is action. Action with purpose. Action with commitment. Action with intention. Action with focus . . . action combined with the eye of the tiger.

It is true: When the student is ready, the teacher will appear. Although Emily Dickinson calls hope "a thing with feathers," I preferred to see myself in a breastplate with a horned helmet. Amazing and miraculous things happen when a woman moves her hope into action and then transforms it into commitment. Unlike hope, commitment is not something that occurs naturally in the human spirit. Commitment is a choice you make. You choose to win. You choose to stop being a victim and start creating your own reality.

"We do not see things as they are;
we see them as we are."

— ANAIS NIN

When you make a commitment, you accept accountability. You take responsibility for yourself and your own life. As women, we tend to be very good at taking responsibility for other people's lives, other people's problems, other people's weaknesses, and that can be a great obstacle to realizing our own potential. But when we take responsibility for ourselves, our whole lives are changed. Dreamers become doers. Golda Meir said that self-responsibility is not a burden but an opportunity for freedom. In life, taking responsibility affords us an incredible opportunity for both personal and financial freedom. Of course, accountability doesn't necessarily come easily.

"Failure is not in the falling down,
but in the staying down."

— MARY PICKFORD

We know that in life, rejection comes with the territory. To thrive requires a character of mind that is impervious to negativity. When I want a snapshot of that attitude, I think of Helen Keller, who said the only real risk in life is not risking, that life is either a daring adventure or nothing at all. Lucille Ball was told for years that she had no talent and should give up, but she believed in herself and went on to become the first lady of comedy. Golda Meir would have risked her own life to save just one child from the concentration camps. She was undaunted by what seemed like overwhelming opposition. The word "quit" was simply not in her vocabulary. And I think of my own mother, who carried herself like a queen in our Bronx city project, and who made three small children's lives abundant in every way that was important. It never even occurred to her that I shouldn't have a college education, even though our household income barely covered essentials. She was the first person to remind me that every day we spend above ground is a great day.

"Work is love made visible."

— KAHLIL GIBRAN

One of the greatest women of all time, Mother Teresa, called herself *"a little pencil in the hand of a writing God, who is sending a love
letter to the world."* This is a woman's relationship to her work. Her
work is an expression of her heart. And the heart is the seat of our deepest desires. Women know that when our work is congruent with our
deepest desires, in any worthwhile pursuit, success is already unfolding.
Then we are ready, as Elizabeth Barrett Browning says, *"to light tomorrow with today."*

Sandy Elsberg is referred to as the "lioness with a heart," and nowhere
is her reputation more evident than when she walks her audience
through what it really takes to earn a multiple six-figure income. "It
can be hard for many people to relate to a six-figure income when
they've been scrambling under the sofa cushions for milk money."
Sandy has taught thousands of people no-nonsense, hands-on, how-to
techniques that empower women and men alike to become a master
copy worth duplicating. Sandy's experience is not theory — her genius
and expertise come from being at the top of seven companies, personally training hundreds of thousands of people worldwide. She is
the best at what she does! Sandy can be reached at (714) 920-9412,
sandy@sandyelsberg.com, www.sandyelsberg.com.

Thank God
I Was Fired by Fax

LARRY THOMPSON

I was considered a legend by some and a pioneer by others. As co-founder of Herbalife International, I dedicated myself to an upstart industry and helped usher in dynamic success for thousands of people . . . including myself. I was confident, diligent, and completely immersed in my work. This story is not about those extremely focused times, however, but about the most devastating day in my life — a day for which I am now eternally grateful!

On January 15th, 1993, while at the top of my game, I was literally fired by fax from the company to which I had given my entire identity — my entire being. Instead of receiving an attractive severance, I was written out of the company history. I didn't get a royal send-off and a thank you for all my dedication and hard work; I had to pick up my personal items from a bonfire-like pile they threatened to throw out. I was abandoned by friends and colleagues, left instantly and painfully alone. How did I not see this coming? Looking back, this was much more of an existential domino than a simple vocational termination.

Out of spite, I started a competing company that would "stick it to them." Although the company grew in numbers, I was unable to make the enterprise profitable. I guess a company built on a bitter foundation is ultimately doomed from the start. It was bad enough having to shut down Lifetronics, but the worst part of all was that I really did not like the person I had become. . . . Yet even this was nothing compared to what happened next.

To say my life completely fell apart may sound like a cliché, but it's actually an understatement. My signature confidence eroded. My marriage fell apart — eventually leading to divorce. A $20 million construction project failed. Most tragic of all, my health gave out. Chaos was everywhere, and I seemed powerless to stop the dramatic inertia. Hope began to fade . . . and I am still shocked at how far I sank. By 1999, I was bedridden and officially diagnosed with Chronic Fatigue Syndrome [CFS]. Few things are as emotionally painful as the feeling of utter hypocrisy. As a leader of a "health advocate" company, I promoted well being, healthy living, and control of one's own destiny — yet I could not even get out of bed. I thought I had reached the end of my life!

Often little, seemingly inconsequential, events impact one's future with a "butterfly effect." Just when my life was at its most tragic, my luck finally began to change. Strangely enough, two simple introductions made all the difference: Two people came into my life at exactly the right time.

My sister first introduced me to a beautiful woman named Taylor, who was looking for help with her business. Although we had an immediate and obvious connection over the phone, we had a major hurdle to overcome. She lived in Texas, and I was physically unable to get off my California Serta to travel and see her. Out of desperation, I finally confided in Taylor regarding my condition. Instead of running away, Taylor helped me get back on my feet both literally and figuratively. I sold my assets and regrouped in Texas with Taylor and my two daughters, Lari and Leah. Although things were finally looking up, I still had a significant health issue to overcome. Again, fortune smiled upon me the day I met Dr. Floyd Westin. He introduced me to an incredible shark liver oil product from Norway that not only got me on my feet again but completely rejuvenated my body. Seemingly overnight, I felt energetic and healthy for the first time in years. Just as important, I was amazed at the number of people with different health challenges (diabetes, cholesterol, etc.) who had similar results.

Everything seemed to come together at the right time — a new life, a new home, a new bride, and a new mission. My brain started thinking about how to create a company that could help people, using my expertise but with a focus on mission more than on profits. People had to know about the shark liver product, and I simply loved promoting health and helping others. Seabiotics was created with this mission focus, but in truth, it was really born years before through a series of humblings I wouldn't trade for the world.

When I think back upon my life, I am often struck by how much I have changed. I used to preach and believe that spiritual and family values should come before business, but I had lost this focus. I bought into the myth my success provided and lost myself along the way. I guess that saying is true: "There are two types of people, the humble and those about to be humbled." I have reconnected with my spiritual side. I now have a wonderfully rewarding family life and the perspective to appreciate it. As I have grown in my ability to empathize and understand the struggles we all experience, I have become more powerful and therefore more valuable to my family and community. My experiences have allowed me to reconnect with my integrity in a deeply spiritual way.

Best of all, I now get up each day immersed in gratitude. I am . . .

. . . grateful for Robert Depew, my first mentor, for giving a twenty-three-year-old his first opportunity and the confidence in myself that came with it,

. . . grateful to Dr. Westin for providing me with the life-changing product that completely transformed my health,

. . . grateful to my beloved Taylor — without whom I can honestly say I might not be here. She is not only my inspiration but my best friend, business partner, and greatest advocate! One could easily say this is just as much a love story as a story of redemption or transformation,

. . . grateful to my two wonderful daughters, Lari and Leah, for providing me with stability and love during the time I was most in need of both. (You will always be my little girls.)

. . . And finally, I am grateful to Mark Hughes, my former partner and imagined "tormentor." Without Mark, I would never have been able to help as many people as I have been blessed to serve.

Mark not only helped me along my initial path, but by firing me by fax, he indirectly gave me the greatest gift of all, the humility to appreciate life. I shudder to think who I might be today without this life-altering gift. From time to time I am reminded of those early years and the man I used to be. Each time, I whisper to Taylor, "Thank God you did not know me then!"

♥   ♥   ♥

Known as the "Mentor to the Millionaires," Larry Thompson has worked with numerous companies, most notably Herbalife International. He can claim forty-plus years of experience in direct sales and the network marketing industry, encompassing dozens of different product lines and compensation plans. He is experienced with ground-floor companies, and has a broad background in maintaining the longevity of direct sales organizations over long periods time. He has been directly responsible for training thousands of people who have made millions of dollars over the last forty years. His timeless philosophy and teaching has revolutionized the direct sales industry, and the training concepts he developed are included in many network marketing seminars over the past twenty years. He has recently come out of retirement to launch a new segment of the wellness industry in marine biologicals.

Join the *Thank God I...* community online to share your story and chat with the authors at **www.thankgodi.com**

Thank God
My Best Friend Died

MY FRIEND JANICE, A ROSE FOR US ALL

SUSAN BURGER

ey, Suz?" It was my good friend Michael on the phone. "They can't find Janice. Have you heard from her?" It was May 1982. A few months earlier, I had moved from the Philadelphia area to Chicago to go to chiropractic college, and my best friend Janice was to come and visit me in a few weeks. We had met in 1973, when I got a job at a local newspaper after graduating from high school. Janice and I worked together in the complaint department and became fast friends.

We both loved to travel, dance, and go down to the Jersey shore. We did crazy fun things, such as driving to Montreal for the 1976 Olympics despite having very little money. We found a place where they rented cots to sleep on at a big gym, and bought a big box of crackers and a jar of Cheez Whiz to eat for dinner, and breakfast, and lunch . . . ! Another year we visited a relative of hers in Miami, and after several days of rain that didn't look like it was letting up, we decided we weren't going to waste our vacation! We called a travel agent and asked for the cheapest tickets to someplace sunny we could fly to . . . and the next day we were in Cancun.

Janice was a "hot pants girl" for the Philadelphia Phillies baseball team. Our boss got two tickets to a World Series game . . . and for some reason he gave them to Janice and me. We went to what turned out to be a winning game, and it sure ticked off the guys in the department that we got those tickets!

The year before I moved to Chicago, we took a road trip in her new black Camaro, driving from Pennsylvania and not stopping to sleep until we reached South Dakota. As we continued through the western states, to save money some nights we'd sleep in the car. That car was our home away from home for a few weeks. It also took us many times to the Jersey shore and back. Camaros were known as "cool" cars back then, and we had lots of good memories of fun in it.

We were two girls looking for adventure. My parents would worry about us because of all of the places we'd go. After all, isn't it safer if you just stay closer to home and not take so many chances?

While our lives went in different directions, we remained close friends. So when Michael called me that day with a strange sound in his voice, we were both concerned. Janice hadn't shown up the night before for a date and had been reported missing. I hadn't heard from her, and being out in Chicago, there wasn't much that I could do to help find her. I was sure that she'd show up soon and I'd find out she was O.K. At least, that was what I'd told myself.

It was later that night that a deep sense of foreboding struck me at the oddest time. Some friends and I had decided to go out dancing. Disco music was playing loudly; many of the songs were those Janice and I danced to when we had been out in the years past. The bass beat of the music was pounding, the strobe lights flashing, and the song "Born, born, born . . . born to be alive," echoed in my ears. It was a song that in the past made me feel energetic and happy, but this night as I danced, I felt weird. In the pit of my stomach, I knew something was really wrong.

The next day, the police found the black Camaro abandoned, with no sign of Janice. The day after that, Michael called to tell me that some fishermen had found her body in a nearby park. I remember just doubling over. "And the big story on Action News tonight: missing local girl's body found in woods." Within a couple of weeks after that, a sixteen-year-old boy was arrested for her murder. Ironically, with all the places we had traveled and circumstances we had been in that could have been unsafe, she had been stabbed twenty-five times while she was sitting and eating lunch outside at a picnic table behind the newspaper office where we had worked together. Who would ever imagine that this would happen in such a benign place and time? Why would this troubled teen do such a thing? He apparently wanted her car. He couldn't just ask her for the keys?! She would have given them to him . . . he didn't have to take her life.

He was tried as an adult and sentenced to life in prison. (I later heard that, ten years after that, he hanged himself. That didn't make it better. It was all so sad.) Now I can look back and still wonder why, but I have learned not to expect an answer to that question. I was so shaken as I prepared to fly home from chiropractic college for her funeral. I was at my locker putting some books away and preparing to leave when Jim, a good friend of mine, came up to his locker, next to mine. Looking at him, I said tearfully, "I don't know if I can do this."

He looked back at me and calmly said, in a matter-of-fact tone, "Of course you can."

He probably never knew how grounding that simple statement was. "Of course I can," I said to myself . . . and left for home.

Seven months later, I was home again for Christmas vacation. Janice's parents hadn't been able to get themselves to clean out her bedroom, so I went over one day to do it for them. It was this process that helped me to begin to see all I had learned, and would continue to learn, from this experience. Rather than feeling angry and sad, I found myself reliving the fun I had with her. In her closet were some cute outfits she had loved to wear when we went out dancing. There were boxes of pictures from trips she had taken, many of which we took together. How grateful I felt to have had a friend like her during such important years (from ages seventeen through twenty-seven) in my life. I did have the strength to deal with it, all of it.

I looked back and saw that her death taught me as much about myself as did the times I spent with her when she was alive. For years I have been, and continue to be, involved in activities promoting peace and non-violence. In my twenties I wondered if I would ever be able to defend myself, or if I could kill another person even in self-defense.

I know now that if my family, children, loved ones, or friends were seriously threatened, that indeed I would defend myself, or even kill. A strange revelation for me.

An old friend from my childhood, whom I hadn't seen in years, sent me a letter. We were in a church youth group together for a while when we were teens. I left the group, but she chose to go to bible college and wrote asking me if I had known if Janice was "saved," and if not that I should have done more to be sure that she was before she died. At first I was angry: How dare she try to make me responsible or guilty! I realize now that she meant well, and am grateful for her letter; especially because it made me do some soul-searching regarding my beliefs about death. While I had drifted away from organized religion, I found a spiritual knowing inside of me that helps me see and feel gratitude.

This experience also taught me that in this society we often misinterpret how well people are handling things. So many of us are walking around with smiles on our faces but tears just below the surface. Even when we do find and feel gratitude, the healing still continues. Just because "she seems fine" doesn't mean she is. It usually means the person is just controlling their emotions so that other people around them feel better. A phone call, an opening to share or even just a hand on the shoulder can be important. We all need to continue to love and be there for each other, even if "it's been twenty-five years." For me the lessons still present themselves. We can experience deep healing and find a heart full of gratitude, but that doesn't mean we have forgotten.

Since Janice died, I periodically get a strong sense of her presence: when I was married, had my kids, later divorced, and as I venture into new relationships, and especially when I travel. There were times that I may not have thought about her for a while, and then at just the right time she comes up in my thoughts, or a song comes on the radio, for me to know there is someone sharing things with me and supporting me from afar, but not really so far . . .

As I thought about writing this story, I asked my friend Rudy, a gifted chiropractor, to do some N.E.T. (Neuro Emotional Technique — a way of releasing buried emotions from the body) with me. I was feeling stuck. There were so many thoughts rumbling around in my head and heart. The first thing that came up with the N.E.T was that at some level I still felt guilty that I wasn't there to "save" her.

Next, there was the issue of anger that I didn't realize I still held onto in my body. I was angry that she had deserted me. As I connected to this feeling and went through the release techniques, I found myself saying to myself, "Damn you, Janice!!! You son of a bitch . . . ."

Immediately, I sensed her there looking at me, smiling, and I saw and heard her say, to my surprise, "Good for you!!!" All these years I didn't want to be mad at her, it wasn't her fault. And now as I acknowledged, felt, and expressed this anger, I see again that she is fine and wants me to be happy. She wants all of us who loved her to live our lives better and stronger because of her. Whatever we feel is fine, but she doesn't need us to feel any of it. One year for her birthday, I wrote out the words for her to one of her favorite songs, "The Rose," sung by Bette Midler. There is a line in that song that says, "It's the one who won't be taken who cannot seem to give, and the soul afraid of dying that never learns to live." I didn't know how much more significant those words would become to me. I feel that I honor her every time I live my life to the fullest, every time I step out and live my life with courage and joy.

The last verse ends, "Just remember, in the winter, far beneath the bitter snows, lies the seed that with the sun's love, in the spring becomes the Rose." Somehow things are as they should be. Thank God I knew Janice — she has become a Rose for many of us. I look forward to seeing what else I will learn because of her influence.

Janice, you were my best friend then, and in some ways, you are still my best friend now.

❤   ❤   ❤

Dr. Susan Burger has been the owner/director of Riverside Chiropractic & Vitality Center, a holistic multipractitioner center in Morrisville, Pa., for over eighteen years. She teaches workshops on many aspects of natural healing and tapping the power of conscious intention to live our lives in balance in mind, body, and spirit.

She is a founding member of the Greater Bucks Peace Circle, an interfaith group that offers events and resources for the community, and promotes conflict transformation, understanding, and action for change. Dr. Burger is the mother of two teenage boys, who add another delightful dimension to her life. The principles in her story and this book, gratitude for all that is, and living with love, are values that she hopes to inspire in her boys, just as so many have inspired her, and continue to do so each day.

Thank God
My Wife Cheated On Me!

JASON THOMAS KICINSKI

*H*ow could a man who teaches others about relationships be so powerless in his own marriage? I'd been taught that all of life is a gift. What good could possibly come from losing the most important person in my life right in front of my eyes? How could life be so brutal and brutally unfair? Humiliation engulfed me. It was a clear-cut case of "physician, heal thyself."

Seeing my wife in another man's arms was one of the most surreal moments in my life. It seemed to confirm every negative judgment I had of myself. A volcanic eruption of self-defeating thoughts and emotions saturated my consciousness at the sight of my beloved kissing another man. "Impotent loser . . . cowardly failure!" What had I done to deserve this?

When I experienced this most personal of betrayals, my life immediately felt so overwhelming, I would have welcomed any other distraction — including intense physical pain. Unanswerable questions plagued me: What did I do wrong? Why do I feel guilty? Why do I feel like a failure when someone else's actions put me in this situation? *Why? Why? Why?*

On top of these deeply emotional questions, other big-picture questions splintered my mind. *What drives someone to betrayal? What must I learn about myself while enduring these chaotic times? How will I grow if I can make it to the other side? Will I ever feel vital, loving, or vulnerable again? Will I ever get rid of this numbing sense of detachment, which is my only refuge from the agony of misguided Eros?*

I saw my parents grow through their own personal divorce hells, yet they were clearly better off after their separation. I experienced their divorce as a painful yet necessary part of our family's sanity. I counseled couples and individuals who dealt with personal relationship and divorce issues. I was supposed to have all the answers on healing relationships . . . yet my own marriage crumbled. I could not escape the sense of hypocrisy, the cruel torment. *Why me?*

My melodrama began in high school. I began dating the girl who became both my wife and then my ex. She was my first real girlfriend — and the first person with whom I shared any real intimacy. Dating this beautiful girl immediately gave me a sense of my manhood. I no longer felt like the unmanly nerd girls viewed as only a friend. I got to play hero, help her with her "stuff," and even attend the prom. I truly began to connect with the opposite sex in a way I had always dreamed. It wasn't all wonderful, though.

When my girlfriend returned from college orientation she told me she wanted the freedom to see other people. I couldn't eat, breathe, concentrate, or study. I'd successfully maintained the masculine power role up to this point, now I groveled and begged her to take me back. It felt more like pity when she relented. Without question, this event altered the power structure within our relationship and foreshadowed its eventual grand finale.

As college graduation neared, my attachment to her grew even stronger. Over Christmas break, she agreed to marry me. Soon we were living together as fully functioning adults in a new city. I excelled at work, which led to another move, another new city, and another setting. This setting became the stage for my first — but not last — intense humbling.

After a series of successes at work, everything changed . . . seemingly overnight. Just a few weeks prior I was the conquering hero at work; then suddenly I fell out of favor with management. Work instantly became a nightmare. I turned even more to my wife for my sense of manliness and worth. (Do you notice a pattern here?)

I worked intensely on myself to understand why things had gone wrong so quickly. I changed jobs, attended seminars all around the world, and read as much as I could. During these times of painful growth, my ex underwent her own series of trials and personal realizations. She continued to take classes and finally found her vocational calling. While my future filled with confusion, hers now filled with hope and clarity — I am clear the timing was no accident.

Fortunately, I found a series of teachers who helped illuminate my path through the turbulent darkness. They taught me in ways that integrated my spiritual curiosity with my logical engineering left brain. I discovered I had a natural ability to teach others what I learned. While still working a full-time job, I began speaking and helping others through seminars and consultations. In hindsight, it happened rather quickly, yet I felt completely alive and vital while working with clients.

My wife was initially enthusiastic about my newfound career. This enthusiasm was short-lived, however, as her desire for an identity outside of "my shadow" grew and grew. Simultaneously, I began to have doubts that we were on the same path. We each benefited so much from our experiences, yet neither of us could find a sense of peace in the relationship. Although very successful in helping my clients, I didn't have the client volume to make a full-time transition out of corporate America. My wife was about to graduate from college and — as I found out soon enough — from me.

I noticed a major change when she spoke of her classmates. One particular person always seemed to be in all her stories. I was truly happy and excited for her success in school and her new career, yet the more I tried to be a part of her future, the more she pushed me away. She was confused about her place in our marriage. She spent more and more time with her friends from school. I became more and more frustrated that I could not get my business off the ground full-time.

In a flash, the house of cards came tumbling down. I suspected this one particular classmate was more than just a friend, so I followed her to his home one morning. I caught them in full lip-lock. I was stunned, angry, sad, and yet strangely glad to know exactly what was going on. I learned a lot about my ex in the next few weeks. What followed for me was not a blame dynamic, however, but one of extreme personal abuse. I stood by her through her tough times, apparently I wasn't worthy of loyalty in return.

Despite all my training, my success in helping others, and all the benefits I experienced from my parents' divorce; intense feelings of inadequacy, futility, and impotence overtook me. Every self-defeating thought I'd ever had about myself rushed to the surface. When I discussed this situation with my wife, she told me *he* had every one of my good qualities yet none of my bad ones. She had found her Prince Charming, her soul mate. I found only . . . myself. (Writing this paragraph hurts!)

Many things in life are simple, yet not easy! I could not shake an intense feeling of hypocrisy. I was supposed to have all the answers. Yet, in truth, I *did* have all the answers — I knew them from all my studies, clients, and experiences. Despite all the pain, suffering, and melodrama, I knew intuitively and intrinsically that we were better off apart. I knew life was my mirror, and that life's challenges were really gifts. I knew I wanted only to be with someone who wanted to be with me. Yet none of this mental understanding seemed to alleviate the unrelenting emotional turmoil.

During an intense meditation something began to shake the confusion from my consciousness. As always, a series of questions moved me through my dilemma: "Do I love her more like a daughter or a wife?" whispered my unconscious, eerily similar to that famous scene in *Field of Dreams*. I could not deny the truth — which was immediately confirmed by my recollection of something she had casually mentioned before: that she cared for me "like a father and teacher."

I immediately listened to and answered other questions that flowed to and through me: "Is she really the right person for me and my future?" (No! But *why?*) Then, with this little bit of momentum, I really began to consult myself in a bizarre Spinoza-like self-analysis. I was at peace mentally with the relationship ending, but how would I pull myself from the emotional insanity? What questions broke me from my cage?

In working with clients, I always worked from a series of Universal Truths. *These truths were the only tools I had to tame my internal melodrama.* As they are truly universal, they help anyone in times of crisis. These truths consist of a few clear ideas:

1) Life is a Mirror. What we judge in others is our own reflection — Our own "Stuff"
2) All things have an inherent balance of supportive and challenging energy.
3) All things serve!

(Of course I cannot relay all of my self-analysis here, but here are the key questions and realizations that transformed my experience.)

First question: What really, truly hurts about this breakup? The answer? *Betrayal!* I had given her so much . . . I sacrificed . . . I would have done anything . . . yada yada yada.

Second question: Who have *I* betrayed? Who feels I have betrayed them? While I could see the answer included a few people at work and in my family, and my wife to a small extent, freedom flowed from the realization that I'd betrayed *myself* for far too long! How does one betray oneself? I had not been true to my path, my wisdom, and my own value system! I had sublimated my inner calling in order to live a temporarily less painful — more normal — life. I'd denied my own manhood, masculinity, and self-worth. Is it any wonder the person closest to me did me the greatest service by showing me the folly of my ways? This was in truth her greatest gift to me. She forced me to find, love, and appreciate myself in a way I'd yearned to do throughout the first thirty years of my life!

Third question: Why was I infatuated with her? What did she provide me that I felt was missing in myself? Beauty, sexual power, and a sense of "manliness" were the prime answers. As I began to really dig for these answers — the answers I had helped so many of my clients find previously — it became obvious that our relationship had quite successfully taken each of us as far as it could. I also made sure that I owned every trait I perceived in my ex's new lover.

Finding my mirror in my wife's new lover was quite challenging, yet it became a truly profound event in my life. What form did my attractiveness, youth, vitality, power, and so on take? Finding my masculinity was the biggest challenge, however I learned from Deida's *Superior Man* that a man cannot truly feel successful (and manly) unless he feels he is on purpose. Once I realized that I clearly was on purpose — albeit clearly not patient enough — the other discrepancies began to vanish. I found the people in my life who saw me exactly as my wife saw Mr. Right. I also got back to working out, eating properly, and studying again.

As I sat there, I found myself feeling strangely guilty, considering the circumstances. Yet when I got 100% clear that I had provided my wife with the same assistance in finding herself — in loving herself — the guilt dissolved. You see, guilt in these dynamics usually stems from one of two ideas: either "that SOB did something horrible to me," generating the victim illusion, or, somewhat more unconsciously, "that SOB actually gave me more than I gave in return." I was able to clear both of these issues, using the wisdom of the Universal Truths I stated above.

Not all relationships are meant to last forever! Despite our best intentions and vows, the truth is that people — and therefore relationships — change over time. My ex gave me a tremendous, albeit tremendously painful, lesson in the nature of unconditional love. She gave me everything she had left to give. She walked the plank and took the courageous road, in retrospect, though few would see it that way. She could have stayed in an unfulfilling marriage offering security but little joy; but instead she chose the more difficult road. I still have a profound love for her today.

Looking back, there were a million signs that my marriage was not meant to be a permanent one. Still, I have found tremendous value in the pain of my circumstance. I have found myself. To say it has allowed me to empathize and understand my clients better would be a significant understatement. And yet I have received so much more . . .

FREEDOM: to fully explore the edges of my mind . . . to travel wherever I wish with whomever I wish . . . to never have to ask permission to go or do as I please . . . to spend countless hours in self-analysis and realization . . . to move near the ocean . . . to meet new people . . . to find the next love of my life, one with a value system more resonant with my own. *Thank God my wife cheated on me!*

PUSH: to consciously get back on track of my MVP (Mission/Vision/Purpose), to finally love the parts of myself that were screaming for attention over the years, to capture the lessons I learned, so that I would be able to help others more profoundly, to break the cycle of stagnation. *Thank God my wife cheated on me!*

LOVE: to detach her issues from my own . . . to end a dynamic I did not have the strength to end myself. In addition to an extremely amicable divorce (we both understood the need to own our own shit), the greatest gift she gave me was the space to live the life I was meant to live — and truly could not have done while married to a woman with her value system. *Thank God my wife cheated on me!*

I could go on and on — and have already spent countless hours doing so — but the key points are hopefully clear. I leave you with a few relationship truths:

- Feelings of loneliness are usually calls to find and appreciate oneself again.
- Feelings of loss are usually a sign of an infatuation stemming from a denied part of one's own psyche or personality.
- The beauty of the pain that bubbles to the surface after a relationship ends is the opportunity to find and love parts of oneself previously denied.

CAUTION: If you do not take the opportunity to find and love these aspects of yourself, you will absolutely, unequivocally attract another relationship that will yield the same opportunity — with a little extra pain incentive!

One's quality of life — and relationships in particular — is proportional to one's aptitude for appreciation. If you are looking to transcend a certain relationship vibration, ask the type of questions I asked myself. My growth, personal evolution, and ontological perspective have primarily sprung from my life's great humblings. Without question, I have seen that personal realizations release one from individual personal "hells." I am truly grateful to God, my ex, and her lover, as they gave me myself! Love and appreciation are the answer. Find them and you shall find the freedom you seek.

❤   ❤   ❤

Jason Thomas Kicinski graduated from Carnegie Mellon University with a degree in Chemical Engineering, and has worked with corporate and professional organizations since 1995. He founded Kicinski Breakthrough Artistry [KBA] to facilitate corporate breakthroughs and personal transformations. KBA offers a series of lectures and seminars as well as coaching and consulting services that empower people to take inspired action. Areas of focus include divorces & stressful relationships, prosperity consciousness & wealth attraction, and unclear purpose for life as well as the 3 corporate pillars of personnel management and organizational excellence: Motivation, Communication, and Devotion. Jason also provides ghostwriting services including many of the stories in this book. Jason's first book, *Breakthrough Secrets to Live Your Dreams* and acclaimed audio program *The Mirror: An Audio Guide to Seeing, Owning, and Transforming Your Life* can be found through the KBA Website: http://www.breakthroughartist.com. He can also be contacted at his office: 219-629-5614

Thank God
I Was Fat

TRICIA GREAVES

*F*atty Patty went to town, rolling her blubber up and down. First she stopped at the candy shop, and then she bought a lollipop." That's one of the self-effacing songs I made up about myself in my youth. I was a chubby kid, with a huge roll of fat on my stomach, which I used to collect in my two hands and squeeze in an attempt to measure it. It protruded from my body in a way that made me look like a pregnant eleven-year-old . . . a freak of nature. My mother did her best to get me to suck it in, sometimes by physically putting her hand on it and pushing. I hated her for that intrusion, of course, and just used it as an excuse to eat more. On Sunday nights, I would routinely get up in the middle of the night to vomit all the junk I'd stuffed down over the weekend . . . popcorn, pizza, brownies, and doughnuts. (I had a weak stomach, but with enough practice, I got over it.)

How would you feel, being so fat . . . and suffering the consequences? I loathed it. I was one of the last picked for games at school; I was ugly; the boys I obsessed about weren't interested in me; I was sluggish and asthmatic in sports; and I couldn't even understand why my friends would want to hang out with me. On top of that, my personality was a little off. I was loud, obnoxious, and a clown. I liked to tease others in "good fun" but often went too far, causing pain. Ironically, I was also a "people-pleaser" and would do anything to get people to like me. This drove my self-esteem down to subterranean levels.

What I wanted most was to be thin and have a boyfriend. Yet adolescence brought more weight gain. My face was as round as a pumpkin. I knew I had a social disadvantage, so I compensated for my "handicap" by doing things to be noticed and to be liked. I was on the student council, I had many "popular" friends, and I was involved in many activities. In high school, my weight increased in proportion to my sexual activity. I was pretty messed up sexually due to early childhood sexual abuse, and I used food and the protection of fat to cope. I was obsessed with sex, masturbation, and boys, and suffered endless shame and guilt because of it. I drowned the guilt with alcohol and blackouts and created more shame in the process.

I used food to quell my many nameless fears. I lived in fear — afraid of what others thought of me, afraid of failing, afraid of succeeding, afraid of my feelings, afraid of the responsibilities that came with being alive! Food brought me comfort. I would forget my fears when I was overeating and full. I wouldn't feel a thing. For example, I played goalie in lacrosse, and there wasn't a day that I wasn't terrified of having those balls whipped at me. (It never occurred to me to play another position . . . I was hooked on the extra attention, and after all, the team needed me.) On game days, I was anxious, tense, and full of dread, but macaroni and cheese, French fries, and cookies fixed that. I would stuff myself at lunch and waddle out to the field to gear up. In full gear, I looked like the Michelin man!

I determined that I would be different in college — I was going to be thin and popular! (Why I thought a change of location would change who I was and how I reacted to life, I have no idea.) The only thing that changed was that I was away from my mother's critical eye and could therefore eat and drink with abandon. I joined Overeaters Anonymous in my second year of college and loved the camaraderie of the meetings. I finally found "my kind": people who were as weird about food as I was! After three years in OA, however, nothing had significantly changed. My weight continued to yo-yo. I needed something more, yet convinced that OA was the "last house on the block," I despaired of ever finding a true solution.

One day I heard a woman share who suffered from hopeless bulimia. I saw her struggle for nine months, and then in two weeks she was free from the obsession to overeat. I was stunned. I had witnessed a miracle, and I wanted the same miracle for myself. She gave me the phone number of a man who specialized in helping people who have "tried everything" to overcome their compulsive eating and were out of options. With this man's gift of love, time, and attention, I was able to finally look under the hood of my food obsession and discover the underlying soul-sickness that plagued me. I followed a formula of healing called "Metasteps" that successfully healed my compulsion to overeat — and to engage in any other self-destructive action.

Why am I grateful for the experience of being fat? Because I suffered in a way that makes me sensitive to others who still suffer. I understand the pain of self-loathing. I understand the powerlessness of not being able to stop when my body has long since indicated it's time. I know how it feels to perceive myself to be the ugliest person in the room, whom no one would desire. I understand the despair of having it "together" on the outside and writhing in psychic pain on the inside. I know these things. Only someone who has experienced this unique pain can truly understand. And because I have found a way up and out, I am uniquely qualified to help others discover a way out, as well.

Snippets of advice like "follow a plan," "join a gym," "just cut back," or (my favorite) "everything in moderation" aren't going to work for someone like me. These well-meaning suggestions from doctors, family, and friends only made me feel like a bigger pariah. Fortunately, I am able to offer something much deeper and lasting to those I have the opportunity to help. There is a language of the heart that can actually heal another's compulsion. That language healed me, and through my work, I do my best to share it with others.

Searching for an answer to my food problem led me to address the deeper pain from which I suffered, pain which had nothing to do with food or weight. Little good could come to me if I didn't heal the dissatisfaction I felt about myself. I learned that excess food served two functions for me: painkiller and punishment. When I overate, I experienced a calming, numbing sensation, a safety from the storm. But since I couldn't stop myself from eating too much, the food I ate quickly became a punishment, a way for me to hurt my body and hate myself for my lack of control. Why did I need the comfort of a pain-killer? Because the thoughts churning inside seemed too hard to feel. Why did I inflict punishment on myself? Because at some level I felt, I deserved to feel bad and suffer. Addressing the feelings inside, as well as the deep-seated worthlessness was my only hope of experiencing lasting weight loss.

Both the pain and the self-loathing came from many aspects of my personality that are typical of emotional eaters. For instance, I rarely honestly expressed my emotions for fear of how I would be perceived. This caused me to use food to bury my unexpressed feelings alive instead. Another example was my habit of trying to get people to like me by denying my needs in favor of theirs. As a result, I'd burn with resentment and console myself with food. Furthermore, my per-sistently low self-esteem drove me to seek validation from bosses and coworkers for my Herculean efforts and extended hours at my job. I routinely ended my long day feeling burned out and attempting to refuel with a binge.

How could any weight-loss scheme tap these root causes (and there are many more than I've mentioned here)? The truth is that they couldn't. My process of recovery involved building an entirely new relationship with myself and with others. When I came to see how closely my disordered eating mirrored my disordered living and think-ing, I realized the necessity of going within. Diets or a gastric bypass weren't going to change my head, my heart, and my reactions to life. Being fat has led me to seek wisdom and love beyond nutritional expertise and skinny jeans. It has transformed my life and given me the opportunity to help others in their own transformation. In addition, through the grace of God, it has delivered me to freedom from the vise grip of emotional eating . . . one day at a time.

❤   ❤   ❤

Tricia Greaves is the founder of Be Totally Free!, a non-profit offering hope and a real solution to those struggling with eating disorders, emotional eating, weight loss, and many various addictions. Having lost fifty pounds and overcoming several addictions herself, Tricia offers the unique, patented "*Metasteps*" solution, which addresses the underlying causes of all addictions, and which is based entirely on her personal experience of what actually works. People who have tried "everything" to stop are able to finally experience total freedom through Be Totally Free! To learn more and to receive your own Free "JumpStart Kit," visit www.betotallyfree.com.

Thank God
I Lost My Father

OR I WOULD NOT HAVE LEARNED OF LOVE

ROBERT JOSEPH IWANIEC

*T*his is a love story . . . a love story about loss, gain, and ultimate love. Fifteen years ago, when I was twenty-six, we were about to have our first child. My wife was very pregnant. I'd describe how she looked, but it would be in my best interests not to. Our family had amassed for the annual Thanksgiving Day celebration. That morning, November 28th, my father and I had decided to go out hunting. It was a family tradition of sorts, I guess dating back to the time of the Pilgrims. I really didn't want to go, but if you knew my father, you would have known what a pain in the ass he could be. I got dressed in six layers of clothes, (it was cold!!), and we headed out to a friend's apple orchard, about a fifteen-minute drive.

As usual, he dropped me off at the best spot and continued on about another five hundred yards. I watched him painstakingly make his way up the knoll, and his orange parka slowly disappeared from my view. There we were, alone in the woods though together. Hunting, they call it. For me it was like a meditation, a place to sit and think about life. Most hunters would agree that the solitude is as much a part of hunting as the camaraderie or the actual taking of game. So there I was, freezing my ass off (so much for the meditation!), when I heard a noise. Crack! I don't know if you have ever been in the woods on a cold day (why would you?), but the woods are usually quiet. The cracking of a fallen branch under the weight of a deer sounds quite alarming. I turned toward the sound and there he stood, a magnificent eight-point buck. I slowly drew my gun up toward him but had to wait a bit for the fog to clear from my scope. (Here's a hint for you future hunters: You will get excited when you see a great deer in the woods. If it's cold and you start to breathe heavily, just don't huff and puff on your scope.) I waited a few moments — which felt like hours — for the fog to clear, and then I steadied the crosshairs and gently squeezed the trigger on my .303. Bam! Funny thing — as loud as the gunshot must have sounded in the silent woods, I don't remember hearing it. The buck dropped in an instant, and I let out a couple of expletives. Out of joy, of course.

My father and I agreed earlier to wait until noon to meet, but on his hearing my shot, he quickly made his way back down the mountain. It still felt like an eternity to me. When you shoot a big deer, you just can't wait to show it off. It's a male ego thing. What a hunt, what a day! Boy, were things about to change. We dressed and then dragged the deer back to the truck. It was heavy, but on the way in we had placed an old orange sled under a pile of leaves. (How's that for optimism?) It took us about twenty minutes to make it down the mountain. We placed our gear into the truck. By now, I had removed four of the layers — you sweat a lot when you drag a heavy animal through the woods. As my father bent over to place the tag on the deer, he collapsed with a massive heart attack.

I was in a daze, but thank God, there were other hunters at the scene. We began CPR and quickly called for an ambulance, but to no avail. Two hours later, they pronounced my father dead at the young age of fifty-one . . . two months before the birth of his first grandchild. The hospital where he had been taken called my family, and I met them there. Needless to say, it wasn't a very grateful Thanksgiving.

There is the loss.

The next year was very difficult. As much as my father and I loved each other, we had never said it. The expression of feelings among men was just not macho. Honestly, I had a difficult time dealing with his loss. I held a lot of guilt, for he and I would often go at it. We had been two know-it-all Polacks (is that an oxymoron?), and I felt incomplete after his passing, for I had not communicated to him exactly how much I loved and appreciated him. It was affecting my work and my relationships, as well as my role as a new father. So how did I get out of it? How did it all turn around?

Here is the gain.

By the grace of God, I came in contact with a man who knew how this grieving thing worked. His name is not necessary for this story, but his love and wisdom are. He sat me down and asked me about my father. He asked me, "What do you think your father would want you to do right now? Would he want you to continue to suffer, or would he want you to go on with your life?"

I answered, "Of course he would want me to go on."

He said, "You love your father, don't you?"

With tears welling up in my eyes, I replied, "Of course!"

"And he loved you, too?"

"Yes," I replied.

He handed me a tissue, reached into his black leather case, and pulled out a sheet of loose-leaf paper. "I would like you to do a little exercise with me. First, do you believe that you are your body? If I were to cut off your arms and legs, would you still be you? Would all of your thoughts and feelings and memories of life still be there? Of course, they would. You are not your body. Your father was not his body. He doesn't go away with the loss of his form; he just changes. Spirit (energy) cannot be destroyed or created. It can only be transformed. What you feel is missing — your father — exists in a form unrecognizable to you. Now, before we find him, I want to ask you a few more questions. Are you nice?"

"What do you mean?"

"Are you nice all the time?"

"No."

"Was your father?"

"No, not all the time."

"Are you selfish?"

"Sometimes."

"Was your father?"

"Sometimes."

He followed with another twenty or so questions that I felt almost guilty admitting to. Most were of the negative aspects of my father's and my own personality. He reminded me that we all have both sides. When loved ones pass, we grieve for the loss of the good parts. But we tuck away the bad parts, for we feel guilty in admitting to them. And here lies the problem of incompleteness. When we don't honor our loved ones in their totality, we close off our only means of communication, our open heart.

So I listed on paper twenty traits, both positive and negative, about my father, and which of those traits I had as well. I began to cry.

He told me that unconditional love has no boundaries. When we can truly open our hearts and love whomever we wish for their magnificence, in their totality, we can connect, for lack of a better word, with them any time, any place, whether living or dead. Yes, it was a little freaky.

So there I was, closing my eyes and seeing my father telling me that he loved me. It felt real. As real as it feels when someone tells you while your eyes are open that they love you. I told him that I loved him too, and that I was sorry that he didn't live to see the birth of his grand-daughter. He quickly responded that he had greater vision now, and that he saw it all — and that she was as beautiful as I was. I thanked him for all that he had done for me, and most of all for being a great father. By now the tears were dripping down to my chin. Then I opened my eyes and just sat there. I bent over and placed my tear-drenched face into my cupped hands. It felt like an eternity of time had passed. Yet it was only about an hour since I had begun the exercise.

What an experience . . . if you would call it that. I didn't know what to call it. I knew only that I had just experienced a heart-opening moment with my father. I felt complete. I felt relieved. I felt twenty pounds lighter. I thanked the man. I asked him if it was real. He reiterated, "Unconditional love has no boundaries." In fact, what I had just experienced was more real than the love that most people think they share everyday. He then told me that there were still a few things to do. He had me write a list of everything that I had thought was missing since my father's passing. I wrote down about fifteen things . . . the first being, of course, my father himself. The man instructed me to find my father now. He asked, "Who is playing the role of your father now? Look hard. Nothing is ever missing. It has only changed form." Again, tears welled up. My mother was dating a fine gentleman who was indeed a great father figure. I went down the list, loss after loss, and indeed there was nothing missing.

Last, the man instructed me to find out the benefits of my father figure in the new form versus the old form. After some difficult searching, I truly felt that I had not lost a thing. I was complete with my father. I let him know exactly how I felt. I was able to get out of my feelings of loss. Now I could go on. Just as I knew my father would have wanted. Just as your loved ones would want you to.

Here is the love.

The gentleman packed up his case, hugged me, and told me that of all the things that matter most in this world, none stands before love. "In truth, love is all there is. All else is illusion." When we love others, truly love them for who they are, they can never go away. Oddly enough, his words of wisdom reminded me of a little joke I once heard: How can I miss you if you won't go away? Hmm, maybe it isn't a joke at all. Thanks for the lesson, Dad. I love you.

GREATER LOVE

sometimes things don't work out in life
so other things can
it's as if we're guided by a greater love
to greater love
God's will for man

RJI

❤   ❤   ❤

Dr. Robert J. Iwaniec, a professional speaker, chiropractor, author, poet and success coach, has dedicated his life to the study of health and human performance. He is the author of several books including, *Breakthrough Secrets to Live Your Dreams, Inside Out, Pieces of Eight, Charm, Four, Nonsense and Retrogenesis.* He has also authored two children's books, *Flowers* and *Billy Burka and the Burka Trees.* Dr. Iwaniec resides in Clifton Park, New York with his wife Diane and their three children, Jenna, Robert, and Nicholas.

Thank God
I Am the Product of Rape!

LADY

As a very young child, I sensed "something" was in charge of, watching over, or orchestrating, everything that was. I just didn't know what that something was called. As I reflect on my earliest childhood memories, I realize that my spiritual journey began far earlier than my ability to articulate the experience. I was taught that the "Something" was called God and that He hears all and answers all. When my pleas seemed to go unanswered, I came to believe either God viewed my problems as too insignificant, or that God was just not listening. I recall asking myself the same question everyday of my young life and especially throughout my teen-age years . . . *"God, Why did you choose this life for me?"* How many people do you know have asked that very question, *"Why me?"*

My mulatto (Irish/Black) grandmother was over forty years old and suffered with hypertension when she gave birth to my mother. Family legend has it that my Bahamian grandfather possibly had syphilis, which might be the reason my mother was born moderately mentally retarded. Grandmother was in denial about my mother's mental capacity and enrolled her in school for "normal" children. What Mother had in her favor was that she looked normal and could mimic any behavior or action if she witnessed it repeatedly. After a time though, it became painfully obvious that my mom could not keep up with the other children her age. She was removed from the public school system. When my mother was older, she attended a day program for those mentally challenged. While attending this special program, she met up with an employee she remembered as a former classmate from her early days in school. He was not mentally challenged, simply morally corrupt.

Due to my mother's obesity as well as her mental capacity, it is unsure if anyone in the family knew she was pregnant. Mother didn't understand sex or pregnancy, so it's clear she wasn't aware of my pending arrival. My grandmother died August 1, 1964. I was born just 9 days later.

My great-aunt, Vivian Lett (my grandmother's sister and lovingly known as Ma-mom), told me the story of my birth. She visited the hospital, and discovered my mother had not yet seen me. When she inquired as to why, she learned that because of my grandfather's age and physical health, along with my mother's mental capacity, the hospital performed a tubal ligation on my mother, and put me up for adoption. Ma-mom was outraged that the extended family had not been consulted. My aging grandfather, who was still grieving the loss of his wife, couldn't fathom how he would care for my mother and a newborn baby, so he gave the approval.

Ma-mom was a strong woman of principle; she refused to allow her niece to be sent away, never to know where she came from. With the help of my godmother, my aunt wrapped me in a blanket, stole me from the nursery, and took me to my mother, so she could see me for the first time. She told my mother not to worry — that she was taking the baby home, and that she would return for her. My aunt made clear to the hospital that should the hospital pursue kidnapping charges, she would file legal charges against them for making decisions without consulting those in our extended family. No charges were filed. Because of Ma-mom's courage, I stayed with my mother.

When I was old enough to realize that everyone had a father but me, I asked, "Where is my real daddy?" They told me that my birth was the result of a rape. I didn't understand the information. In my head I would question over and over again. *"How does one get raked? And, how does a baby, come from it?"*

Ma-mom lived next door for a few years and would come over to cook and try to clean for us. She helped as much as she could, but she was married, had eight children of her own and worked full time. There was no one on the planet I loved more than this woman, who called me 'Shug' until the day she died.

I grew up in Central Philadelphia and learned very early on what poor was, and that we were it. Our home was filthy. None of my friends' homes looked like mine on the inside. None of my friends wore old dirty clothes or shoes like mine. None of my friends were ashamed to have me come into their home. We lived in a 940 square foot two-story row home with two bedrooms and one bath. We had roaches, bedbugs, rats, and water bugs. After a while, the rats and bedbugs became so abundant that I would even have nightmares. Trying to alleviate my fears, my grandfather hung a cross above the bed where I slept. When I was between four and five years old, my mother and I started sleeping downstairs on the couch. Because of my mother's obesity, I only had a small place at her feet to sleep.

At some point mother began to have seizures, which was a bone frightening experience for a small child. I remember the first time I actually witnessed her seizure; I wet myself out of the sheer terror of it all. I awakened to the feeling of my mother jerking in her sleep. I called to her and there was no answer. She rolled off the sofa and onto the floor as I sat up screaming "Mommy". I will never forget the horror of watching her body stiffen as her muscles contracted. Then her back and neck arched, she foamed at the mouth, bit her tongue, wet herself, and jerked her body violently. As her eyes rolled back in her head, her arms flailed around uncontrollably. She turned blue and made grunting sounds as she gasped for breath. Although the entire episode only lasted for 2 minutes, it felt like it lasted for hours. This vision is burned into memory bank for the remainder of my life.

My mother's doctor instructed me in what to do in the event she had another seizure in my presence. I was to place a warm washcloth on her forehead and place a tablespoon in her mouth to prevent her from swallowing her tongue. I kept these items on the end table by the sofa. Each time she jerked in her sleep, I would be in a state of panic, knowing a seizure was about to strike. I was afraid to go to sleep or even wake her to take me to the bathroom, which was a frightening trip all on its own. Because of broken plumbing, we couldn't use the tub. To flush the toilet we would have to fill a bucket with water. The smell was horrific. I was convinced — God hated me for sure!

I attended a public school for kindergarten and soon encountered racism and cruelty. When Mother walked me to school, Caucasian kids would scream, "Nigger!" at her and ask what she was doing with a little white girl (how I hated being called "white"). The rocks they'd throw bloodied her face. Mother defended me, but because of her slurred, child-like speech, the teenagers became even more enraged and their attacks became even more brutal. Their words cut as badly as the rocks that hit my mother in the face. I would plead with her to ignore them, to not say anything, in hopes it would hide the fact that she was retarded.

My family agreed to pool their money together to send me to the Catholic school on the other side of town to keep Mother and me out of harms way. But, the screams and torment of racism never stopped. My mother was dark-skinned and I was very, very light with extremely dark, long, curly hair. To Caucasian people I was white. I longed for darker skin. I longed for a different life. I secretly wished my great-aunt had allowed me to be adopted; by a normal family with a mother and father who would have a house that I wasn't ashamed to say was mine. I never shared this secret with anyone I knew. Ever! I hated being in my neighborhood, my home, my life and most of all I hated being me!

One night when I was six or seven a knock on the front door woke me up. My mother opened the door a crack, and I heard the voice of my best friend's brother. He pushed his way in, breaking the chain off the door. I hid under the blanket on the couch. As he shoved my mother to the floor, he shut the TV off so it was dark. The only light was coming in thru the window curtain. I heard my mother scream "stop", then I heard him hit her and tell her to be quiet or he would hurt us both. I heard her clothes being torn. He raped my mother on the living room

floor as I pretended to sleep on the sofa. I could hear my heart pounding in my chest and I cried, afraid I might be next. Pulling on all my
courage, I ran for the bathroom. At this, he got up, grabbed his clothes,
and ran out of the door. When mother turned the light on in the bathroom, I saw that her clothes were torn and her face bruised.

The next day I told Ma-mom and grandfather about the incident.
They were angry with my mother for opening the door. This same man
tried to molest me one day when I was eight and was visiting my best
friend's house. I managed to run out of the house. I thought it was my
fault, and since nothing apparently happened to him after what he did
to my mother, I feared nothing would happen if I told someone, so I
kept it in my box of many secrets. I never entered my best friend's home
again.

Eventually my grandfather's health began to fade; I was ten years
old when he died in his sleep. I moved in with my aunt's oldest daughter, along with her five-year-old. I didn't realize then how difficult it
must have been for her, to take care of us without any financial help.
Although I know she loved me very much, she was extremely strict
and physically punished us often, at times for the most absurd reasons. I'm grateful for this experience because I know it's the reason I
won't hit my children today. I now realize that she took her frustrations out on us, and this probably was the only way she knew at the
time to cope with the pressures of providing for two, one of whom
wasn't even hers. We all do the best we can, and I know some of my
best qualities are a direct result of living with her.

At age twelve, I had my first and last encounter with my biological father. I was playing jacks on the neighbor's porch with friend. A
man came over with his mother to visit his sister, my friend's mother.
My mother and godmother, on the porch down the street, saw him
approach the house. By this time, Mother knew about sex and that
babies resulted from it. She told my godmother that he was the one who
raped her those many years ago and that he was my father. My mother
and godmother went around the corner to my great aunt's home. A
few minutes later all three came back, told us to stay outside, then they
walked into my friend's home. I heard him speak to my mother, then
arguing broke out between him and my aunt. He stormed out of the

house, his mother following. As she passed me, she touched my head, and with tears in her eyes said, "You are such a lovely girl". Then they drove away. I never saw him again.

My aunt, mother, and godmother took me home and explained what happened. This man admitted knowing my mother, and that they did go to school together. He admitted working in later years at the school she attended. My great aunt then told him I was his daughter, but out of fear of legal ramifications he denied it. My great aunt said she just wanted me to know my father, but his own fears made that reality impossible.

I stayed in Catholic school from first grade through high school. We were obligated to take Religion classes, and the lessons taught perplexed me. In second grade I raised my hand to ask a question. The teacher told me not to question God's word. I raised my hand to ask this question again, believing she had not understood my query the first time. This time she smacked me in the mouth for asking. Needless to say, I never raised my hand to question anything in my Religion classes again. During my remaining school years, my quest for truth began. My spirit knew I wouldn't find it in the Catholic faith. Over the following years I went to Episcopalian, Baptist, Lutheran, Seventh Day Adventist, Pentecostal, and Presbyterian churches. I even learned a bit about Islam because one of my cousins converted to Islam.

At eighteen years old, I married my high school sweetheart and left Philadelphia as fast as I could. He said he loved me eternally and seemed to be on his own spiritual quest for truth. To my eyes, he was a savior and superhero. But in reality he did not know how to behave as a husband. Because of this, my self-esteem suffered many deaths; but my search for truth never faltered. Although my family was in Philadelphia, God always sent angels disguised as friends to be my local family and support me in my unending times of trouble. Living in California and not seeing my mother regularly was the catalyst that helped me understand why my childhood was designed perfectly even with all the pain and turmoil it brought. Becoming a mother truly changes you. With the help of my uncle, who had named me Lady, I moved my mother five minutes from my own home, so she could be close to her grandchildren and me.

The next ten painfully long years of marriage brought many changes in my life. I decided to completely remove myself from any affiliation with standardized religion, including no longer celebrating any Christian holidays. My son and daughter never celebrated Easter or Christmas. I determined that the traditions passed down from generations had no real connection to spiritually. I remained married for nine more years which brought me more pain than can be shared in this short story, but also granted me clarity, grace and gratitude that might not otherwise have been found.

Only after giving birth to two beautiful healthy children of my own, did I discover that amidst the chaos is perfection. The mother that I am today is a direct result of lessons learned from being raised by my cousin, and having so many mother figures at crucial periods of my life. Not having a father or a strong mother figure caused me to seek my own truth in ways I may have never considered if I'd had "normal" parents. What would have been the catalyst for me to question my very existence if my parents were normal? If not for the many years of pain, what would have been the purpose of the many sister/angel friends who loved me through some of the toughest times of my life and who enabled me to find the strength to rise above it and shine? If not for the pain and turmoil what would have been the basis for my quest to find if there was any truth to what I had been taught to believe about our creator?

Being raised by my mentally challenged mother brought me a deep understanding that a mother's love surpasses any IQ score. It taught me to see beyond anyone's disability, physical or otherwise. I gained the knowledge that we are eternal and not just the vehicle we now occupy. It took me until my forties before I finally reached a place of gratitude for the experience of those years of pain with an understanding and humility that I could not have imagined in my younger years.

With every tear, a prayer was answered and the journey from there to here would not have become a story. Without it all, would I have honestly come to the place of believing that I was deserving and worthy of a truer love than I was currently experiencing? That my life's purpose was not to take care of my mother or be a stepping stone for a husband who took me for granted in everyway a person could. Would I have become a woman who stands up for herself without fear, and encourage other women to find their strength by listening to their own inner voice? Without all of it, would I have ever found the strength to walk away from a nineteen-year marriage with children in hand, and the knowing that God would definitely provide a means for us to survive? I think not.

One morning, the truth screamed loudly in my heart: If you want something to change, you have to change. If you expect things to be different, you must do things differently. If you are to demand respect, you must first start by respecting yourself. I left my home, my husband, and my job all in the same day. I was a property manager, and my apartment was included with my job. I left, not knowing where we would sleep, other than inside my car. I had asked my husband to leave many times. He refused every time, saying that if I was so miserable, I could leave. I had a job pending as a leasing consultant with a luxury apartment complex, but they had not yet found an apartment for me. The pay was considerably lower than what I was used to earning. Still, I left on faith that God would provide a way and God did!

I slept at a friend's house for three days; another friend paid for a hotel room for two; and then the complex called and said they had an apartment for me and my two children (who were nine and four at the time). Through it all, I knew God would take two steps toward me if I took just one step towards Him on faith. I filed for divorce and never looked back. Life got much harder before it got easier. My income dropped; I had two cars repossessed and much debt. But with every book I read, with every question I asked, God spoke to me, in such clarity that all would be okay. I was all I needed. I was More than Enough! The more I believed I would be okay, the more I was okay. The more I believed it would get better, the better it became. The more I sought to find the truth, the more books of wisdom found their way to my hands, and as the saying goes "when the student is ready, the teacher will appear", which was so abundantly true in my case.

When I needed to know I was not alone in my beliefs, God sent another angel, disguised as my boss, who in days became one of my very best friends. In God's perfect time, in Spirit's perfect way, less than one month of our knowing each other, she said to me, "You are so

Agape," and of course I had no idea what she meant. Who knew that the answers to all my childhood and life long questions were about to be answered by one source. One Sunday she picked me up and said, "Just trust me and don't worry. It's not church." When we arrived at the Agape International Spiritual Center, the Agape African Orphanage children's choir was singing. Every cell in my body began to shake. They were not singing in English but my heart and soul instinctively knew their voices were projecting words of love. Within minutes the congregation lifted their hands to offer newcomers a blessing. I have never cried so hard in public in my entire life. To this day, I cannot discuss it without coming to tears.

I knew God had led me home. The journey, regardless how difficult, felt sweeter, fuller, and richer because of every tear I shed along the way. You would never truly appreciate the warmth of the sunshine if you never felt so wet and cold from many days of rain. I am never as alive at any other time as I am in the presence of those angels. How amazed I was to discover an entire community just ten minutes from my home, practicing daily and teaching what I came to believe as truth for most of my life! My heart didn't seem big enough to contain all the love pouring out of me for my best friend, the founder, Rev. Michael and his Spiritual Center. Since my quest for Truth ended that day, I have never been the same and I truly Thank God for it.

I dedicated my life to being a beneficial presence on the planet and being in service to Agape, along with my dedication to my fiancé and my beautiful children. The woman I am today, in my community, to my children, at my place of employment, as a writer and as a member of my spiritual community would not exist if it were not for me being my mother's daughter. In January 2007, I decided to finally put my unique story to paper to share my gratitude with the world. I wrote the first chapter of my book with no idea of how it was to be published, and no idea if anyone really would be interested in reading it. But I knew from experience that if I took one step in faith, believing God would meet me more than halfway, then I had nothing to fear. Within forty-eight hours of finishing the first chapter, I was at Agape waiting for the event coordinator. I saw a flyer with the information about the book series, *Thank God I . . .* , and their search for inspired authors. I laughed out loud. I lifted my head to the sky, closed my eyes, and said, "I knew you would meet me halfway, Lord. Thank God I showed up!"

♥ ♥ ♥

Author of "Thank God I Am the Product of Rape," Lady resides in California. She is the proud mother of two, a ten-year-old daughter and a fifteen-year-old son. Her second marriage will take place in April 2008, and she will gain three beautiful stepdaughters. Lady is a speaker and career advisor.

Thank God
I Have Herpes

UMOH NTUK

I sat half-naked in a cold, artificially bright doctor's office, listening to her clipped accent telling me what I already knew. My stomach dropped, my eyes filling with tears and my mind with horror. The family doctor I had been seeing all my life was not very sympathetic. Her detached, matter-of-fact disposition exacerbated my humiliation and intense embarrassment. As a young, insecure girl, I took this as her silent condemnation. This was the beginning of years of guilt, shame, lying, and hiding the fact that I had herpes. Herpes . . . just the word conjures up all sorts of disturbing connotations. It's something comics on HBO joke about other people having. It's something that happens to promiscuous, dirty, irresponsible people. Or at least, that's what I thought.

I felt like a slut and saw myself as damaged goods. I couldn't imagine anyone would ever want to have sex with me again, let alone love me in my permanently flawed state. I needed sex to validate myself, to feel safe, to feel alive, and to release the intense passion for life that I had nowhere else to channel. I was broke, failing in school, didn't see where I fit in the world, and had no relationship to speak of with either of my parents. My lofty goals and aspirations frightened me into paralysis. I derived a sense of control and security based only on the fact that plenty of guys were always eager to have sex with me. And so I lied and I kept having sex. I lived in a constant state of denial.

I never told my boyfriend. I didn't know if I had gotten it from him, but I suspected I had given it to him. Of course, the relationship didn't turn into a storybook romance. What I thought of as protective and assertive turned into jealous and possessive. I'm sure my lies didn't help. Shortly after we moved in together, he slapped me across the face, and the violence continued from there. Even though I had seen all the after-school specials on domestic violence, I stayed. He would follow me and question me about any man I talked with. Even after he hit me repeatedly, (and I knew it wouldn't stop) I stayed. I loved him, but more importantly he loved me despite the fact that I probably had given him an incurable STD. I ignored the voice screaming inside me, "Get out, and get out now!" I convinced myself that I was helpless. I couldn't afford to move out and had nowhere to go. I chose to believe that his apologies and promises meant something.

One morning we were lying in bed talking about our future. I said I didn't want to move to San Bernardino, where he wanted to live. He flipped out, pushed me out of bed, and started throwing things at me. A gallon of water hit my chest, and I looked up just in time to avoid being hit in the head with a rock. When I saw the look in his eyes, I gathered the sheet around me and ran out the door. As I crouched behind somebody's bougainvillea, listening to his footsteps race by, I finally woke up. I still had a very low opinion of myself and didn't think anyone else would ever love me. But I also finally decided it was better to be alone than dead. I left, sleeping on my grandmother's couch for the next six months.

After he and I broke up, I continued to have sex with people without telling them I had herpes. I felt terrible but didn't believe I could live any other way. I knew it was selfish and violated people I really cared about, and so I tried to compensate. I became vigilant about monitoring my body for signs of an outbreak. I did research about ways to suppress symptoms and did my own experiments. One of my greatest fears was giving herpes to someone else. I also feared anyone finding out that I wasn't telling anyone. People always thought of me as a nice person and complimented me on how kind and considerate I was. I desperately wanted to be perceived as that sweet, thoughtful person, even though I believed I was evil because of what I was doing. So I thought about it as little as possible . . . until I had my spiritual renaissance.

I had dabbled with God here and there but at that point, I was a firm believer in nothing. I thought that God had to come with religion, which I had long ago rejected. Twelve years of Catholic school convinced me I wanted no part of religion. I hadn't envisioned any other way to be connected to God. One night, a few friends and I were sitting around talking. Someone gave me a copy of the *Tao Te Ching*. I stayed up all night, smoking weed and lying in bed reading the book. I found it fascinating and read each page over and over until I grasped the full meaning of it. I feel asleep with universal connectivity and the nature of reality swimming around in my dreams.

The next day, I woke up and drove to San Francisco to see a guy I was dating casually. He and I took some Ecstasy. It was like nothing I had ever imagined or any other drug trip I'd experienced. I saw his aura glow with the most beautiful golden light. I found myself floating out of my body and being forcefully drawn up into a vast, indescribable mass of darkness and light. I was cloaked in the most intense experience of love, joy, and completeness that I've ever experienced. It frightened me because I was losing myself in its intensity. I knew from a deep, primal familiarity that this was God. I struggled to separate myself from its mammoth beauty and maintain my humanness.

After this, I knew what nirvana meant, and I knew there was nothing to fear in this life. I stayed high for a week, and a new person was born. I cried the day I came down because I had thought I would stay in that enlightened state forever. I saw a spider and got scared. I cried because I didn't want to be afraid ever again, because I knew my fear wasn't real. Once I got over my sadness, I understood this experience was to show me the way, to open a door for me. I couldn't expect a drug to do the work for me. I would have to create the magic for myself.

Shortly after that, I fell in love for the first time since my abusive relationship. He was exquisite, angry, and wounded. He had an innocence and vulnerability about him, a gentle charisma. He believed in fairies, loved animals, did yoga, sold drugs, and beat people up. I related to his duality and understood his pain. He opened my heart like no one else, and I felt safe in letting him in. I knew I had to tell him my secret, and I was terrified. After we had been together for a month, I cheated on him. It was because I didn't want to have to tell him that I was diseased and had compromised him without telling him. I was being self-destructive and hoped he would break up with me so I wouldn't have to deal with it. But he didn't. My newfound connection to the cosmos would not let me continue to hide.

Everywhere I went, I saw signs that I should tell him the truth. Finally I decided to tell him that I had herpes, but I pretended that I had just found out. I told him I had to tell him something and to meet me at the park. I remember sitting in the car watching the shadows move across his face right before I told him, the genuine concern in his eyes. I turned away as I uttered the words, "I have herpes." It was the first time in my life I said it out loud. Lightning did not strike. The earth did not open up and swallow me whole. Tears poured down my face as I stared out the window into the trees. I braced myself for his rejection, but it didn't come. I couldn't believe it. The weight of carrying this burden for years was lifted. I felt loved, really and truly, for the first time.

I discovered that fear lives in dark places. All secrets revealed lose their power. Bringing them to light releases us from their bondage and peels them away to reveal deeper, richer levels of joy, peace, and existence. It augments meaning in our lives and the expression of the self. I allowed myself to think about what it meant to have herpes after that and why it had come to me. I was learning that there are no coincidences.

I knew it had to do with my relationship to sex, which was complicated to say the least. It was related to my dysfunctional childhood and how I felt about being a woman. Underneath my hedonistic expression of sexual freedom was a repressed Catholic girl who had been sexually abused. She was dying to retreat from all things sexual and intimate. She felt safe only within many great walls. But I had ignored, denied, and shoved her down so deeply, I was scarcely aware of her existence. I believe that contracting herpes was partly about bridging the gap between her and my conscious self. I started to understand the depth of my wounds. I decided it was time to tend to the festering sores of my soul, so they wouldn't have to show up on my body for me to acknowledge them.

I spent more time in nature, to take my shoes off and connect to the earth. Feeling the cool, moist grass beneath my feet while walking home from work nourished me. I would feel all the stress melting out of my body through the soles of my feet. I would sit and listen to the waves crash. At the park, I would lie down and stare into the night sky. The stars would wink at me, and the moon would blanket me with her light.

The deep appreciation I had for nature was being rekindled. In these quiet moments, I could hear the whispering of my own voice. The force of my spirit was being activated. I let the gentle voice lead me. I started to take better care of myself, stopped smoking weed, and eventually broke up with my boyfriend. He was doing more drugs and less of anything else. This time I didn't want to leave. I felt like I was leaving a piece of myself behind. But I knew he wasn't able to grow with me the way I wanted to and needed to now. At least this time I had a sliver of hope that there was more out there for me.

I opened up more actively to inner guidance. I listened to my dreams, went to therapy, developed a rock-solid relationship with my intuition, and attended personal growth seminars. My imagination became my tool instead of something with which to torture myself. I began healing my relationship with my parents. I understood that part of my self-loathing stemmed from that relationship. How can you hate where you come from without hating yourself? I started to dance. It was something that had always interested me. I had taken a class several years earlier but dropped out because I felt so inept. I signed up for a belly dancing class at the park and unveiled a new channel for my passion. Moving my body in this way opened up pockets of blocked energy and taught me how to experience sexuality in a different realm. I was actually pretty good. This nurtured a new source of faith in myself. I decided to go back to school and major in dance. I started writing again, which was another forgotten source of nourishment.

The things that happen to us in our lives are reflections of who we think we are. Surprisingly enough I found my strengths hidden in my shadow and weakness masquerading as talents. Healing the "weak" parts of myself has given me boundless opportunities to grow and expand the reality of who I am and what I am creating in the world. I became aware that the way I felt about myself because I had herpes (dirty and defective) echoed feelings I had about being molested, being a woman, and feeling unwanted by my parents. Having herpes allowed me to experience what was deeply suppressed and needing to be healed. These feelings, not any authentic lack within me, had caused the voids in my psyche and in my life. If I never had herpes I am not sure when or if my journey to recover the self would have ever begun.

Actually herpes has given me many wondrous gifts. Having herpes has also allowed me to understand why people do horrible things, and to be less judgmental of others as well as of myself. It has granted me the opportunity to experience the tremendous power of truth. It will set you free. After I started being honest about having herpes, no one rejected me because of this. Now I am married to an amazing man whom I respect, admire, trust, and love deeply, and who feels the same about me. He knows my "secrets" and accepts me as I am. I've been dancing for six years. I'm writing and learning how to share my intuitive abilities with others.

The most magical, delectable, and exhilarating addition to my life is my beautiful, perfect newborn daughter. She would never have been born if I didn't have herpes. I have had numerous medical issues with my reproductive organs and was told it was highly unlikely that I would ever conceive. Because I was trying to purge the herpes virus from my body I made numerous lifestyle changes. I did fasts, took supplements, adopted a healthier diet, meditated, and visualized my body, especially my reproductive organs, in perfect health. In January I went to the desert alone to do a vision quest and expunge some of my personal demons. I left many of them there and cleared tons of sexual debris from my inner rooms. I felt clearer and more certain about who I am, what I want, and what I deserve. My periods became regular for the first time in my life, and within four months I was pregnant. I was bestowed the most precious of gifts, the opportunity to create and nurture a new life.

Yesterday I was sitting on my couch holding our baby next to my husband, who was playing his harmonica. At that moment I felt an all-encompassing wave of peace, gratitude, and understanding. I let the almost palpable flood wash over me and fill my soul. I realized I was inspired and content with my life.

It sounds simple, but this experience frequently eludes us, or at least it had eluded me. Nothing about my life or me needs to be altered or eradicated. I don't have to postpone enjoying my life for any reason, and all the aspects of my past and present are perfect, clean, and steadily guiding me toward my destiny.

Thank God that I got herpes.

Umoh Ntuk, a small-business owner with a pet services business (Fetch Pet Care), is also a belly dancer and has done extensive study of the spiritual realm and universal laws. As well, she is an intuitive energy reader and a channeler. She is the mother of an eight-month-old baby.

Thank God
I Was a Polygamist's Wife

WHITE DOVE

Near the tail end of my third marriage, from which I had five children, I poured my heart out to God, pleading to understand. "We go to church, I pay my tithing, and we have family home evening. Why is it, if I'm doing everything I'm supposed to, that my marriage sucks and my kids are out of control?"

I got an immediate response, clear as day: "Because you're not praying or reading enough."

That answer pissed me off, so I went to sleep. The next morning, I woke up with the same feelings, the same thoughts, and my same life! I looked up and said, "OK, what do you want me to do?" I read scriptures and studied and really prayed. Not just prayed as I used to, but prayed truly wanting answers, guidance, and help. I became obsessed with right and wrong. If the very church that I was raised in had changed policies and veered from the truth, I wanted to live the true Principles, to do what I knew my Heavenly Father wanted.

There was a Last-Days Group gathering in a small town in Utah whose members experienced the same questions that I had. It was as

if we had all tapped in to the same radio station. My oldest daughter
was married. My son was on a church mission, my second daughter
had moved out, and my fifteen-year-old had run away with her boyfriend. I took my eleven-year-old son and moved to Utah. Divorcing
my husband, I joined an apostate group that basically wanted to live
the original laws established by the First Church. Immediately, my son's
father took our son and left me to fight him in court.

No one had taken a plural wife as yet. But slowly, as the Temple
garments were being prepared and more and more people were moving
in from everywhere, the marriages began. I became the second wife
to a family with ten kids. My new husband, whom I will call Joseph,
positioned himself up in the new Council. He was a performer. He'd
get up in front of others and keep them entertained with his incredible
knowledge. He kept himself available to put out fires. Because he knew
the doctrine, because he knew his scriptures, everyone seemed to be
attracted to his strength of knowledge. I know I was!

My new sister-wife had broken her leg some years earlier and
ever since then would yell to get someone's attention. She was always
involved, and in the middle of everything. She'd butt into conversations.
She could sit around all day and yak and yak and have everyone do
everything for her and never move . . . except to go to the bathroom.

The oldest teenagers were basically the parents.The parents were
mainly unavailable. No one ever talked or listened to the kids. The kids
were flinging themselves off the walls. If any one of them wanted to
go anywhere, it was a Big Deal! They couldn't just go. It was an emo-
tional/mental beating. "Go ask your mother." "Go ask your dad," and
he'd tell them to go ask their mother again. She'd say, "Well if you can
get someone to take over your chores, then maybe . . . come back and
ask me again later." The kids were always on hold. It was insane trying
to talk to parents who were constantly behind the bedroom or office
doors; two parents engaged and absorbed with The Group, always talking about the laws to live, but totally oblivious to living them; having a
second wife was part of living those higher laws.

I quickly learned the rules of the house. I became invisible. I stopped
talking. Every time I would start to say something, my throat would
close off. I would literally lean my head back to let the words come out

of my mouth. I learned to keep my mouth shut because I was constantly being shot down and invalidated. The second wives in The Group were like zombies. We all just went through the motions. We were put upon by the first wives. I wasn't allowed to be alone with Joseph unless my sister-wife let me. Jealousy frequently raged throughout the house.

Joseph was a spineless coward. He would quote scriptures and rant on about eternal damnation to lead his family to exaltation. It was my sister-wife who wore the pants. Clearly she was the boss!

We three slept in the same room for the first week or so. I felt so traumatized and abused, I moved my things to a room upstairs with the children. I knew my sister-wife was ecstatic to be rid of me, although she couldn't stand the thought that now she had lost sight of me. That caused even more contention. One day, feeling so broken, I went to the older kids, and I cried. "How do you survive your parents? I can't do this!" Two of the teenagers rolled up their sleeves above their wrists and showed me scars. At the time I had never heard of "cutting." I thought they had tried to kill themselves. We all cried and hugged each other.

The oldest boy then told me that he had straight-out asked his mother, "Why do you hate her?" She answered, "I don't hate her." He said she went on and the things she was saying convinced him that "she really does hate you." The words of the parents did not match their actions. My sister-wife would say that she loved me and was glad I was in their family. Of course — who wouldn't want someone to watch the kids, make meals, and do the laundry?

I felt very connected with the children. They were good kids, having a hard life. We all bonded because we all were abused and neglected by The Parents. Kids just want attention, recognition, and affection. They were so loving and lovable. Many times, when I was trying to 'just understand', I would get a comforting thought: "Be with the children. Love the children." I could see in my mind the picture of Christ with the little ones around his knee.

We were kicked out of the house because the rent had not been paid for three months, so we moved to someone's backyard and lived in tents. It was outrageous! It was pathetic! We were known as "Tent City" by The Group and were an even bigger joke to the whole town. The parents could be found many nights at the local bed & breakfast, spending the night caretaking when the owners were out of town. So again it was me and the kids, left at Tent City.

Journal entry:
   Well, it's Saturday night. I am sobbing myself to sleep. I do not understand, and I'm pleading to God to help me to get on track. Because my pain is so deep, I told God, "Never mind about me wanting to be at the next level . . . I'm failing miserably at this one! I'm tired of being alone all of my life. So, forget it . . . I just want to be like everybody else." Then I'd sob some more and hurry and say, "Forgive me, God . . . help me to understand." The Holy Spirit manifested to me that I needed to start reading again, and that would keep me on the right path. I felt my whole body shift! It was an actual physical, emotional, and mental happening.

I missed my own children so much. I missed all that I used to have. I missed being me.

Journal entry:
   My children,
   I want you all to know I love you all very much. I wanted every one of you, even before you were conceived. I loved having my babies. You were all great children. There had to be some bad times, but I can honestly say I can't remember anything but good. Everything still would be pretty good if I hadn't started talking to the Lord and asking for His guidance back to the Celestial Kingdom, instead of coasting with the church. That's when I started to lose everything in my life as I had come to know it. All I wanted was my children. I prayed and prayed, "Father, where do I go to save my family, and get my children out of Babylon?" And I lost my children. "Father, I wanted to be married (to my last husband) forever. To be married in the temple. I lost my husband, the temple, the church, my children, my home, my things, my car, my cat, my reputation, my self-worth and esteem, my family, my mother, my sons, and I ask

myself . . . why? Why God? Why, when I started to follow the Lord, I started to lose everything? Now I struggle to just hold on to my life."

I'm writing this so that if I do give up that struggle . . . at least from this life . . . you, my children, might somehow read this and know I love you. I love all five of you. The pain of not having you near me is so tremendous. I have often felt my heart cracking open. I miss you all so much. To marry into a plural situation, I gave up having an exclusive relationship, motherhood, manners, etiquette, quiet, common courtesy, a house, meals together as a family, compassion, and love as we showed it. Father does not forgive suicide . . . not for a long, long time. I want to believe that despite the hell spent for such action taken, that I will know why I'm in hell. I don't know why I'm in hell right now!"

I lasted seven weeks as a plural wife. I knew I was going to Hell! I was breaking my vows and sacred covenants, and I knew God would not forgive me. I was so broken, I absolutely did not care and would take my chances. Thank God being a polygamist's wife was the most unusual thing I've ever done! It was also the gateway that opened my world, my mind, my perspective, my heart, and my possibilities to really know myself. To understand I was no different and no better than the family I entered into in a plural marriage. It was mirroring my own family that I had given up on. I was angry that the parents would abuse and neglect all of us. My children spent a whole childhood being neglected. My ex-husband and my kids stopped talking, just as I did in my plural marriage. I had treated my ex-husband like one of the kids. What better opportunity could I, as an adult, have to learn how a child feels when being treated with no regard, than to be a second wife?

I am grateful for this experience. I am so thankful for the insight and love I now have for people. This experience allowed me to apologize to my ex-husband, re-connect with my children and my family, and connect with my parents, who have passed on from this life. I have been married over twelve years now to a man of peace. He allowed me space to heal and mend. He didn't push his agenda on me. He gave me a soft place to land. He has taught me so much about being kind and finding peace within. God is not the God I grew up fearing. Life is a journey. It's a series of choices, intentions, and living life on purpose. I give thanks and wish well-being to the family that taught me so much. I pray that they too are in a better space of knowing and learning their lessons.

♥   ♥   ♥

White Dove is the mother of five, grandmother of twelve (and counting), and the wife in a marriage that's still happily working. She is a graduate of Southwest Institute of Healing Arts, in Arizona, and is a certified life coach, reiki master, and hypnotherapist, specializing in teaching others to "live their lives on purpose." She currently conducts "well-ness weekends" and health classes in beautiful St. George, Utah.

Thank God
I Lost My Dream Job . . .
and Found My Dream

STEVE BHAERMAN

*N*ext time you utter the phrase, "a funny thing happened," consider this. Maybe that "funny thing" is just an example of the Universe's sense of humor, where you think you're headed down one path and you're really headed down another. Like the time I thought I was a college professor, but a funny thing happened . . . and I ended up becoming a comedian instead.

The story began when I found my dream job. Actually, "found" is not the right word. From the moment I heard there was something called the Weekend College where I could teach autoworkers as part of Detroit's Wayne State University, I "stalked" this job. I knew this job was mine, and every week I called the department head to ask if I'd been hired. I must have been such a nudnik that the guy hired me just so I'd stop pestering him. The day I found I'd been hired, I literally cried with gratitude.

The job was even better than I imagined it would be. I had a knack for making the classes I taught — like Labor History and Ethnic Studies — interesting as well as educational. Sometimes the men would bring their wives to class, because apparently it was the best edu-tain-ment around. More than one student told me I was the first professor they'd ever had who actually spoke to them like a person. They leveled with me on the first day. "We're just in it for the money," one of them told me. Apparently, under this program their stipend from the G.I. Bill was higher than their tuition, and they got to keep the difference. "Well then, I'm in it for the money too," I replied. After all, I was being paid more than I'd ever been paid to teach before. "Tell me," I asked, "do you have to pass your courses in order to get your stipend?"

They admitted that they did. "Well then, we have some work to do, eh?" Those men worked very hard that year and were proud of what they learned and accomplished. They also found many more valuable reasons for being there than just the money. How popular was I? Toward the end of that first year I traded in my Ford Pinto for a new Honda — consid-ered a traitorous act in Detroit — and no one torched my new car.

That summer there were no classes, and I took off to research a book I was writing on education, expecting to have my job when I returned in the fall. And that's when the not-so-funny thing happened. Wayne State needed to replace the part-time employees with tenured professors — most of whom hated the notion of teaching the auto-workers as much as I enjoyed it, I was out of a job. For a semester, I tried to piece together other freelance teaching jobs, but it didn't add up to a living.

Meanwhile, I had moved to Ann Arbor. I decided I needed to get a job, and that's when I saw the ad in the paper. The Ann Arbor Depart-ment of Parks and Forestry was looking for an equipment operator. Since I had operated farm equipment before, I was hired. My job was helping to take down trees that had Dutch Elm Disease, and this had my Jewish mother from Brooklyn a little concerned. She was afraid I might catch Dutch Elm Disease. Seriously.

I assured her that people didn't get Dutch Elm Disease, although dogs get it. "Dogs get it?" she asked, concerned about Buster. "What happens to dogs?"

"They lose their bark," I told her.

For the first several months, the job was great. I enjoyed being out-doors, using my body, and giving my brain a rest. At night, I worked on what would be my second book on education. My first, an account of my experiences starting an alternative high school in Washington, D.C., had been published by Simon & Schuster and had been widely reviewed. Even without a teaching job, I figured, I could get back in the game with another book. As summer gave way to fall and then winter, I started getting depressed. It's one thing working outdoors in the summertime. But in September, the college kids who'd been working part time returned to school. Then there was me — college professor and published author — and here I was getting up each cold, dark morning, putting on a jump suit, and spending the day chipping brush. At least I had a job, but not one my mother was likely to brag about.

I did have one ace in the hole, and that was the book I was writing. It would be a way to get my untracked career back on track. But the book didn't seem to be working either. Simon & Schuster passed on it, and my agent was having trouble selling it elsewhere. Nonetheless, I persisted, writing every night. I was sitting at the dining room table one cold night working away at the book, when I distinctly heard a voice. I'm not accustomed to hearing voices, particularly when they are not attached to people, but I heard this one. "Let go of this book," the voice said. "The book is your past, and you need to focus on the future." "What's the future?" I asked. The voice was silent.

I was at work a couple of weeks later — a bone-chillingly cold February day — and they put me with a new guy, Larry, who turned out to be a brilliant psychologist disguised as a truck driver. As we rode and worked together, Larry came up with an idea. "You're a writer," he said. "Let's start a little newspaper." And so, for the sheer fun of it — and to alleviate the boredom — I said, "Sure." It was a decision that would change my life. Larry and I ended up producing an anonymous humorous biweekly publication for the twenty-five or so people we worked with. We called it States Wire Service, and our masthead slogan was "All the News Before It Happens, Guaranteed to Be Fallacious If Not True."

The premier issue — typed and reprinted at the campus copying shop — was surreptitiously dropped off by a girlfriend and left on the lunch table before everyone cruised in for lunch. I walked in, ignored the papers sitting there, and walked to the men's room. All of

a sudden I heard a whoop. And then another. The guys had discovered
the paper — and it was all about them. For the next two years, we
continued to tell the truth through humor. We created what could best
be described as an ongoing, interactive situation comedy. We would
write something in the paper, and our fellow workers would respond
to it. We started a rumor in the paper that one young and ambitious
groundsman was "campaigning" for foreman. We even wrote a speech
for him in the paper. One morning, I came to work and there he was,
standing on one of the lunch tables, dramatically delivering the speech
we had written for him.

Other times, guys (I say this because it was an all-male workplace)
would try to do things that would get them in the paper or at least
mentioned briefly in our gossip column, which we called — because
of the general sci-fi, outer-spacey tone of the paper — "News From
Uranus." During this time, our nemesis was Foreman Don. A former
marine, Don was tough, tough, tough. He was a man of few words, and
as soon as the paper appeared, he became a man of even fewer words.
One day, he was out on the work site and remarked, "Every time I say
anything, it gets in that damn paper." Naturally, in the next issue we
reprinted that very quote.

A few years ago, I had a reunion with my friend Larry, who had
stayed on to become union local president. "You know," he told me,
"over the years, Foreman Don and I became friends, and you know
what he said? He said, 'I loved that paper. Boy, do I miss that paper!'"

As per the ritual we developed, foremen were not allowed to
be seen buying the paper and had to give their quarter to a worker
to buy it for them. Each time an issue came out, a different worker
sold it — so the entire shop felt they had ownership of it. At a place
steeped in habitual unconscious behavior, all of a sudden there was
a spark of creativity. Two of the workers — both highly intelligent
but illiterate — returned to school to learn how to read. Those who
worked in other city departments would get hold of the paper, and
wished they, too, could have a crazy newspaper about them. Within
months, I'd forgotten about that serious book I'd been writing, and
it forgot about me. I discovered two important things: The first thing
was, for the first time I recognized the power humor has to generate

sanity, balance, and creativity. The second thing I realized was, I was really good at it. One day, while generating material for the paper, a funny name flew into my head . . . Swami Beyondananda.

A year later, after I'd "pre-tired" (that's when you leave a job before you get really tired of it) from the Forestry Department, a friend and I decided to start a publication to reach Ann Arbor's newly forming holistic community. We knew that people took their health, growth, and spirituality way too seriously, so we decided the paper needed humor. We gave Swami Beyondananda the inside back page feature, and the Swami's been running the show ever since.

Very quickly, the Swami became the most popular feature in our magazine. Swami's early columns like "Teach Your Dog to Heal," "Tantrum Yoga," and "Everything You Always Wanted to Know About Sects" made their way into syndication around the country. In late 1986, my wife, Trudy, and I took to the road with the comic Swami act, and the Swami and I have been inseparable ever since. We've met wonderful people, been to great places, and watched thousands and thousands of people laugh. It turns out the joke was on me, and a fortunate joke it was.

My good fortune reminds me of the young immigrant who came to America from a little Jewish village in Poland. He needed work and, being a very religious young man, he went to the local synagogue and applied for a job as a shamus — a janitor. He almost got hired. But when he revealed he couldn't read or write, he was turned away. Desperate yet resourceful, he bought a little pushcart and sold cheap items on the street. He sold a little more, he bought a horse and wagon . . . and finally, he opened a storefront. Long story short, after twenty-five years he owned a huge department store. Still religious, he made a large donation to the synagogue. There was a big ceremony, and the successful businessman handed the rabbi a check — which was signed with an "x." The rabbi was surprised. "You can't read?" "If I could read," the man said, "I'd be a shamus."

How fortunate I was to have a job I loved, and then lose it only to find a truer calling. Thank God the universe had a bigger plan for me than I had for myself. Thank God I lost my dream job and found a dream I never would have dreamed.

❤   ❤   ❤

Steve Bhaerman is a writer who performs comedy internationally as
Swami Beyondananda, the Cosmic Comic. As the Swami, Steve is the
author of *Driving Your Own Karma, When You See a Sacred Cow Milk
It for All It's Worth, Duck Soup for the Soul,* and *Swami for Precedent:
A 7-Step Plan to Heal the Body Politic and Cure Electile Dysfunction.*
Steve is currently working on a more serious book with cellular biol-
ogist Dr. Bruce Lipton, called *Spontaneous Evolution: Our Positive
Future Now,* to be published in fall 2008. He can be found online at
www.wakeuplaughing.com.

Printed in the United States
112753LV00001B/1-93/P

9 780981 545301